Routledge Revivals

Where Do We Come From? Is Darwin Correct?

First published in 1911. The first chapter in this fascinating study devotes itself to a short preliminary introduction to Darwin's ideas, and some remarks on the thoughts of the ancients on the subject and how matters stood in the period immediately preceding the appearance of Darwin himself. The second and third chapters discuss Darwin's theory and a suggested alternative hypothesis. The concluding chapter is devoted to the philosophical aspect of the case, and to some general reflections after a close perusal of Darwin's works.

Where Do We Come From? Is Darwin Correct?

A Philosophical and Critical Study of Darwin's Theory of "Natural Selection"

by Herbert Morse

First published in 1911
by Kegan Paul, Trench, Trübner & Co., Ltd.

This edition first published in 2018 by Routledge
2 Park Square, Milton Park, Abingdon, Oxon, OX14 4RN
and by Routledge
711 Third Avenue, New York, NY 10017

Routledge is an imprint of the Taylor & Francis Group, an informa business

© 1911 Herbert Morse

All rights reserved. No part of this book may be reprinted or reproduced or utilised in any form or by any electronic, mechanical, or other means, now known or hereafter invented, including photocopying and recording, or in any information storage or retrieval system, without permission in writing from the publishers.

Publisher's Note
The publisher has gone to great lengths to ensure the quality of this reprint but points out that some imperfections in the original copies may be apparent.

Disclaimer
The publisher has made every effort to trace copyright holders and welcomes correspondence from those they have been unable to contact.

ISBN 13: 978-1-138-49646-0 (hbk)
ISBN 13: 978-1-351-02142-5 (ebk)
ISBN 13: 978-1-138-49651-4 (pbk)

WHERE DO WE COME FROM?

IS DARWIN CORRECT?

A PHILOSOPHICAL
AND CRITICAL STUDY OF DARWIN'S THEORY
OF "NATURAL SELECTION"

BY

HERBERT MORSE

B.A. OXON., AND LINCOLN'S INN BARRISTER-AT-LAW

LONDON
KEGAN PAUL, TRENCH, TRÜBNER & CO., LTD.
DRYDEN HOUSE, 43 GERRARD STREET, W.
1911

CONTENTS

PART I

DARWIN'S LAW OF NATURAL SELECTION

CHAP.		PAGE
I.	INTRODUCTION	3
II.	PRELIMINARY OBSERVATIONS	20
III.	DARWIN'S THEORY. WHAT IS IT!	38
IV.	AN ALTERNATIVE HYPOTHESIS	53
V.	TWO FATAL OBJECTIONS	72
VI.	MAN AND THE MONKEY	86
VII.	THE LAW OF HYBRIDITY	110
VIII.	TRANSITIONAL VARIETIES, AND THE GEOLOGICAL RECORD	127
IX.	CENTRES OF CREATION, THE ICE-AGE, AND MEANS OF DISPERSAL	148
X.	NATURA NON FACIT SALTUM	174
XI.	THE MENTAL AND MORAL QUALITIES OF MAN AND THE ANIMALS	190
XII.	MISCELLANEOUS OBJECTIONS	212
XIII.	SEXUAL SELECTION	220
XIV.	THE LAW OF EVIDENCE, AND GENERAL OBSERVATIONS	227
XV.	SOME CLOSING OBSERVATIONS	251

PART II

THE TREND OF DARWIN'S PHILOSOPHY

XVI.	DARWIN'S PHILOSOPHY, AND REFLECTIONS THEREON	267
XVII.	CONCLUSION	341

PART I
DARWIN'S LAW OF NATURAL SELECTION

CHAPTER I

INTRODUCTION

I WAS chiefly prompted to write this criticism on Darwin's theory of "Natural Selection," so strenuously advocated in his two great works "The Origin of Species" and "The Descent of Man," by the re-awakened interest that the very numerous and very laudatory articles which appeared on Darwin, as a man, a naturalist, and a discoverer, on the occasion of the centenary of his birth, created and excited in the public mind.

One and all, with hardly an exception, eulogized Darwin to the skies. He was at once a great man, a great naturalist, and a great discoverer. His "Law of Natural Selection," so they asserted, in its main outlines still held the field, though certain minor modifications might be necessary here and there, to bring it more thoroughly into line with recent discoveries and subsequent and more exhaustive speculations on the subject.

For many years past, like most other fairly educated men, I have been acquainted in a general way with Darwin's theory as a whole, with the main contention that underlies it, and with the nature of the evidence that he was enabled to adduce in its support. But I had never, until prompted to do so by the reopening of the discussion, and the renewed interest in his works, which the celebration of the centenary of his birth inevitably provoked, made a deep and first hand study of those works for myself.

If you wish to understand a man's writings, go straight to the fountain head; think out and ponder over all he has to say, and never turn aside or be influenced by criticism, from however exalted a quarter it may come, until you have formed your own opinions on the meaning, and contents, of the work by original study.

Read the criticisms afterwards, and the more of them the better, especially if they proceed from all points of the intellectual compass. Keep an open mind, and let them confirm, modify, or reverse your opinion as the case may be. But read the original first. The majority of people,—if they read at all—especially such works as "The Origin of Species," read the criticisms first, form their faith second hand, and never really reach the point of original perusal.

The opinion even of the man in the street—and I claim for myself no higher authority than that—is always worth listening to, on any subject within his knowledge, and comprehension, provided that opinion is really his own, and is an honest and fearless expression of the conclusions he himself has arrived at.

I remember many years ago, when a student

in the chambers of an equity lawyer, a man of the old school, with the mind of a judge, and the heart of a gentleman, now long gone to his rest, that the old lawyer would occasionally come in with a bundle of papers, and would say, " I wish some of you youngsters would read this, and see what you can make of it " : not, he would add significantly, that you are cleverer than I am, let there be no mistake about that—we may, or may not have been, but he most assuredly did not think so—for he would add it is astonishing sometimes what light a fresh mind will occasionally shed on even a difficult subject. Out of the mouths of babes and sucklings wisdom does sometimes proceed, and things are occasionally revealed to them, which are kept hidden from the wise and prudent, and even from the discreet and learned ministers of the law.

Not that to criticise such works as " The Origin of Species " and " The Descent of Man " needs any apology. They are well within the compass—when one is once acclimatized to the rather high-sounding phraseology in which they are couched—of any man of ordinary understanding. Anyone who can read and write, who has the ordinary powers of reasoning, and is possessed of some knowledge of the nature and value of evidence, is as capable of passing as sound an opinion on the value of the theory, that, that evidence endeavours to corroborate as any scientist of them all. It needs no laboratory preparation, no special knowledge of science in any single department, for the theory enunciated in these writings is really simplicity itself. And what is this wonderful theory of Darwin's that has made such a commotion in the world, and on the strength of which many of Darwin's most illustrious disciples, have assigned Darwin a place beside the great Sir Isaac Newton himself? A child could understand it, if there were anything in it really to understand. It is a poor frail ghost of a theory at the best. For it must always be remembered, that the idea of Evolution is not Darwin's at all. It was well-known and thoroughly thought out and discussed by many of the ancients, such as Epicurus, Lucretius, and others. Indeed, it is one of those self-evident truisms that any observant boy might discover for himself. Again, as regards the Struggle for Existence, and the Survival of the Fittest, other self-evident truisms, the ideas were first propounded by Malthus, who applied them only to humanity, and Darwin merely took the ideas over and applied them to all organic life. What then remains of this revolutionising and epoch making theory, which Darwin can claim as peculiarly his own? Nothing but his idea of Natural Selection. And what is Natural Selection? Not evolution certainly, nothing but the method, means, or agent, by which evolution is enabled to persist; a mere tendency in nature to preserve what already exists, and which is worthy of preservation. It implies only the preservation of such variations as arise, and are

INTRODUCTION

beneficial to the being under its conditions of life! Those are Darwin's own words, there can be no mistake about them, and with this very feeble and inadequate instrument, he endeavours to establish the tremendous proposition that all organic life, man himself included, is descended from a common " stirps," " stock," or " progenitor," which appeared at any time between sixty million, and twenty million years ago upon the surface of the earth, in the shape of a piece of gelatinous substance, called by the chemists protoplastic proteid, and which contained within its prolific womb the seed of every living thing from the smallest microbe to man himself, which from that day to this has appeared upon the globe.

The idea is conceivable, but the conjecture is a wild one, and from the very nature of the case incapable of even approximate verification, or from ever passing beyond the limits of legitimate, or one might almost call it illegitimate, speculation.

As to what took place twenty million years ago as regards the origin of life can at any rate never be anything but mere guess work. Twenty million years! The human mind reels at the thought. And it must be remembered that in this matter the powerful, and far-reaching, arm of mathematics is quite unavailable. We are thrown back then on ordinary evidence. And what evidence is Darwin able to produce in support of his now famous hypothesis? Of positive or direct evidence there can be none;

it is precluded by the very nature of the case. There only remains then inferential or circumstantial evidence, the argument from analogy, and the assertion that a single act of Creation fits in with the nature of things, and is in harmony with what has sometimes been called, the Law of Least Action.

Now, by the Law of Least Action I suppose is meant that Nature will not be at the expense of effecting in two strokes, what she can equally well accomplish in one, that her rule is simplicity rather than complexity, economy rather than extravagance. But this itself is a quite unverified hypothesis, and it is always dangerous to endeavour to buttress up one uncorroborated theory, by another equally unproven. Of course, in a sense there is a unity in all nature. The universe itself is one, or rather one, multiplied by infinity. But in this unity there is endless diversity. Variety in creation, variety in operation, and variety in manifestation. My point is that Nature by no means always acts with simplicity; sometimes her operations are very complex. There is extravagance, and waste enough in the birth, life, and death, of all organic life. There is nothing really in the nature of things why Nature should prefer one act of creation to many. If Nature preferred the many, it would be as likely to exhibit the Law of Least Action as the one. The many in this particular case may be the least action possible.

And again, as regards the argument from analogy. Analogy is the last refuge of proof. And however convincing and attractive analogies may appear at first sight, they are after all but imperfect inductions, and the induction nearly always stops short, and breaks down at the very point where its aid would be invaluable. And Darwin's analogies, clever as some of them are, are no exception to the rule; unfortunately they are in many respects misleading, and consequently, as evidence useless and ineffective.

There remains then only the evidence from inference; the only evidence in a case like this which is worth anything at all.

There is a fundamental unity in all organic life, a resemblance sometimes obvious, and proximate, sometimes remote and hardly to be detected; varying as you ascend, or descend the scale, in organic life, in the main outlines, organs, conformation, and structure of every living thing.

And this fundamental unity, this common resemblance, points conclusively, says Darwin, to a community of descent. From the common properties you infer the common ancestor. If there was no other way of accounting for these resemblances, there certainly would be much in the contention. But there are other and more satisfactory explanations, as I have endeavoured to show, in the subsequent chapters of the book. And how about the discrepancies and dissimilarities in organic life. They have to be accounted for. And here it is that the Law of Natural Selection comes in and finds its true field of operation. But the Law of Natural Selection no more adequately accounts for the difference, say, between the brain of a tadpole, and that of a man, or the physique of a mole, and a mammoth, than the law of gravitation itself.

And here, perhaps, while on this question of evidence it would be as well to point out, that in the "Origin of Species," which is really the ark of the new dispensation, Darwin directs nearly his whole energies, not so much to evidencing and establishing the theory itself, as to clearing obstacles out of the way. But merely to clear obstacles out of the way of a theory, is not necessarily to advance its proof. And how great and formidable those obstacles are perhaps only Darwin himself fully realised. But he never satisfactorily succeeds in either demolishing, surmounting, or circumventing them, and he seems at times painfully aware of it.

This frail bark of Darwin's called "Natural Selection" is all through the "Origin of Species" labouring in a heavy and tempestuous sea, and not all the resources and ingenuity of its celebrated captain, nor all the skill and seamanship, of such dexterous and experienced pilots as Huxley and Tyndall, were able to bring it safely into port, or to find for it a safe and permanent anchorage, in the reason, still less in the heart of man.

And here be it remembered I am not quarrelling with Darwin's facts; it would be an impertinence on my part to do so. Darwin was a great naturalist;

INTRODUCTION 11

I am none. He is welcome to all his facts and as many more of them as he pleases. But if his facts were multiplied a thousand times, and were all relevant to the issues involved, I should still maintain that they would be quite inadequate to support the gigantic theoretical superstructure which Darwin endeavours to place upon them.

Not that a theory is necessarily untrue, merely because there is no evidence to support it. For years, there was no evidence to support the idea that the earth travelled around the sun, and not the sun around the earth, but the theory was true nevertheless. But until the theory was established by evidence, or at any rate by its inherent probability, it was nothing more than an idle dream.

It has always been a mystery to myself—it may be that my brain has not undergone sufficient modification by variation to enable me sufficiently to appreciate the situation—how such great thinkers, and reasoners as Professor Huxley, Tyndall, and Wallace, to say nothing of a host of others, could assert so confidently as they did that the evidence in support of Darwin's contention was overwhelming. To my mind the evidence as exhibited in the "Origin of Species" and "The Descent of Man" overwhelms nothing but the theory itself. The "Origin of Species" is itself the severest blow that the theory of "Natural Selection" has ever experienced. It seems almost sacrilege to harbour such a thought in the Temple of Science, even to whisper it, still less to write it down, but I sometimes wonder whether the above learned professors ever really read the "Origin of Species" at all.

There appears to have got abroad in some quarters the very erroneous impression, that Darwin was a mere patient and laborious student of nature, who was concerned chiefly with facts, was rather indifferent as to theory, and inclined to let the facts speak for themselves. The facts, were everything to him, the theory a matter of indifference. But the " Origin of Species " quite disposes of this notion. It is highly contentious and argumentative from the first page to the last, and Darwin is his own most strenuous advocate.

But facts are stubborn things and refuse to be driven. Darwin and his facts remind one of a drover and his pigs. Everyone must have observed what difficulty a drover sometimes experiences in getting his pigs through a gate. They are unaccommodating and perverse, they go beyond the gate, behind it, they hark back, jostle together, and tumble into the opposite hedge. They take every turn but the right one.

And so it is with Darwin and his facts, reason, amplify them, and manipulate them, as he will, he can never get them through his theoretical gate.

I will only give two instances here to show at once that I do not speak altogether without warrant—

INTRODUCTION 13

and they are by no means the most intractable and recalcitrant set of facts with which Darwin has to contend—to illustrate what I mean by unaccommodating facts—which Darwin with all his ingenuity cannot bend to his will. Take the question of Species. What is Species? Darwin, it will be remembered, in the earlier part of his career was firmly convinced of the immutability and stability of Species; it was only later on when his law of Natural Selection had to be established at all costs, that he was converted to the idea that Species were mutable and interchangeable.

Now, to say the least of it, it is a remarkable fact that Darwin nowhere gives a clear definition of what he means by Species. It is true that he here and there loosely describes it, and gives what he considers some of its essential attributes. But he frequently uses the word interchangeably with "varieties." The distinction he draws between such words as "orders," "genus," "families," and so on, are mere arbitrary classifications, and their meaning varies with different naturalists, but there is never any real or vital line of demarcation, whereas the true definition is close at hand.

A "Species" is "any set of living organisms that refuses to interbreed with any other set of living organisms." It is an incontrovertible fact, that there are not merely two, or three, but thousands of such sets of organisms that refuse to interbreed, and the more distant they are from one another in the scale of organic life, the more impossible is it for them to intermingle.

This fact simply cannot be got over, it is within the common knowledge of humanity through all historic time. All breeders know it, and everyone however slightly acquainted with animal life. Take, for instance, the case of the horse and the donkey, animals, be it remembered, very nearly allied and both belonging to the order " *Equidæ.*" It is true they will produce offspring, but there it stops; the mule is banned with sterility and can never propagate its kind except with the original stock.

Darwin endeavours to get over this difficulty, but the evidence he is able to produce in its support, is so insignificant as to be absolutely worthless.

Nature, for obvious reasons, has placed her barrier against promiscuous intercourse between species; and why Darwin objects to the barrier and endeavours to get rid of it is this. It points to the fact that all species have an ancestry of their own, an independent and original progenitor, and are not all descended from a single and common " stirps," and if that is the case Darwin's theory of a common ancestor, and a single centre of creation, as against multiple ancestors, and multiple centres of creation, falls at once to the ground. It is fatal to his whole theory.

Take one more illustration, the case of man himself. It must be remembered that the Law of " Natural Selection " operates on and affects all

INTRODUCTION 15

organic life, from the gyrations of the rotifera in the village pond, right up to the finest, the most subtle, and most sensitive emanations, of the brain of man. Natural Selection is the instrument—according to Darwin—that directs and gives permanence to the various molecular actions and reactions acted on by pressures, some physical, some chemical, some electric, which, according to science are the agents that give vitality and expression to the brain.

But there is at any rate one vast distinction—one only among many—one great gulf fixed, between man and the rest of organic life. Man is a self-improving organism, no other organism is. Every other organism is the mere sport of nature, at the mercy of environment, a mere physical puppet, incapable of controlling its surroundings, still less the great laws of Nature that gave it life. But man is not. Man is capable by his own unaided exertions, of almost limitless expansion and advance. No other organism ever improves even with the assistance of the educating and fostering hand of man himself. Here and there they may appear to do so, certain of their functions may appear to do so, but there is no, so to speak, inner or appreciable advance along the whole line of their being.

Take the case of the dog. The intelligence of the domestic dog is not a bit above that of the wild dog, its progenitor, notwithstanding its long association with man. It seems incredible that with this deep line of cleavage between man and all other organisms, to say nothing of many others —almost equally deep and remarkable,—that they should both belong to a common stock and owe their origin to a single progenitor.

It is essential to Darwin's theory, and he is quite aware of it to prove that this is the case, but his efforts to do so are quite unavailing, and the evidence he adduces in the " Descent of Man " is weak and inefficient in the extreme. He simply has not a shadow of a case. So this is another fatal flaw in the theory, another stubborn fact which, manipulate it as he will, he cannot drive successfully within his theoretical gate.

It is a pity Darwin did not leave theory alone altogether, a theory which, let scientific men argue as they will, can never get beyond the region of the purest conjecture. More men, more institutions, and more communities have been wrecked by a blind adhesion to theory, than this world dreams of. But perhaps someone will say: " Well, but no one ever supposed this theory to be anything more than a speculation," but men no less eminent than Huxley, Tyndall, and Wallace, and a host of others only less illustrious than themselves, have asserted, and some of them do still assert, that this theory is established by almost irrefragable evidence, that it will stand the test of time and is founded on a basis almost as secure as the Law of Gravitation itself.

INTRODUCTION

To say the least of it, it inculcates a very downgrade biology, which carries with it its own condemnation.

There are many theories that have been invaluable instruments in promoting the intelligence, the prosperity, and the happiness of man. But this cannot be said of Darwin's theory of Natural Selection, even if it were true, which is highly improbable. It serves no good end, and is disastrous in its teachings to the higher interests of the race. It degrades man and places him on no higher level than the brute creation.

Man, according to Darwin, appears on this earth merely to struggle for existence, to keep his place in the ranks if he can, to procure himself a mate, to propagate his kind, and when the specialisation of his functions and those of his race are complete he, like all other organisms, disappears for ever, he goes down into the pit, and with him his thoughts perish. To say the least of it, that is not a very encouraging or cheering Gospel, with which to console suffering humanity.

If that were all, one wonders why Darwin was ever at the trouble of writing the " Origin of Species " at all.

But it is too late in the day to attack Darwin generally or merely on philosophic grounds. The ball of assertion and negation has been banded backward and forward long enough. It is impossible to prove a negative, especially a negative twenty million years old. Darwin's idea of the origin of things may be true. My contention is that there is no evidence to prove it. At any rate, it is not to be discovered either in the "Origin of Species" or the "Descent of Man."

There is an old legal maxim, "Dolus latet in generalibus"—there are snares, and pitfalls, in generalisations. So I purpose here to leave generalities largely alone, and to discuss some of Darwin's leading propositions, by means of which he endeavours to establish his theory of Natural Selection.

To adopt any other method with so powerful, so observant, and so close a reasoner as Darwin, would be to court disaster and expose oneself to ridicule; and for this reason it has been necessary for me to quote Darwin very largely, otherwise I should lay myself open to the charge of having either misread, distorted, or misrepresented his views. I am not consciously aware of being guilty of any of these three. I have wrenched no text from its context, neither have I expanded his meaning in one direction or narrowed it in another, merely for the purpose of controversial accommodation.

The first chapter is devoted to a short preliminary survey of the situation; and some remarks on the thoughts of the ancients on the subject and how matters stood in the period immediately preceding the appearance of Darwin himself. The second and third chapters discuss Darwin's theory and a suggested alternative hypothesis. In the subsequent chapters, I come to close quarters with the leading features of Darwin's hypothesis, and the concluding chapter is devoted rather to the philosophical aspect of the case, and to some general reflections, which naturally arise, and suggest themselves to the mind, after a close perusal of his works.

For if Darwin's contention is true, then the horizon for man both individually, and as a race, is bounded by this life; for him, and for it, there is no hereafter. Materialistic logic can, I admit, make out a powerful argument for that view. But logic is not everything. And even the strong chains of a mathematical demonstration, if such demonstration were possible, would not be sufficiently powerful to fetter for all time, still less to extinguish for ever, the higher aspirations, and ultimate hopes of the race of man.

In this case as in all others a chain is no stronger than its weakest link. In this chain there are many weak links and some of them are absent altogether. Our old friend the monkey is only one of innumerable missing links, which it is necessary to make good, if this long chain reaching through twenty million years is to preserve an unbroken continuity.

CHAPTER II

PRELIMINARY OBSERVATIONS

BEFORE proceeding to discuss Darwin and the evolutionists, it is necessary to clear the ground by reflecting a little on the origin of things. There are only two hypotheses open as to the origin of matter and of life. One is that all matter and all life, at some infinitely remote period of time, were brought into existence out of nothing, by the fiat of an Omnipotent Creator. The other is, that all matter, and all life, have existed from all eternity, and that they will exist to all eternity, and that both alike are indestructible. That their quantity can never be increased, and can never be diminished. I believe I am right in saying, that this latter hypothesis, is the one that the majority of scientific men of the present day are really inclined to, however much for appearances' sake they may endeavour to conceal it. It was certainly the undisguised opinion of Tyndall, and Huxley, if not of Darwin himself. Though Darwin, as far as I am aware of, never quite commits himself to so bald a statement of the case But as regards this latter theory there is a qualifying factor, which must never be lost sight of; that man is tethered to his own intellect, and that beyond that he cannot go, and the true value of his own intellect he is quite incapable of appraising. Relatively as regards his surroundings his estimate of it may be true, but as regards absolute and eternal things, such as " time " and " space," he may be wrong about them altogether. All knowledge is purely relative to the medium of the organism through which it passes, whether that medium be the brain of man, or the brain of a lower organism. Of course that argument tells equally against creative power; but at least we can cry " quits " and are even with the materialists.

But further than this, the possibility of spontaneous generation has been ruled out of court altogether; and by spontaneous generation I suppose is meant, the creation of a living organism, without an antecedent living organism to produce it. Both Tyndall, and Pasteur, conclusively proved, at any rate to their own satisfaction, by the most refined chemical experiments that were in their day available, that no evidence was forthcoming to give countenance to this method of creation. So man denies to Nature this power of spontaneous generation; and yet so strange a thing is man, that at this present time some of the ablest of living chemists are exerting all their ingenuity, and straining every nerve, aided by all the resources of chemical manipulation, to bring about the very result which they refuse to Nature, the power to perform; Nature, a far subtler chemist, and a far more skilful manipulator than any chemist of them all.

But the most probable explanation of the origin of organic life on the earth is, that every particle of matter of which the earth is composed, ever since the earth took on a separate existence, and commenced its course in space as a satellite of the sun, has been animated with some life, however elusive, however obscure, however refined, however incapable of detection by the human mind, or inconceivable by the human imagination, and that this particle of matter with its attendant life, only required a favourable environment, the approximation of chemical ingredients adjusted to a nicety, in an atmosphere, temperature, and locality favourable to the operation, to enable it to pass from the inorganic to the organic stage. But what is this method but the method of our old friend " spontaneous generation."

So here the scientists have apparently transfixed us on the horns of dilemma, from which there is no conceivable avenue of escape. For if there was a time, and a very prolonged time too, and the majority of scientific men maintain that there was, when, due to physical causes, organic life was an impossibility on this earth, and if organic life could never have been created or spontaneously generated, the whole argument is a *reductio ad absurdum* of the most ridiculous kind.

As a matter of fact, the speculations of men of

PRELIMINARY OBSERVATIONS

science on ultimate things, are no more to be trusted than those of the theologian. The opinions of the greatest of them, on the most momentous questions, in every department of scientific activity, vary and change from generation to generation. The Dreadnoughts created in one age are speedily displaced, and cast upon the scrap-heap; the scientific idol of one era, is not infrequently treated by its successors almost with scorn, and regarded as a sort of robust but misguided infant in the intellectual childhood of the world.

To give an instance of what I mean: until quite recently the nebulous theory and the igneous cooling down of the earth after its final detachment from still greater masses of combustible material, were regarded as axiomatic and indisputable propositions.

But there are already signs of a change, there are murmurs in the camp, a new and different theory is being advanced that, of a little earth growing up on what is called a meteoritic hypothesis. Physical theories are undergoing a change. Kelvin and Arrhenius are now inclined to believe that the cooling down of the hot crust of the earth was not a long process but an unexpectedly rapid one. Well may Professor Henry Armstrong exclaim in recent publication: "After all we scientific workers like women are the victims of fashion: at one time we wear dissociated ions, at another electrons: and we are always loth to don rational clothing: some fixed belief we must have manufactured for us : we are high or low church, of this or that degree of nonconformity, according to the school in which we are brought up—but the agnostic is always rare among us, and of late years the critic has been taboo."

When one contemplates these mysteries, such as man's origin, purpose, and destiny, the human mind reels beneath the strain. The endeavour to grasp the meaning of a million years even from a purely mathematical point of view, almost overwhelms the imagination; but when one takes this million years, or as many of them as you will—for to science a million years is but as yesterday—and endeavours to utilise it as a thread by which to link together all down the ages the whole process of organic life, and this is a task that Darwin has set himself, at any rate in outline, to perform, one stands amazed at the audacity of the undertaking. My meaning is that to endeavour to realise a million by its concrete application in a set of living pictures, is a far greater strain on the understanding than the abstract idea of a million itself.

After all what is man, what is man's brain, and what its value, that he should venture upon such mysteries as these!

The brain of man we have been recently informed is largely composed of proteids, in its turn made up of compounds known as " amino acids," which are brought into self-consciousness by some mysterious process called " reflex action." That may be true, it sounds well enough; but there is still and ever will be a "*tertium quid*" that no one ever has been, or ever will be able satisfactorily to account for. " You have not gained a real height nor are you nearer to the light, because the scale is infinite."

It is as plausible a speculation as are many of those of scientific men, that there are beings somewhere in space as far surpassing man in understanding and knowledge, as the brain of man surpasses that of the tadpole in the neighbouring pond.

Supposing the Newtons, the Darwins, and Huxleys among the tadpoles in this neighbouring pond were to set themselves to write a work on the origin, destiny, and nature of man, I should imagine that when this work was brought up to mankind for presentation it would be received with a smile of credulity. Mankind would probably detect errors here and there. So, likewise, if our Newtons, Darwins, and Huxleys were to present their works to those beings as far above themselves as they are above the tadpoles, their works would meet with a very similar reception.

The old theory of creation as propounded in the Book of Genesis, can possibly no longer be very satisfactorily maintained. Poetry and mythology is its proper department and to that department it must be relegated :—

" The Book of Genesis, says Professor Tyndall, has no voice in scientific questions. To the grasp of geology, which it resisted for a time, it at length yielded like potter's clay; its authority as a system of cosmogony being discredited on all hands by the abandonment of the obvious meaning of its writer. It is a poem, not a scientific treatise. In the former aspect it is for ever beautiful: in the latter aspect it has been and will continue purely obstructive and hurtful."

I suppose no educated man in these days, who is even remotely cognisant of the great and divergent thoughts, that are stirring humanity to its depths, unless caught young and when the brain is most plastic and impressionable, and brought up in the most rigid and secluded sect of ecclesiastical thought, could really give credence to the story, that some visible or invisible arms came down from the skies, moulded man and woman like a potter out of the clay, breathed into this clay the breath of life, and gave them the lease of everlasting life, conditional on good behaviour, in some fairy land of the poetic imagination.

The idea is incredible and not to be entertained. But at the same time, though in many respects inaccurate and erring, it is extraordinary how nearly in other respects the account given in the Book of Genesis approximates to the views of modern thought and even to the Darwinian theory of evolution. Man, we are told, was taken out of the dust, or, in scientific phraseology, evolved from some lower organism; the created groups indicated are few;

and the sequence of their production with some few material discrepancies might satisfy even Darwin himself.

Perhaps the most remarkable text relative to this account to be found in the Book of Genesis, and one that may even yet prove of significance to mankind, is: "But of the tree of the knowledge of good and evil thou shalt not eat of it."

Oh this tree of knowledge! Is it not after all rather weary and unprofitable work to be for ever plucking the apples, however enticing, from its inexhaustible and perennial stem? To be for ever "climbing up the climbing seas," to be for ever ascending the staircase of a temple that has no end and the pinnacle of which is for ever unattainable. To some minds the very thought of it is a burden unendurable. In science there is no finality. And is it not this craving for finality that gives religion her chief charm, and is one of her most powerful sanctions!

But there is no suppressing or silencing the curiosity of the human mind. Onward and upward, is its motto, and onward and upward, it will go. Therefore being there, it must be there for some good purpose, and to subserve some divine end. So man will go on until his race is swept away, or until some unexpected development entirely alters the constitution of his brain, and with it his whole mental outlook.

But how about the ancients; had they any thoughts on these things; and have they contributed in any way to our enlightenment? As a matter of fact, there were some few of them who had some definite and distinct scientific conceptions. One at any rate among them, the great mathematician Democritus, not merely made a guess at it, but actually formulated the atomic theory in a way that would have satisfied a modern chemist. Empedocles, a man of more poetic nature, declared that the atoms experienced love and hate, to account for their combination and separation. And as matter is being run now so closely into life and thought, perhaps he was not so very far from the truth; but he went further than this and asserted that it lay in the very nature of suitable atomic combinations to maintain themselves, while unfit combinations must rapidly disappear. Here we have a man anticipating by two thousand years the almost identical doctrine of Darwin's "Natural Selection."

And what about Aristotle, that master mind that dominated the world, and directed human thought long after his ideas in the scientific direction were exploded? Aristotle's "Ethics" may be immortal, but his conceptions of natural science were radically unsound. He was, as Professor Tyndall points out, a great systematizer and a great collector, but he was not possessed of the true scientific insight and intuition which enables a mind to knit together the concrete knowledge he amassed with appropriate abstract conceptions. His method of reasoning was in some directions right, and in others

PRELIMINARY OBSERVATIONS 29

entirely mistaken. He all too frequently substituted words for facts. He made the universe a closed sphere, in the centre of which he fixed the earth, proving to his own satisfaction that no other universe was possible, and it required the scientific imagination of a Bacon in one direction, and the scientific knowledge of Copernicus in the other, to burst the bonds that had so long held Europe in bondage.

And to a student of history, and to one who can read the progress of human thought aright, this tardy breaking away from preconceived ideas is not to be wondered at, still less to be despised. It is a tribute to the stability and innate reverence of the human mind. When we reflect on the immense power and tenacity that preconceived ideas, inherited and inculcated from generation to generation, imbedded in the mind at its most plastic and receptive stage, exercise on the best and truest understandings, we shall appreciate, and not till then, what a long process of disintegration must be gone through, before the new solvent has done its work, and the last snap occurs which separates finally the old thoughts from the new. It requires a great, a powerful, one might add an almost evil mind to inflict the final stroke.

Evil is a strong word perhaps, but I use it advisedly, for does not a feeling of shame, nay almost of treachery, pass over the mind, when at the voice of the discoverer and the pioneer a man deserts for ever the old ways for the new. Let us alone, let us alone, we are happy where we are, begone and enjoy your Land of Promise all alone! Is not that the feeling a man experiences, when at the voice of truth he turns his back upon the past, and plunges into the unknown waters of speculation? And yet the step seems inevitable, for the law of change is greater, even than the law of love. We know what it takes to make a bird forsake her brood, she would die rather than desert them. Yet so powerful is this law of change, that when the period of migration comes again, the impulse is irresistible; go she must, and go she does, and her offspring are left to perish.

But how about Darwin's immediate predecessors! Was the idea of evolution peculiarly Darwin's own, or was he anticipated in thought by any of his contemporaries! The idea of evolution generally as a workable hypothesis of the progression of all organic life was, as Darwin candidly admits, familiar to many minds besides his own. Indeed, he enumerates a list of them in his " Origin of Species," and himself confesses that he had appropriated the idea of the " Survival of the Fittest " and the " Struggle for Existence " from Malthus, and applied the theory of Malthus to the whole of organic life. On page forty-seven of his " Origin of Species " he says :—

" It is the doctrine of Malthus applied with manifold force to the whole animal and vegetable kingdoms : for in this case there can be no artificial

PRELIMINARY OBSERVATIONS

increase of food and no prudential restraint from marriage. Although some species may be now increasing, more or less rapidly, in numbers, all cannot do so, for the world would not hold them."

Of course the idea of evolution, as popularly understood, is a self-evident truism, and needed no philosopher to enunciate and drive home the fact. So again with the doctrine of the "Survival of the Fittest." If Nature thinks a man fit to survive he does, and if she does not, he dies. Professor Wallace, a contemporary of Darwin's, and a coadjutor, and discoverer, with Darwin himself of the idea of "Natural Selection," confesses as much, for in an article on the "World of Life" in the March number for 1909, he says: "The theory of 'Natural Selection,' commonly called 'Darwinianism,' is one of the most simple and easy of comprehension in the whole range of science, yet after fifty years of continuous exposition and study, there is perhaps none that is so widely and persistently misunderstood."

. . . . .

The struggle for existence, and the survival of the fittest, then, are self-evident truisms; but Darwin's theory of "Natural Selection," which is the method, according to Darwin, that Nature has selected to work out her process of evolution, though a truism in one sense, is in another sense, as I shall presently endeavour to show, hardly fit, from any evidence that there is to support it, to rank even as a plausible hypothesis, unless Darwin means nothing more by it than that Nature preserves what is worthy of preservation. This seems a bold assertion, but I hope before this essay is concluded to make good my contention.

It must always be remembered that the survival of the fittest, does not necessarily mean the survival of the best; quite the contrary: let me show what I mean by illustration. If you could have taken, say, Sir Isaac Newton and set him down in the cannibal islands, there is a high probability that Sir Isaac would have perished, and the cannibals survived, and why? not because the cannibals were higher and better beings than Sir Isaac, more useful to the race, or fitter members of society, but because for the immediate environment, the particular locality, and the surrounding circumstances, the cannibals were more in harmony with Nature and with Nature's laws. So Nature selects the cannibals and rejects Sir Isaac. The latter perishes, and the former survive.

Or to give another instance. Let us suppose that the celebrated billiard player Stevenson elects to play a billiard match with some accomplished amateur. It is admitted on all hands that Stevenson is generally a far better and fitter player than his opponent; but owing possibly to some momentary break down in Stevenson's nervous system, the usual correlation between his hand and eye will not work, the light is bad, the table does not suit him, or his opponent is more lucky, and Stevenson loses the game. And why, because his opponent is the fittest for this particular occasion, and this particular game. The amateur survives, and Stevenson disappears.

But let no man flatter himself that he survives on account of some innate superiority of himself to his fellows. Quite the contrary, very frequently, the superior beings perish all round, while the inferior remain to propagate their kind. One man may meet with what we call, and rightly so, an accident—though nature, if we could only see far back enough into space and time, knows of no such thing as accident. With one, a mere slip of the foot may turn the scale, another may have to contend not only with his fellow-men, but with other and hostile groups of organic nature, at one and the same time; a third may succumb to the forces of the atmosphere, or climatic conditions, from all of which others are exempt: but nature heeds not, the one set of men are chosen, and the other left. All down our lives, and during every instant of our lives, we survive as long as we do, merely because, for some inscrutable reason, nature requires us, and not another, however useless and even hurtful our existence may appear.

And here, at the commencement of the tale, it may not be altogether out of place to take a glance at the man Darwin himself. What manner of man was he, what his education, and what his mental equipment?—not perhaps for the task he set himself to perform, for at the outset apparently he had no clear ideas as to where his natural proclivities would lead him, but for the great work that he ultimately accomplished.

As far as educational evidences go—though they do not count for much—he does not appear to have been naturally gifted with an intellect or a mind much above the average of his fellows. But he was one of those men who have a strong bent towards the study of nature, who are inquisitive and curious about her ways, and are always endeavouring to unravel, classify, and account for her actions, whenever, and wherever, they may occur. This love of nature probably began with Darwin as a hobby, and grew into the habit and occupation of a lifetime, on which he concentrated his whole mind and his great powers of observation. Such men in their beginnings at any rate are common all the world over. Generally one or more of them are to be found in every school, in every village, and in every community; but the cares of this life, if not the deceitfulness of riches, choke most of them off, and they bring no fruit in this particular direction to perfection. Moreover, Darwin was possessed of powers of intense, and continuous application, such as few men possess, and fewer still whose nervous system will admit of the strain. He had an intimate and first-hand acquaintance with almost every fact that he recounts; he had read deeply and in many languages, most of the works that had any bearing on his subject; he always drew from the most reliable authorities, and was the last man to be hoodwinked by untrustworthy information. Add to these qualities a dignity that never deserted him, and a humility that was almost sublime, and one understands how at last Darwin had greatness thrust upon him, and was acclaimed as one of the great ones of the race. He pursued, whether knowingly or unknowingly, the inductive method, which is peculiarly the right method of reasoning to pursue, in a subject like his own, that is to say he reasons from the particular to the universal, and not from the universal to the particular. The hypothesis which he afterwards launched upon the world, only dawned upon him as an explanation of the working of certain facts which he could not otherwise account for. He did not of set purpose invent an hypothesis, and then inflate it with all sorts of irrelevant matter to give it an imposing appearance. He was, moreover, a man of noble and generous instinct: science never seemed to have had on him that baneful effect that it has on meaner minds, of hardening him into a groove of moral scientific coldness, and precision, leading first to indifference, and ending in cruelty. Humanity at large owes Darwin a debt of gratitude for the following noble passage, taken from his work on " The Descent of Man " :—

" The aid which we feel impelled to give the helpless is mainly an incidental result of the instinct of sympathy, which was originally acquired as part of the social instincts, but subsequently rendered in the manner previously indicated, more tender and more widely diffused. Nor could we check our sympathy, even at the urging of hard reason, without deterioration of the noblest part of our nature. The Surgeon may harden himself whilst performing an operation, for he knows that he is acting for the good of his patient: but if we were intentionally to neglect the weak and helpless, it could only be for a contingent benefit, with an overwhelming present ' evil.' "

How different is that sentiment to those expressed by many of our new philosophers. Darwin, had he turned his powers in that direction, would have been as great a moral philosopher as he was a naturalist. To destroy another you degrade yourself, and the physical convenience or ease thereby obtained is not commensurate with the moral loss.

As a writer, when he is sure of his ground and master of the situation, his style is easy, graceful, and entertaining; but when he sees adverse theories, and stubborn facts looming up against him, it becomes turgid, and involved, and not infrequently obscure. It may be said to vary in the inverse ratio of the complexity of the subject that he has under discussion. Darwin's was perhaps not quite the mind to put tersely or unravel with lucidity any abstruse, or complicated piece of reasoning. It is amusing to watch him when in difficulties. He reminds one of some old hound when baffled and at a loss for the scent. One can almost hear alternately his grunts of disappointment, and bays of hope. When he hears the crack of the whip of reason, he is off in one direction, and back in another. He points, he pauses, he hesitates, he covers the ground again and again, and when finally baffled, and unable to run his quarry to earth, he picks up another scent and is off again.

As to the greatness of his personality, only those who knew him are entitled to speak: that he was great as a naturalist is conceded by all; but that he was great as a discoverer is open to question, and posterity will probably deny him the award.

CHAPTER III

DARWIN'S THEORY. WHAT IS IT!

THE main outlines of Darwin's theory may be briefly summarised in the following four propositions :—

(1) All organic life—that is all life that is capable of reproducing its kind—that lives now or ever has lived on the earth, of whatever nature, from the lowest protozoa to the highest mammal, owes its origin to one common ancestor, in a single locality, and that this common ancestor consisted of a gelatinous substance, called by the chemists a protoplasm chiefly consisting of proteids.

(2) That the development, and numerous ramifications of the progeny of this common ancestor, owe their evolution through the ages, chiefly to the agency of the Struggle for Existence, and that this agent was the great promoter and agent of variation.

(3) Natural Selection, which is a tendency in nature to preserve favourable variations in the individual and species.

(4) Sexual Selection, when acted on by Natural Selection, aided by the attractions of what Darwin calls secondary sexual characteristics.

Now, in the above four propositions are to be found what is called Darwin's theory of evolution, and on

DARWIN'S THEORY. WHAT IS IT! 39

which his great reputation, not as a naturalist, but a discoverer, has been built up.

But it is necessary to criticise and expand somewhat fully these four propositions, as without a right understanding and proper grasp of their true meaning and significance the reader will never properly appreciate either the strength or weakness of Darwin's contention.

Perhaps I shall best bring home to the mind of the reader what Darwin means, when he says that all organic life has a common progenitor, by the method of illustration. Let us then imagine a pyramid whose apex is A, and the area of its foundation B, C, D, E. A is the common ancestor, and on the floor of the pyramid stands all organic life as we see it at this hour, of whatever that life consists, from the lowest protozoa to the highest mammal, whether insect life, plant life, the life of fish, birds, or mammals. Draw down from the apex A, inclined lines to every class of living organisms on the floor, and let every one of those inclined lines represent a genealogical tree with collateral branches, reaching down in every direction to the classes and variations below. That gives, I trust, a vivid picture of how, according to Darwin, all life, to speak metaphorically, has issued from a common womb. Or to start at the base and work upwards, if you only continue the process long enough, that is anything under one hundred million years, all life will meet again, and discover its origin in A, the apex of the pyramid.

Now, to be perfectly fair to Darwin, as he approaches very closely to A he hesitates and stops short: he only dare complete his journey by leaning on the uncertain, and dangerous arm of analogy.

> "Analogy would lead me one step further, namely to the belief that all animals and plants are descended from some one proto-type. But analogy may be a deceitful guide. Nevertheless all things living have much in common, in their chemical composition, their cellular structure, their laws of growth, and their liability to injurious influences."

It has been finely said that "Providence hangs great weights on very thin wires!" Well, Omnipotence itself could hardly make Darwin's extremely attenuated thread support the superstructure he endeavours to place upon it. As a matter of fact this thread snaps and gives way all along the line, as I shall presently endeavour to show.

And now to turn to the second point, "Evolution" and the "Struggle for Existence." Let us consider for a moment this question of Evolution generally, without reference to Darwin's particular definition. Regarded from a scientific and philosophic point of view, both Matter and Life are eternal; that, is they never had a beginning and will never have an end; the quantity of each is never increased and never detracted from. So what happens when a child is born into the world? The

DARWIN'S THEORY. WHAT IS IT! 41

parents do not, strictly speaking, create the child, that is they are not the authors of the life and matter of which the child consists, for these constituents already pre-existed: they are merely the channels of a new combination.

The parents are no more the authors of the child than the tailor is the creator of the material out of which a suit of clothes is made. The tailor is the creator of the suit but not of the material. But the child grows and increases. It has been calculated that a full-grown man is three million times as heavy as the seed from which he sprang. Then surely some one will say the matter of the Universe has been added to. Not at all! Precisely as the child increases so does the surrounding matter from which it draws its weight and sustenance decrease. And so the child lives and grows till it reaches its meridian, and then first in this direction, and then in that, the combination begins to break up and disappear, till the matter rises up and returns to its place, and the spirit also goes its way.

Now the foregoing is, I think, a very good illustration of what is understood by evolution generally. The law is everywhere present, and everywhere whole, always, and for ever in operation. I should prefer to call it the law of "Change," which every observant and educated man must long ago have discovered for himself, without the illuminating assistance of any philosopher whatever.

It is a true, but paradoxical utterance, that there

is nothing new under the sun. Regarding nature from the standpoint of unity the saying is true. But in that unity there is a multiplicity and inexhaustible variety, presenting ever fresh and shifting combinations. The combinations and colouring formed by the kaleidoscope of nature are as delicate, as beautiful, as varied, and as infinite, as is nature herself.

But I am digressing. The Evolution of Darwin is brought about by the Struggle for Existence. It was the theory of Malthus that the food-supply regulated the life-supply. Malthus was the man to broach the idea, but applied it only to mankind. Darwin took over his theory and applied it to all organic life. Now, as all creation, if given a free hand and relieved from the pressure of external dangers and cares, tends to multiply exceedingly, and with extraordinary rapidity, unless perpetually restrained by innumerable checks, the whole world would soon be overrun and overstocked. Man is a slow-breeding animal, one of the slowest on the earth; yet by a very simple sum in arithmetic it can easily be shown that from a single pair, in twenty generations, no less than a million direct descendants can be produced. Or again, take the case of the elephant, the slowest breeder of all known animals: yet Darwin has computed that its minimum rate of increase, after a period of seven hundred and forty years, would be nearly nineteen million elephants, descended from the first pair.

Now the greatest of all checks on this increase,

though of course there are other factors to be taken into account, is the Struggle for Existence, brought about by the insufficiency of food to maintain so inexhaustible a multitude. Not that the struggle need be a physical or bloody one, it very rarely is; for when the food-supply falls short in any large area, such as our Indian peninsula, the majority die, either of starvation, inanition, or their results, and the struggle is most severe, and the competition most keen, not between one class of organic life and another but between the members of each class "*inter se.*"

The struggle is always more severe between species of the same genus if they come into competition than between species of different genera.

But not to misinterpret or misrepresent Darwin in any way, it may be best to give his own definition of what he means by the Struggle for Existence; though his definitions are not always very lucid or precise, and it must be confessed that his style, in the "Origin of Species" is at times, at any rate, very laboured, and involved, and has the appearance of being written in a hurry.

"I should premise—he says—that I use this term in a large and metaphorical sense, including dependence of one being on another and including which is more important not only the life of the individual, but success in leaving progeny. Two canine animals in a time of dearth, may be truly said to struggle with each other which shall get food and live. But a plant on the edge of a desert is said to struggle for life against the drought, though more properly it should be said to be dependent on the moisture. A plant which annually produces a thousand seeds of which only one on an average comes to maturity, may be more truly said to struggle with the plants of the same and other kinds which already clothe the ground. The mistletoe is dependent on the apple, and a few other trees, but can only in a far-fetched sense be said to struggle with these trees, for if too many of these parasites grow on the same tree, it languishes and dies. But several seedling mistletoes, growing close together on the same branch, may more truly be said to struggle with each other. As the mistletoe is disseminated by birds, its existence depends on them: and it may metaphorically be said to struggle with other fruit-bearing plants, in tempting the birds to devour and thus disseminate its seeds. In these several senses, which pass into each other, I use for convenience' sake the general term of 'Struggle for Existence.' "

And this struggle, he adds, inevitably follows from the high rate at which all organic beings tend to increase.

Now it cannot be too often insisted on that this theory of the Struggle for Existence is a thing apart, and not Darwin's peculiar theory at all. Darwin merely uses it as the "corpus," to which he applies his theory, or the field of operation on which his theory acts. The term "Struggle for Existence" is

DARWIN'S THEORY. WHAT IS IT! 45

not synonymous with the term "Natural Selection," but Darwin does use the term "Natural Selection" as synonymous with the term "Survival of the Fittest," for he says—

"I have called this principle, by which each slight variation if useful, is preserved, by the term Natural Selection, in order to mark its relation to man's power of selection. But the expression often used by Mr Herbert Spencer of the 'Survival of the Fittest' is more accurate, and is sometimes equally convenient."

Now what is Darwin's theory of Natural Selection as stated in its naked simplicity! And here it is necessary to proceed with great caution and accuracy, and to let Darwin speak for himself.

"Can it then be thought impossible, seeing that variations useful to man have undoubtedly occurred, that other variations useful in some way to each being in the great and complex battle of life, should occur in the course of many generations? If such do occur, can we doubt (remembering that many more individuals are born than can possibly survive) that individuals having any advantage, however slight over others, would have the best chance of surviving and of procreating their kind? On the other hand we may feel sure that any variation in the least degree injurious would be rigidly destroyed. This preservation of favourable individual differences and variations, and the destruction of those which are injurious, I have called 'Natural Selection' or the 'Survival of the Fittest.' And again :—

"Several writers have misapprehended or objected to the term Natural Selection. Some have even imagined that natural selection induces variability, *whereas it implies only the preservation of such variations as arise and are beneficial* to the being under its conditions of life."

So, strictly speaking, Darwin's theory is nothing more than the method by which evolution works, or a preservative agent of the innumerable favourable variations which the struggle for existence induces. Though it is difficult precisely to discover whether in the first instance Darwin imagines the variation to be a condition precedent, or subsequent, to the struggle for existence : but when once the variations are set in motion they become alternately conditions precedent, and subsequent to the struggle for existence in the various species. On page forty-five of the "Origin of Species," he tells us that *the struggle for existence—not Natural Selection—*induces the variations.

"Again it may be asked, how it is that varieties, which I have called incipient species, become ultimately converted into good and distinct species, which in most cases obviously differ from each other far more than do the varieties of the same species? How do those groups of species, which constitute what are called distinct

DARWIN'S THEORY. WHAT IS IT! 47

genera, and which differ from each other more than do the species of the same genus arise? All these results follow from the struggle for life. Owing to this struggle, variations, however slight and from whatever cause proceeding if they be in any degree profitable to the individuals of a species—will tend to the preservation of the individuals, and will be generally inherited by the offspring."

Quite so, but when and how did these struggles and variations have their origin!

"Looking to the first dawn of life, when all organic beings, as we may believe, presented the simplest structure, how it has been asked, could the first steps in the advancement or differentiation of parts have arisen? Mr Herbert Spencer would probably answer that, as soon as simple unicellular organism came by growth or division to be compounded of several cells, or became attached to any supporting surface, that—homologues—units of any order become differentiated in proportion as their relations to incident forces become different."

The above quotation is couched in somewhat metaphysical language, and its meaning is in consequence a little difficult and hard to understand.

Probably, what Herbert Spencer really means is this: there are two factors to be taken into account, the creature, and the medium in which it lives, or, as it is sometimes expressed, the organism, and its environment. Mr Spencer's principle is that between these two factors there is incessant interaction. The organism is played upon by the environment, and modified to suit its requirements. There is a continual adjustment between internal and external relations.

Not a very satisfactory vantage ground from which Darwin starts off on his long journey down the ages: for in the very next sentence he remarks, "But as we have no facts to guide us speculation on the subject is almost useless." And one could add with perfect truth, there are no facts to guide us all down the line.

So then Darwin's great theory comes to this—
"*That there is a tendency in nature to preserve any favourable variation that may appear in the individual or species.*"

Surely a self-evident truism; nature would naturally tend to preserve what is favourable for her own preservation, or she herself would disappear with the species she has created. And his second proposition is like unto it, that a limited supply of food can only support a limited number of beings: again another very self-evident truism. In fact nothing can be made of Darwin's theory whatever unless you work conjointly the two above propositions. They cannot be dissociated, for the one is the co-efficient and correlative of the other. But

DARWIN'S THEORY. WHAT IS IT! 49

taken together what is their *modus operandi?* Darwin's contention is that certain favourable varieties appear from time to time, both in the individual and the species, induced by the struggle for existence. That these variations, if favourable, tend to spread among any given species, until they affect the whole class, and the variation becomes constant; the variation conferring on the individuals of the species who possess it, a certain superiority, however slight, which gives them an advantage in the battle of life; so that those not possessed of this variation in the same species, being at a disadvantage, tend to die out and disappear. This process of variation is or may be continued in the species from generation to generation, and age to age, until the cumulative effect, or to use the language of mathematics, the integration of these innumerable differentials, alter the species out of all recognition to its original, and practically create a new species, differing later in external appearances, and even functionally, and organically, according as the modifications are rare, or frequent, limited, or far-reaching.

Now Darwin makes the theory of modification by variation, *i.e.* Natural Selection, the prime, and one might almost say exclusive agent and instrument, in accounting for all the differences, divergencies, and variations, whether structural, functional, organic, or mental, that we see in all created things, whether in insect life, plant life, or whether in the lives of fishes, birds, or mammals, that now cover the face of the whole earth. That all the differences between them, from the meanest protozoa, to the most exalted man, are to be attributed chiefly, indeed almost exclusively, to this one great agent and factor, Natural Selection.

This definition of Natural Selection, "that it is a tendency to preserve what is worth preserving in nature," reminds one of a similar definition in another, and very different field of thought, made by a celebrated writer of the last century, "that there is a tendency or a something that makes for righteousness."

It must be confessed that these tendencies, however attractive they may be, are not very satisfactory prescriptions with which to work out one's salvation, in either biological, or theological life. If I were to go to a job-master, and tell him that I had a long road and a difficult one to travel, and that I wanted a "mount" that had some chance at any rate of taking me to my journey's end, and he told me that he had a splendid animal that had "a tendency to make for something," I am not sure that I should be altogether satisfied with the recommendation.

But why should Darwin pin his faith to this very intricate and attenuated hypothesis to account for all the variations all down the ages, in the whole field of biological life? There are other and far more powerful factors immediately to his hand,

DARWIN'S THEORY. WHAT IS IT! 51

ready to elucidate the whole mystery at once. Darwin is perfectly aware of them, but for some inexplicable reason only known to himself, he treats them as quite subordinate and insignificant agents, mere contributory streams, whose action is slight in comparison with the great volume of the main river of Natural Selection.

I allude, of course, to the great agents of transmission by inheritance, sexual intercourse, the use and disuse of parts, physical conditions, the great geographical changes, and convulsions, which take place periodically on the surface of the globe; the action of climate, and temperature, to say nothing of those of chemistry and light.

Now I maintain that any of these if taken singly, much more so if taken collectively, are sufficient to knock the middle wicket of Darwin's hypothesis clean out of the ground.

Darwin always reminds one of a batsman who has knocked his own wickets down, and been bowled out, stumped out, run out, and caught out, over and over again, and yet refuses to leave the wicket. But how was this! How was Darwin so long enabled to maintain his position and occupy the "pitch" unmolested? Well, it must be remembered that the field of operations was a very large one, that the concourse of people assembled round the boundaries were an ignorant and indiscriminating multitude, hardly even acquainted with the elementary rules of the game. They had heard that

Darwin was a "stayer," and likely to run up a long score. By the fielders, and the bowlers, the umpires were appealed to again and again. But the umpires happened to be, or were a short time ago, Professor Tyndall at one end, and Professor Huxley at the other; they were both of them so enamoured of Darwin's performance that they refused to entertain the appeals, however much insisted upon or well merited. Darwin's performance fell in with their own ideas, and their preconceived opinions, as to what such performances should be. Or did they wilfully—after the manner of Sam Weller, who, in the celebrated trial of Bardell *v.* Pickwick, when appealed to by the judge, if he could see his father in Court, fixed his face steadfastly on the ceiling of the Court and declared he could nowhere discover him, —turn a deaf ear and look the other way? But it is really high time that Darwin and his hypothesis were conducted back to the pavilion. The fresh umpires, Professor Wallace and others, are beginning to shake. There are signs that they have their suspicions, that the bowling is becoming too strong, and that Darwin's legs, impede, rather than his bat advances the progress of the ball.

CHAPTER IV

AN ALTERNATIVE HYPOTHESIS

HAVING stated in the previous chapter, what I conceive to be Darwin's theory of Natural Selection, and made some preliminary criticism on the main principles of his contention, I propose to discuss in this chapter a possible alternative hypothesis which, certainly, has not escaped the notice of Darwin himself, but which he objects to solely, as far as one can ascertain, on the ground that it entails multiplicity of creation.

It must be borne in mind that neither the one theory nor the other, has anything to do with explaining the origin of life.

The mystery of life, still lies hidden, as Darwin himself admits, in profound and impenetrable obscurity. Of that we do, and can know nothing. It is with the procession of organic reproduction, when once organic life was established, with which we are here concerned. What form did organic life take in its inception, and what course did its propagation and evolution take, all down the ages to this day?

But before proceeding any further, there are three sets of conditions, which it may be as well at once to refer to, and which go far to paralyse, if not to destroy, Darwin's contention at the outset.

First :—let us suppose for a moment that Darwin's theory is correct—that all life sprang from a single progenitor. What follows! Either this original piece of gelatinous proteid, produced, or gave birth to, similar or dissimilar organisms, low down, it may be, in the scale of life, such as "amœbæ," 'infusoriæ,' and what not. Now if these new creations were all similar at the outset, it seems inconceivable that any period of time, however prodigious, or any set of circumstances however extravagant, could by any process of slow accretion have converted say a flea into a flamingo, or a mouse into a mammoth; especially when we remember that on Darwin's own showing it takes millions of years to make even a single permanent alteration in species. And why should some remain stationary as created, and others alter so amazingly, and into beings of such various, and gigantic dimensions.

On the other hand, if these newly created organisms were dissimilar at the outset, why would not that alone be sufficient to account for the differences, and render unnecessary altogether the law of "Natural Selection."

And secondly, as regards the duration of reproductive life on this earth, the scientists differ among themselves. The mathematicians, the astronomers, and the physicists are by no means at

AN ALTERNATIVE HYPOTHESIS

one on the matter with the chemists and biologists, and the two classes differ not only with each other, but also *inter se*, on the subject. They are by no means all of them willing to concede to Darwin the time that his theory necessitates.

Moreover, the theories as to the age of the earth, are already undergoing a change. Not so very long ago it was laid down as almost axiomatic that the cooling of the earth's crust was a process of inconceivable time. Now all that is changed: in a recent scientific article in "*Science Progress*," we read the following :—

" Again, in the light of present physical theories, we must conceive that of the earth condensed from a gaseous mass, the time elapsing from the first formation of a hot crust, and the cooling of this to something like the present temperature, would not have been long. A solid crust would have formed at somewhere not very far from 1000°, and according to Kelvin and Arrhenius, the time required to cool this mass to below 100° C., the boiling-point of water, was probably but a few thousand years." In sixty, twenty, or any smaller number of million years, all organic life, for all we know, and for anything that science can show to the contrary, may have been created, and recreated, over and over again. So far from having only one place of origin, it may have had a thousand. So far from having emanated from a single piece of gelatinous proteid, it may have traced its descent from a thousand gelatinous substances, of different chemical combinations.

And thirdly, what tremendous convulsions, both external and internal, may not the earth have experienced, from those great agents of geographical alteration, fire, water, and ice? It is idle to speculate on what may have happened, so let us turn to geology, which now takes rank amongst the greatest of the sciences, and teaches something at any rate, by evidence at once unshakable and irrefragable, of what actually did happen. But here I must confine my attention to one point only, as Darwin discusses it at some length. It has an important bearing on the subject, and is utilised by Darwin, as one of the chief agents, in the distribution and disposal of organic life. I refer to the action of ice in the great Glacial Period.

I suppose most people's idea of the Glacial Period, if they ever gave the subject a serious thought, is that, some thousands of years ago, the temperature of the Northern Hemisphere was far lower than it is now, owing to great blocks of ice, issuing hither, and thither, from the northern seas, making their way southward and adding to the general chilliness and discomforture. But the Glacial Period was in reality one of the most magnificent, far-reaching, and appalling catastrophes that the geological record has to reveal.

According to Mr Croll, a geologist whom Darwin greatly affects—partly, one cannot help suspecting,

AN ALTERNATIVE HYPOTHESIS

because his ingenious, if somewhat conjectural speculations, come to Darwin's assistance when in a very tight corner—the last great Glacial Period occurred about 240,000 years ago, and endured with slight alterations of climate, for about 160,000 years. The whole subject is fully discussed in Sir Charles Lyell's "Geology," but the most illuminating and picturesque account of what actually took place is that given by Sir Archibald Geikie in his "Class-book of Geology." After discussing the evidence, he says: "From this kind of evidence it has been ascertained, that the whole of Northern Europe, amounting in all to probably not less than 770,000 square miles, was buried under one vast expanse of snow and ice. . . . Upon Scandinavia it was not improbably between 6000 and 7000 feet thick. It has left its mark at heights of more than 3000 feet in the Scottish Highlands, and over North-Western Scotland it was probably not less than 5000 feet thick. Where it abated on the Harz Mountains it appears to have been still not far short of 1500 feet in thickness.

"This vast mantle of ice was in continual motion, creeping outward and downward from the high grounds to the sea. The direction taken by its principal currents can still be followed. In Scandinavia, as shown by the rock-striæ and the transport of boulders, it swept westward into the Atlantic, eastward into the Gulf of Bothnia, which it completely filled up, and southward across Denmark, and the low grounds of Northern Germany. The basin of the Baltic was completely choked up with ice; so also was that of the North Sea as far south as the neighbourhood of London.

"The Western margin of the ice-fields from the South-West of Ireland to the North Cape of Norway, must have presented a vast wall of ice some 2000 miles long and probably several hundred feet high, breaking off into icebergs, which floated away with the prevailing currents and winds. Northern Europe must have presented the aspect of North Greenland at the present time.

"In Europe no distinct topographical feature appears to mark the Southern limit reached by the ice-sheet; this limit can only be approximately fixed by the most southerly localities where striated rocks and transported blocks have been observed. In North America, however, the margin of the great ice-cap is prominently defined by a mound or series of mounds of 'detritus' which seem to have been pushed in front of the ice. These mounds, beginning on the coast of Massachusetts, run across the Continent with a wonderful persistence for more than 3000 miles. They form what American geologists call the 'Terminal moraine.'"

But to turn to the alternative theory. Why does Darwin confine himself to one act of creative

AN ALTERNATIVE HYPOTHESIS 59

power, and why should all organic life have descended from one common ancestor? And what put this idea of community of descent into the minds of the naturalists at all? This last interrogatory is not difficult to answer.

The more the naturalists looked into nature, the more were they struck with how much every living thing has in common, both in structure, in organism, and in function. The difference in outward appearance was more startling than the difference in their internal economy. Strip off the flesh from the man and the monkey, and their resemblance is greater than when both of them are covered; again, go beneath the bones, and look at their organs and functions, and the resemblance is greater still; but go deeper once more, and regard the embryo in the womb, and the resemblance still holds good. And this similarity, it must be remembered, runs through all organic life. Of course as you work backward, or rather downward in creation, the resemblance becomes less and less close and accentuated, but it is never entirely obliterated. Well, the thought at once suggested itself to minds of the naturalists, "All these living organisms must have had a common origin, it is the only way of satisfactorily accounting for their similarity." So they reasoned, and so far their reasoning was sound. But they still had to account for the extraordinary differences, and divergencies, exhibited in them all. What could be more unlike, than say a bee, and a hippopotamus, both in structure, habits, and reasoning powers? Could they, asks the sceptic, have had a common ancestor? Darwin says, "Yes, they could, and I will show you how it all came about," and then he proceeds to unfold his story of evolution by natural selection.

Now the question that at once arises in the mind, and that one asks oneself, is this: why does Darwin nail his colours to one act of creative power, and to one only, and confine that act to one particular locality? If he concedes, as concede he must, one act of creative power, why does not he concede a thousand, or at any rate sufficient acts, to supply at any rate the great types of organisation with separate stocks of descent? Once concede that and everything becomes plain: the differences and similarities, common to all organic life, are at once accounted for. There is certainly no "*a priori*" reason against it. For when this globe was at the right temperature and chemically ready, and conditioned for organic life at all, what more probable than that organic life should spring up and burst out in many places at once? Let us imagine this globe to be an orange, split up into its component sections, all placed so far apart in space, that any transit of life from one section to another was impossible: do the evolutionists maintain, that life only appeared on one of those sections, and if so on which? For if life appeared on them all, there you have at once your various stocks of

AN ALTERNATIVE HYPOTHESIS 61

descent. It by no means follows that these various progenitors need have been very dissimilar in composition, merely because they had not a common progenitor. They might have had, and probably did have, just such hidden, and different potentialities as would be sufficient, and no more, to account for the marked divergencies in their progeny, which we see all round us at this day, in organic life.

Yes, the evolutionist might answer, that may be so; but would different progenitors produce progeny so similar in their structure, in their organism, and in their functions, and in their habits, to say nothing of their outward appearance? The answer to that surely is that as these progenitors were transformed into organic life on a common globe, and under the same temperature, and practically under the same physical conditions, they must of necessity have had much in common. Their progeny would breathe the same air, see the same light, eat, relatively speaking similar food. They would all possess organs of reproduction, digestion, and respiration; they would all have similar powers of recuperation and progression, and their instruments of attachment, and locomotion, would naturally very nearly resemble one another. Similarity is not identity. And if a man is in some respects similar to a monkey, he certainly is not identical; then why should the progenitor of the one be identical with the progenitor of the other? The chances are that he was not.

The answers that Darwin gives to this solution of the difficulty are exceedingly unsatisfactory and inconclusive. On page 300 of the "Origin of Species," when discussing the single centres of creation, he says:—

"We are thus brought to the question, which has been largely discussed by naturalists, namely whether species have been created at one or more points of the earth's surface. Undoubtedly there are many cases of extreme difficulty in understanding how the same species could possibly have migrated from some one point to the several distant and isolated points where now found. Nevertheless, the simplicity of the view that each species was first produced within a single region captivates the mind. He who rejects it rejects the 'vera causa' of ordinary generation with subsequent migration and calls in the agency of a miracle."

Here I confess I fail to follow Darwin altogether. Why are two creative acts more a miracle than one? Why, if a species appears at point A, is it a miracle; and if it appear at point B it is not! Therefore, what does Darwin mean, when he talks about calling in the agency of a miracle? Moreover, the idea of a species being generated in one place, does not captivate the mind, any more than if it had been generated in another.

Again, in his conclusion in the "Origin of Species," he says:—

"Undoubtedly some of these same questions

AN ALTERNATIVE HYPOTHESIS 63

cannot be answered by those who believe in the appearance or creation of only a few forms of life, or of some one form alone. It has been maintained by several authors that it is as easy to believe in the creation of a million beings as of one; but Maupertius's philosophical axiom 'of least action' leads the mind more willingly to admit the smaller number; and certainly we ought not to believe that the innumerable beings within each great class have been created with plain but deceptive marks of descent from a single parent."

Without any acquaintance with the philosophical works of Maupertius, it is easy to form a correct idea of what he means by the law of "least action." Presumably he means that nature in her actions prefers simplicity to complexity, that she will not fire two shots where one would be equally effective, and that her motto is economy rather than waste. It is always dangerous to buttress up one conjectural hypothesis by another more conjectural still. In the first place nature never creates anything, she merely makes new combinations, and she is making millions of them every day and every hour; indeed it is almost her sole occupation. A thousand combinations are as simple to nature as one. To bring about a given result, a multiplicity of creation may be a more simple plan than one single act of creation. Certainly in the particular instance under discussion, multiplicity of creation would be far simpler in its working out, and results, than Darwin's prolonged, and uncertain, method of Natural Selection.

And is it so certain that nature prefers economy to extravagance? To all appearance nature is extravagant, nay even wasteful, both in life and death.

"So careful of the race she seems, so careless of the common type."

Moreover, there is no necessity for believing that innumerable beings have been independently created, but only sufficient are required to supply the great types of organisation.

Professor Huxley takes the same view as Darwin, and gives him his support, for in a lecture delivered before the Royal Institution on the "Persistent Types of Animal Life," he remarks in a passage not conspicuous for its accuracy or truth:—

"It is difficult to comprehend the meaning of such facts as these, if we suppose that each species of animal and plant, or each great type of organisation, was formed and placed upon the surface of the globe at long intervals by a distinct act of creative power: and it is well to recollect that such an assumption is as unsupported by tradition, or revelation, as it is opposed to the general analogy of nature. If on the other hand, we view 'Persistent Types' in relation to that hypothesis which supposes the species living at any time to be the result of the gradual modifica-

AN ALTERNATIVE HYPOTHESIS 65

tion of pre-existing species, a hypothesis which, though unproven and sadly damaged by some of its supporters, is yet the only one to which physiology lends any countenance."

But the assumption is most assuredly not unsupported by Revelation, on the contrary, Revelation gives it its explicit sanction, for it actually enumerates great types of organisation. Why, moreover, are created types opposed to the general analogy of nature, any more than one created type? They are certainly not opposed to nature, and what Huxley means by the "general analogy," it is not easy to see. Analogy is the last argument that ought to count with a student of nature. And why should physiology withhold her countenance from one scheme more than the other? Physiology has nothing to do with how creation came about, it merely concerns itself with the functions of organic life when created.

If life came down in parallel lines, however innumerable, instead of from a common centre, whatever value Darwin's theory may possess, that theory would be equally effective in its operation, in the one case, as in the other.

It is strange, but unlike the mathematicians, the majority of chemists, geologists, and biologists, have a dislike for and distrust of the idea of creative power. They would rule the idea of creation out of court altogether if they could.

E

This may be partly due to the nature of their calling, "like the dyer's hand" they become subdued to what they work in. The mathematicians take a wider sweep, and have a greater synthetic imagination, doubtless largely attributable to their method of reasoning. They must assume something, and they reason deductively from the universal to the particular, while the inductive reasoners will assume nothing that the witness of the facts themselves will not immediately demonstrate. Being for ever immersed in matter and the proximate laws that govern its many transformations, law must account for everything, the lawgiver, if there is one, is a matter of indifference. The perpetual process of classification and analysis, must to some extent thwart the imagination, and have on the mind a disintegrating and somewhat deteriorating effect. The process is inevitable. What is gained in one direction, is lost in another. Here as elsewhere the great law of compensation is at work, as Goethe has said :—

"In order to spend on one side nature is forced to economise on the other."

My contention, then, is that all organic life came down not from a common centre, but in parallel lines with "stirps," at the head of each. How many those "stirps," were must, of course, be a matter of conjecture. They were probably numerous enough, as all the witness of organic life, whether past or present, living or recorded, bears witness

AN ALTERNATIVE HYPOTHESIS 67

to. As regards four great classes, at any rate, the laws of biology have ever been the same.

The first class embraces the vertebral animals, having vertebral columns and a regular nervous system. It includes all the quadrupeds and bipeds, with man at their head. The second class includes the mollusks, or animals living in shells. The third class are articulated animals having coverings connected by annulated plates, animals like the lobster and spider, and insects generally. The fourth great class are the zoophites or animal plants. In all ages of the world these four great classes of animals have existed.

Now the variations always follow or are approximate to the parallel lines of descent. This need not at all be attributable to Natural Selection; physical conditions, transmission by inheritance, the use and disuse of parts, are quite sufficient to account for any one of them. And when Darwin talks about connecting links it is not always clear what he means. Of course in all nature there is an underlying unity of plan. Similarity, however close, is not necessarily identity either in origin or completion. One organic being may have a strong similarity to another, and yet never even have hit it all down the line of descent. What Darwin calls a connecting link may be a distinct species or genus. To take the case of the monkey and the man. Even if a go-between were found, it would prove nothing, for it might be no true link at all, but merely a relict of a distinct and individual species. So the quest of the missing link is really as idle as that of the philosopher's stone.

To show the absurdity of Darwin's contention, it is necessary to quote here at some length what he calls an excellent illustration of it. On page three hundred and fifty-three of the "Origin of Species" he says:—

" We are next led to inquire what reason can be assigned for certain butterflies and moths so often assuming the dress of another and quite distinct form, why, to the perplexity of naturalists, has nature condescended to the tricks of the stage? Mr Bates has, no doubt, hit on the true explanation. The mocked forms, which always abound in numbers, must habitually escape destruction to a large extent, otherwise they could not exist in such swarms; and a large amount of evidence has now been collected, showing that they are distasteful to the birds and other insect devouring animals. The mocking forms, on the other hand, that inhabit the same district, are comparatively rare, and belong to rare groups: hence they must suffer habitually from some danger, for otherwise, from the number of eggs laid by all butterflies, they would in three or four generations swarm over the whole country. Now, if a member of one of these persecuted and rare groups were to assume a dress so like that of a well protected species that it continually deceived the practised eye of an entomologist, it would often deceive predaceous birds and insects and thus often escape destruction."

AN ALTERNATIVE HYPOTHESIS 69

Now when we remember, according to Darwin's own showing, that to greatly modify a single species, or to convert an old species into a new one, it takes as long as the making of three geological formations, and runs into millions of years, the question naturally arises in the mind, what became of the mocking species during all the ages that these Lepidopteran tailors were making for it this stage suit of clothes. Why were they not long ago destroyed by their many enemies, before they had this mocking armour to protect them ! And what proof has Darwin that birds decide solely by colour, on the form of food that they prefer. And if the mocked form of butterflies could swarm over the whole country, why not the mocking ?

Again, contrast the giants and pigmies of organic life, the great anomalies of size, form, and brains.

Many species of ferns dug out of coal mines reach a height of 40 or 45 feet. And among mammals the case of the dinotherium or the megatherium of South America may be taken as illustrative of size. In this latter we have an animal 12 feet long and 8 feet high with colossal proportions. Its thigh bones, three times thicker than that of the elephant, its tail, and feet, and its spinal marrow a foot in diameter. Or again the ichthyosaurus, a marine reptile, sometimes 30 feet long, or the gigantic birds whose footsteps have been discovered in new red-sandstone of America.

Contrast these giants with such pigmies as the bee,

and the ant, as different in their structure, organs, size, habits, and brain power, as organic beings could well be. The size of the ant is more than compensated for by the magnificence of its instinctive, one might almost say its intellectual power. Most people have heard something of the powers of the ant; Darwin, in his "Descent of Man," makes among others the following observations.

"Ants certainly communicate information to each other, and several unite for the same work, or for games of play. They recognise their fellow-ants after months of absence and feel sympathy for each other. They build great edifices, keep them clean, close the doors in the evening and keep sentries. They make roads as well as tunnels under rivers, and bridges over them, by clinging together. They collect food for the community, and when an object, too large for entrance is brought to the nest, they enlarge the door, and afterwards build it up again. They store up seeds, of which they prevent the germination, and which if damp are brought up to the surface to dry. They keep aphides and other insects as milch cows. They go out to battle in regular bands, and freely sacrifice their lives for the common weal. They emigrate according to a preconcerted plan. They capture slaves, and endless similar facts could be given."

Now, is it conceivable that creatures so diverse as the above, could have obtained such divergence

AN ALTERNATIVE HYPOTHESIS 71

had they all descended from a common progenitor by Darwin's inadequate theory of Natural Selection or modification by variation? Darwin himself admits that countless species have had their day and become extinct, and it would take eternity to work out the various modifications, to account for the difference between say an ant, and an elephant. Moreover there is such a much simpler explanation ready to hand to account for the whole matter. The great variations that have been produced were merely adaptations to the varying conditions of the earth's surface. The earth since its creation has been the seat of several distinct economies of life, each occupying long periods, and then passing away. During each of these periods, distinct groups of animals and plants have occupied the earth, the air, and the sea. The successive groups have been entirely distinct, so that had the different groups changed places with each other they must have perished.

It must be remembered that the fish of the oldest rocks were not, as the development scheme would require, of a low organisation, but high in the scale of fishes. "All our most ancient fossil fishes," says Professor Sedgwick, "belong to a high or organic type, and the very oldest species that are well determined fall naturally into an order of fishes which Owen and Müller place, not at the bottom, but at the top of the whole class."

And what higher authorities could one have than Owen and Müller?

CHAPTER V

TWO FATAL OBJECTIONS

DARWIN's theory of Natural Selection did not suggest itself to him at once, it dawned upon his mind during his intellectual pursuits, as an explanation of the variations, development, and sort of organic progression he saw in organic life. This is clear from a letter he wrote to Sir Richard Hooker after his return from his voyage in the " Beagle." He writes :—

> " I have ever since my return been engaged in a very presumptuous work, and I know no one individual who would not say a very foolish one. . . . At last gleams of light have come and I am almost convinced that species *are not immutable*. . . . I have found out the simple way by which species become exquisitely adapted to various ends."

Now, the general opinion about Darwin's works, possibly even among those accredited with some knowledge on the subject, is that they are a vast and varied storehouse of facts, and information, relating to natural history; that Darwin was a man of too humble a nature to push his theory as it deserved; that he was rather inclined to ignore the theory, and let the facts speak for themselves, and bring the theory to light. That other minds, in some respects greater and more brilliant than his own—particularly those of Professors Tyndall and Huxley—saw the value of Darwin's suggestion, that they worked Darwin's incipient hypothesis for all it was worth, that they fitted on to themselves Darwin's wings, developed them to their full extent, and themselves soared on them into a heaven of genius and popularity.

There is possibly a certain element of truth in this. Tyndall and Huxley have not inaptly been called the apostles Peter and Paul of the Darwinian movement. It must be remembered that Tyndall, and Huxley, besides being great men of science, were two of the most brilliant and lucid writers that the nineteenth century produced, and that without the powerful advocacy of them both, it is more than doubtful whether Darwin's hypothesis would have taken the hold it did on the popular imagination, still less on the scientific world.

But be that as it may, Darwin himself was his own most powerful advocate; no one who has read carefully, his two great works, the "Origin of Species" and "The Descent of Man," can fail to perceive this. The "Origin of Species," even more so than "The Descent of Man," is highly contentious throughout. It is an elaborate and ingenious piece of insistent special pleading, from the first page to the last. In this work, all the energy of Darwin's nature, his great powers of reasoning—which would be irresistible if he had a good case—which he has not—all his array of facts, gathered from all quarters, and from almost every science, all his skill in marshalling and manipulating his facts to serve the end he has in view, are brought to bear, to buttress up, strengthen, and if possible establish on a sure foundation his theory of Natural Selection. But surely he signally fails, not to prove his case, for of course that would be impossible, but to place his theory in the ranks of even a plausible hypothesis. As a matter of fact, the facts are too big for the theory, the theory simply refuses to contain them. It is simply amazing how, in the teeth of the evidence against them, Huxley and Tyndall could have come to the conclusions that they did. Nearly the whole of the evidence that Darwin does bring to bear, is equally available for, and perfectly consistent with, another and wider theory altogether, viz., that which I have discussed in the preceding chapter.

For the more the story unfolds itself in the "Origin" the more must it appear to any candid mind that multiple centres of creation and many progenitors are a more probable explanation of the process of organic life than that all life proceeds from one common stock. The importance of the theory really lies in the philosophic inferences that necessarily flow from it, and are its inevitable sequence.

But before proceeding to discuss two apparently fatal objections to Darwin's theory it may be as well to say a word, to shield oneself from being

TWO FATAL OBJECTIONS   75

accused of unwarrantable presumption on the deference due to authority.

No man should accept authority as final, further than his own reason will take him, though of course he must provisionally act on the faith of authority, until his own reason is further illuminated, or until others have shown him a more excellent way. But how often does one see the flame of one generation, the mere ashes of another, and the genius of one age only the genesis of the next. And whenever the human mind has achieved greatness and given evidence of extraordinary power in one direction, there is always a tendency to credit it with similar powers in another. Darwin was doubtless a great and true naturalist, but was he equally great in his powers of inference, and in the deductions that he drew from his observations, and from the knowledge of facts familiar to his mind!

Let me illustrate and give proof of my assertion by proceeding at once, to two apparently fatal objections to Darwin's whole position, and contention. And for that purpose it is necessary to refer to Professor Russell Wallace's article on the "World of Life." On page four hundred and twenty-nine of the March number for 1909 of "The Fortnightly Review," in endeavouring to answer a common objection made by Darwin's critics, Professor Wallace makes the following observations :—

"Perhaps the best way of explaining how

Natural Selection actually works will be by quoting one of the common objections to it, and showing how the actual facts of Nature afford a sufficient reply. The most common of all the objections to the action of the survival of the fittest, in the production of new species rests upon the strange belief, that variation is a rare phenomenon, that favourable variations occur singly and at long intervals, and therefore can have no effect in producing any important change.

" As a rather recent example of this objection— he proceeds—we may take the statement by the late Lord Salisbury at Oxford in 1894."

After describing how the most diverse races are produced by artificial selection, Lord Salisbury continues:—

" But in Natural Selection, who is to supply the breeder's place? Unless the crossing is properly arranged the new breed will never come into being. What is to secure that the two individuals of opposite sexes in the primeval forest, who have been both accidentally blessed with the same advantageous variation, shall meet and transmit by inheritance, that variation to their successors? Unless this step is made good the modification will never get a start; and yet there is nothing to ensure that step but pure chance. The law of chance takes the place of the cattle-breeder or the pigeon-fancier.

" Here we have it plainly set forth—says Professor Wallace—that advantageous variations

TWO FATAL OBJECTIONS 77

occur simply, on rare occasions, and remote from each other; and that even when they do occur, unless by some lucky accident a male and female should accidentally find each other ' in the primeval forest,' nothing happens, and the ' advantageous ' variations are swamped in the general mass of the species supposed not to vary."

As a matter of fact, in the quotation Professor Wallace here makes, Lord Salisbury does not plainly set forth that variations occur singly, he neither says nor implies anything of the sort, and if he did assert it he is only repeating the very language of Darwin himself.

Darwin himself insists again and again all through his work on the " Origin of Species " on the extreme slowness with which modification by variation works, that at first the favourable variation only occurs in a few individuals of the same species at the same time, and that it takes ages to make any variation, however slight, constant in any given species.

But that there may be no mistake on this point, it is better to quote Darwin's own words on the subject. On pages seventy-eight and seventy-nine of the " Origin of Species " he says :—

" That natural selection generally acts with extreme slowness I fully admit. It can only act when there are places in the natural polity of a district which can be better occupied by the modification of some of its existing inhabitants."

And again :—

"But I do believe that natural selection will generally act very slowly, only at long intervals of time, and only on a few inhabitants of the same region."

Again on page one hundred and twenty-three :—

"For variation is a long-continued and slow process."

So certainly Darwin's kingdom of nature does not come with observation. Indeed, such enormous drafts does Darwin make on the bank of time—a cheque for a million years is a mere nothing—that eternity itself can hardly acknowledge his presentations.

His contention is, that favourable variations arise at first only in a very limited number of any given species, and that it takes ages of time as measured by years, for this variation to assert itself sufficiently to become constant in the species.

That being the case Lord Salisbury's illustration holds good, and is agreeable in every way to Darwin's hypothesis.

Let us assume that there are ten million in any given species, a by no means extravagant number according to Professor Wallace himself; and that 10,000 of these simultaneously exhibited, a practically similar variation—though the chances, I should imagine, were enormously against it—but it is

TWO FATAL OBJECTIONS 79

necessary to assume something like that, to enable Darwin's hypothesis to commence operations at all. Well, the odds here are a thousand to one, against any male with the given variation, mating with a female of the same variation: and if this union did accidentally take place, the whole of the offspring of that union are not at all likely to inherit the variation, and even if they did, they would almost to a certainty again mate with the common stock: in a generation or two the variation would be swamped and die out, and the species revert to its original condition.

But what answer does Professor Wallace make to Lord Salisbury and " such critics." He says:—

" What totally false ideas of Nature such critics must have both as to the number of individuals in every common, widespread, and dominant species, as to the nature and amount of variation, to imagine that the very existence of the organic world during each period of changing conditions should have been dependent on a few scattered individuals."

But does not the learned Professor see that the more you multiply the millions, the less chance is there of those affected with the particular variation ever meeting or having an opportunity of perpetuating the favourable modification.

Darwin himself sees the force of the objection more clearly than Professor Wallace, for on page sixty-six of the " Origin of Species " he discusses this very point. "Nevertheless," he says, "until reading an able and valuable article in the 'North British Review,' I did not appreciate how rarely single variations, whether slight or strongly marked, could be perpetuated."

"The author takes the case of a pair of animals, producing during their lifetime two hundred offspring, of which from various causes of destruction, only two on an average survive to procreate their kind. This is rather an extreme estimate for most of the higher animals, but by no means so for many of the lower organisms. He then shows that if a single individual were born which varied in some manner, giving it twice as good a chance of life as that of other individuals, yet the chances would be strongly against its survival. Supposing it to survive and to breed, and that half its young inherited the favourable variations: still, as the Reviewer goes on to show, the young would have only a slightly better chance of surviving and breeding, and this chance would go on decreasing in the succeeding generations. The justice of these remarks cannot, I think, be disputed."

Darwin frankly and freely admits that this disappearance always takes place in the case of monstrosities, or to coin a more delicate phrase, what I may call "malign variations." For he says on page thirty-one—referring to individuals possessed of them:—

"They would also, during the first and succeeding generations, cross with the ordinary form, and thus their abnormal character would almost inevitably be lost."

So the malign variations disappear, but the benign do not. But even this, according to Darwin's own showing, is not always the case, though I admit it is difficult to classify either the following illustration, under either the head of malign or benign variations. It is difficult to see how it is an advantage in the Struggle for Existence, still less can it be regarded in the light of a Secondary Sexual characteristic, for the performance can hardly be considered as an attraction to the female in man, or even to the females in the lower organisms. On page thirteen of " The Descent of Man " we read :—

" Some few persons have the power of contracting the superficial muscles on their scalps : and these muscles are in a variable and partially rudimentary condition.

" M. A. de Candoble has communicated to me a curious instance of the long continued persistence or inheritance of this power, as well as of its unusual development. He knows a family, in which one member, the present head of the family, could, when a youth, pitch several heavy books from his head, by the movement of the scalp alone : and he won wagers by performing this feat. His father, uncle, grandfather, and three children possess the same power to the same unusual degree. This family became divided eight generations ago into two branches: so that the head of the above-mentioned branch is cousin in the seventh degree to the head of the other branch. This distant cousin resides in another part of France, and on being asked whether he possessed the same faculty, immediately exhibited his power. This case offers a good illustration how persistent may the transmission of an absolutely useless faculty, probably derived from our remote semi-human progenitors: since many monkeys have and frequently use the power of largely moving their scalps up and down."

But is this power so absolutely useless, as Darwin contends, if developed to its ultimate limit, on the lines of progress laid down in his law of favourable variation. It might have enabled the descendants of the common ancestor, to pitch a book in this manner from one end of France to the other.

But to pass on to another and still more overpowering and fatal piece of criticism to Darwin's theory than the last. I refer to the question of the Brachiopods. How is it that if Darwin's theory of modification by variation is true, that this great class of marine bivalves has remained practically unaffected by the theory for a period of at least 60,000,000 years!

Now the Brachiopods, it must be remembered, are no insignificant branch, but an immense and important class in the kingdom of nature. They are a marine bivalve and their scientific name was suggested by two long arms furnished with ciliæ, with which they create currents that bring food to the mouth. "Of all shell fish," says Mr S. P. Woodward, "Brachiopods enjoy the greatest range both of climate, depth, and time. They are found in tropical and polar seas, in pools left by the ebbing tide, and at the greatest depths hitherto explored by the dredge. At present only seventy species are known, but above a thousand extinct species are distributed through the sedentary rocks of marine origin from the Cambrian strata upwards."

Now as the struggle for existence is always going on, in all organic life, and as this struggle for existence is the parent, and great evidence of variation, which natural selection has a tendency to preserve, how is it that if this power is always in operation, the form of the Brachiopods has remained practically unchanged, through all these countless generations.

"It is no valid objection to this conclusion—says Darwin on page two hundred and eighty-nine of the 'Origin of Species'—that certain Brachiopods have been but slightly modified from an extremely remote geological epoch, and that certain land and fresh-water shells have remained nearly the same, from the time when, as far as is known, they first appeared. It is not an insuperable difficulty that Foraminifera have not, as insisted on by Dr Carpenter, progressed in organisation since even the Laurentian epoch; for some organisms would have to remain fitted for simple conditions of life, and what could be better fitted for this end than those lowly organised Protozoa? *Such objections as the above would be fatal to my view, if it included advance in organisation as a necessary contingent.*"

But on page ninety-one of the same work, he says:—

"Natural Selection acts exclusively by the preservation and accumulation of variations, which are beneficial under the organic and inorganic conditions to which each creature is exposed at all periods of life. The ultimate result is that each *creature tends to become more and more improved in relation to its conditions*. This improvement inevitably leads to the gradual advancement of the organisation of the greater number of living beings throughout the world."

Here Darwin certainly makes an advance in organisation a necessary contingent of his hypothesis. So he really stands condemned out of his own mouth, and his theory falls, or appears to fall, to the ground.

It is true that in the above quotation there is one saving term, the "greater number." But why this qualification? The whole object of his work is to prove that the struggle for existence, and Natural Selection are always and everywhere in operation.

"Natural Selection is daily and hourly

scrutinising, throughout the world, the slightest variations; silently and insensibly working, whenever and wherever opportunity offers, at the improvement of each organic being in relation to its organic and inorganic conditions of life."

CHAPTER VI

MAN AND THE MONKEY

BEFORE proceeding to discuss the question of man, and the monkey, and their relationship and connection, if any really exists, a word might not be out of place, on what I may call for want of a better expression " predetermined desirability," or the wish being father to the thought. The balance in no man's mind is perfectly true. There is always a " kink " somewhere in the highest, and the most impoverished intellects alike. Some people have more of these " kinks " in their brains and a greater predisposition to them than others. All classes and all people are affected by them, the men of science almost every bit as much as the theologian. Every man has hidden away somewhere in his person, like Mr Dick in David Copperfield, his " King Charles the First's head." It need not and is not always protruding itself: but there it is; and it shows itself from time to time and sometimes quite unexpectedly. Every man has certain ideas, tastes, and proclivities, and some of them are very pronounced and accentuated. He has a predilection for a particular hobby, a particular theory, or a particular line of thought. His object is to propagate these particular ideas, tastes, and proclivities, and to establish them if he can in himself and in others. We have all of us come across people in life numbering in their ranks many excellent and clever men, who seem to have an infinite capacity for belief. Their credulity is unbounded, they believe almost anything. Give them one cup of miracles to swallow, and so far from it upsetting their digestion, they will immediately cry out for another. They are people to be envied, rather than ridiculed. To believe everything in the heavens above, and in the earth beneath, and in the waters under the earth, is surely a better attitude of mind than to make life one long and querulous negation.

"To bow to ne'er a God except oneself and to one's belly first of deities." But these people might, one would think, at times mingle with this draught of credulity, a little of the water of discretion. But then they would not be true believers if they did. Now this capacity for belief sometimes, and generally, only touches one point of the individual or personality. Some men are as sound and hard-headed, in their business relations, their management of affairs, and their outlook on life as one could wish to see. But get to know them well, and there is always a rift in the lute, a weak spot somewhere. The value of facts, and the common and accepted standard of evidence by which they are usually guided, when they come to the rift disappears and vanishes like the wind.

And scientific men, even the greatest of them, are by no means above the infirmities and weaknesses of their fellows. They reject all miracles but those of their own creation, and though one would not willingly charge them with wresting or perverting evidence to their own use, yet if they have an end in view, or a theory which they think has a future, their sense of the value of evidence becomes if not obscure, at times at any rate very much dimmed, and they eagerly press into their service witnesses whom they would reject with scorn in any other cause but their own. Now the particular weakness of Darwin, Huxley, Tyndall, and the other evolutionists, was the monkey.

They held a brief for the monkey, they were his counsel, they had heavy retaining fees, and it was to their interest and advantage to get the monkey his peerage, and enable him to take his seat among his fellows. Not only that, but they endeavoured to establish the fact, that the monkey, so far from belonging to an order inferior to that of man, was himself man's forbear and progenitor, and that if he had his rights his portrait should be found hanging in the ancestral halls of the very children who rejected him. Here was a " cause célebre " indeed, the trial of Warren Hastings sinks into insignificance beside it. Was man a little lower than the angels, or merely a little superior to the ape? The monkey was on his trial at the " bar " of humanity, and the final verdict of humanity has yet to be given. Personally, whatever the evidence, I abhor monkeys. I disown all connection with them, either proximately, or remote, either in time or eternity. Like Disraeli, " I am on the side of the angels." Now what was the evidence with which the advocates of this hairy monstrosity with a tail, endeavoured to establish their case.

It must ever and always be borne in mind that similarity, however close, does not and cannot mean in the individual identity of personality; and if similarity between two, say men, does not mean identity in themselves, why should it mean or imply identity in their progenitors? Pick up two grains of sand, they have a far greater resemblance to one another, than a man has to a monkey, yet they most assuredly have not a common origin for they are both of them, or at least the atoms of the elements that compose them, and have been from all eternity, independent creations.

The monkey then was duly introduced into court by his illustrious advocates, and they said, " Here, gentlemen of the jury, is a long neglected brother and a man, and if you will not believe our assertion look at the marked similarity, almost family resemblance, between this object and yourselves." This was hardly flattering to the Court, and the marvel is that it did not instantly resent the insult, and commit the monkey and his counsel, and all his adherents, for contempt on the spot. However, the Court of humanity thought differently, and took it, as the saying is, " very well," and they called on Mr Darwin the leading counsel for the monkey to open his client's case.

His speech took the direction which one would naturally expect, he dwelt on the close resemblance, both outwardly and inwardly, structurally and organically, physically and physiologically, between man and his client. It is notorious he said :—

" That man is constructed on the same general type or model as other mammals. All the bones in his skeleton can be compared with corresponding bones, in a monkey, bat, or seal. So it is with his muscles, nerves, blood-vessels, and internal viscera.

" The brain, the most important of all the organs, follows the same law, as shown by Huxley and other anatomists. Birschoff, who is a hostile witness, admits that every chief fissure and fold in the brain of man has its analogy in that of the orang : but, he adds, at no period of development do their brains perfectly agree : nor could perfect agreement be expected, for otherwise their mental powers would have been the same. But it would be superfluous here to give further details on the correspondence between man and the higher mammals in the structure of the brain and all other parts of the body."

It should be observed here that the structure of the frame, and folds, and fissures, of the brain, are merely analogous; a loose phrase that is capable of a very wide interpretation. If you made a facsimile of a monkey in wood, all the parts might be analogous to the corresponding parts in a living man, and yet no one would argue from the similarity that they were descended from the same " stirps." Nor is it surprising that, roughly speaking, all animals have some resemblance to man, some more, some less remote; that the main outlines of their structure, organs, nerves, and tissues, are fashioned in a very similar mould. The mere fact that they inhabit the same earth, and have to get their living in much the same way, would fully account for this without any evolution by descent from the same progenitor.

Moreover, one would like to put this question to Darwin and the evolutionists. Do they assert that if the whole human race were at once swept off the face of the earth, and that the monkeys, being the next highest being in the scale of creation, were left in possession of the field, that they would ever develop into man, give them what extension of time you will? I trow not! And if not, why not? if the theory of the evolutionists is true.

Again, if man were to domesticate the highest monkeys and keep them under his instruction, care, and protection for a million years, would their sagacity improve, and would they ever become more than they are? It is very doubtful!

It is very doubtful if the dog, who has been domesticated now for thousands of years, has mentally developed one fraction in general understanding. I say in general understanding, for what powers he has may have been improved by concentration in some given direction, but only at the expense of his general intelligence.

From the stories related of wild dogs, their intelligence is every bit as great, and in some respects greater, as their natural powers of intuition are less impaired by disuse, than are those of the domesticated animals.

One of the most remarkable stories of the intelligence of the wild dog I ever remember reading was that of a certain wild pack, I believe in South Africa. The pack for hunting purposes, were for ever crossing and recrossing a great river infested with crocodiles. The crocodiles were always on the look out for their passage; the dogs were quite alive to their intentions, and to deceive the crocodiles whenever they wanted a clear passage, they would run loudly barking down the bank of the river. They would then suddenly become quiet, turn aside inland, hark back to the point from which they started, and cross the river with impunity in the rear of the crocodiles.

It has yet, moreover, to be proved that the monkey is superior in intelligence or nearer man in brain power, than the ant, the elephant, the dog, or the parrot.

And then Darwin goes on to discuss some points of correspondence not obviously connected with structure.

"Man is liable—he says—to receive from the lower animals and to communicate to them certain diseases, as hydrophobia, the glanders, cholera, etc.; and this proves the close similarity of their tissues and blood, both in minute structure and composition, far more plainly than does their comparison under the best microscope, or by the aid of the best chemical analysis. Monkeys are liable to many of the same non-contagious diseases as we are. . . . These monkeys suffered also from apoplexy, inflammation of the bowels and cataract in the eye. The younger ones when shedding their milk teeth often died from fever. Medicines produced the same effect on them as on us. These trifling facts prove how similar the nerves must be on monkeys and man, and how similarly their whole nervous system is affected."

This may be all very true, but are the diseases precisely the same? or are they mere equivalent diseases in animals to those in man! But the argument carries you no further than the mystery of pain. Animals suffer pain, so does man; but that does not help one very far on the road to identity of origin.

There is another great fact to be born in mind when discussing this question of descent: that conceding for one moment Darwin's theory of community of descent: even if man and the monkey were evolved from the same original life, they may have from the first proceeded down parallel and collateral branches and never have hit each other anywhere all down the line of descent.

There is a difficulty at first in discovering whether Darwin meant, that man was connected with the monkey merely " quâ " natural selection, that is, that the process of natural selection proceeded much further with man than the monkey; that the monkey, so to speak, was left behind, and man proceeded onward to his present stage of development; or whether man had directly descended from the monkey, by the ordinary process of generation. But judging from Darwin's remarks on page one hundred and fifty-three of the " Descent of Man " it can hardly be doubted that he means the latter, for he says:—

" Now man unquestionably belongs in his dentition, in the structure of his nostrils, and some other respects, to the Catarrhine or Old World division: nor does he resemble the Platyrhines more closely than the Catarrhines in any characters, excepting in a few of not much importance and apparently of an adaptive nature. It is, therefore, against all probability that some New World species should have formerly varied and produced a man-like creature, with all the distinctive characters proper to the Old World division: losing at the same time all its own distinctive characters. There can consequently hardly be a doubt that man is an offshoot from the Old World Simian stem : and that under a genealogical point of view, he must be classed with the Catarrhine division."

And on page one hundred and fifty-five Darwin continues :—

" As a man from a genealogical point of view belongs to the Catarrhine or Old World stock, we must conclude, however much the conclusion may revolt our pride, that our early progenitors would have been properly thus designated. But we must not fall into the error of supposing that the early progenitor of the whole Simian stock, including man, was identical with or even closely resembled any existing ape or monkey."

The last sentence in this paragraph is very important as it opens up a double possibility. For if we are not to fall into the error of supposing that the early progenitor of the whole Simian stock, including man, even closely resembled the existing ape, then why should he not resemble man, and the monkey be himself a degenerate specimen of humanity. The one alternative is every bit as arguable as the other, and quite as probable. But Darwin dislikes this idea because it conflicts with his dictum that modification by variation is always beneficent, and that it never promotes deterioration or takes a downward course. Nature, according to Darwin, disapproves of a downgrade biology, every bit as much as Spurgeon disapproved of the same action in theology.

But is this true? Is nature for ever levelling up, and never levelling down? Her process may be and probably is during the whole line of life and time, one of general advance and improvement: but there are ebbs and flows in the tide, and her action in this respect is not invariable.

Among the invertebrate animals are numerous examples of the deterioration of a race. M. Alcide D'Orbigney, one of the most accomplished of Paleontologists, speaks as follows of the cephalopods found in the oldest rocks:—

"The cephalopods, the most perfect of the mollusks, which lived in the early period of the world, shows a progress of degradation in their generic forms. We insist on this fact relative to the cephalopods, which we shall hereafter compare with the less perfect classes of mollusks, since it must lead to the conclusion that the mollusks, as to their classes, have certainly retrograded from the compound to the simple, or from the more to the less perfect."

And if this action can take place in one department of oranic life why not in another? It is quite conceivable, and by no means improbable, still less impossible, that a monkey is a degenerate member or branch of a common stock. The thought is weird, wild, and terrible, and fit for the imagination of a Dante, that in long past ages, and in the twilight of the days when man, or whatever being then represented humanity in organic life, when his powers were not so developed as they are to-day, nor his self-control so strong, may either through the powers of nature, the hardships of life, or through long-continued abuse of his moral nature, in one direction or another, have lost his possibilities of progressive development and parted with his birthright of any intellectual advance. The common stock may have split up into the Cains, and Abels, the Esaus, and Jacobs of the world. Some may have prevailed, others may have succumbed and deteriorated—to borrow the picturesque phraseology of the Psalmist—to the terror by night or the arrow by day, that ever lie in wait to destroy all organic life. And when once this deterioration had set in, their race may have been cursed with it for ever, and their intellects permanently dimmed though through the inherent forces of nature, they may, for a time, have been allowed to continue and propagate their kind! Who can tell?

Darwin having stated generally the biological case for the monkey, hands over for a time his "brief" to Professor Huxley, who examines the case, and marshals the evidence, for his client from the physiological and embryological standpoint. Of course his argument must of necessity take the line of physiological and embryological parallels, precisely as Darwin's did that of biological.

Professor Huxley naturally lays great stress on the resemblances and parallels between the brain of a monkey and the brain of a man. By a predetermined desirability, by a natural bias, and by a scientific ardour to make good his contention, he probably stretches the common properties of each a little further than the circumstances warrant. If you want to see a thing you generally do see it, and the eye of faith recognises no limitations. But be that as it may no one can deny that the resemblance is startling. In general structure, and in the number and conformation of their convolutions the brain of man and that of the higher apes very nearly correspond. Let Professor Huxley speak for himself:—

"There remains then no dispute as to the resemblance in fundamental characters, between the ape's brain and man's nor any as to the wonderfully close similarity between the chimpanzee, orang, and man, in even the details of the arrangement, of the gyri, and sulci, of the cerebral hemispheres. Now turning to the differences of the brains of the highest apes and that of man, is there any serious question as to the nature, and extent of these differences. It is admitted that man's cerebral hemispheres are absolutely and relatively larger than those of the orang and chimpanzee: that his frontal lobes are less excavated by the upward protrusion of the roof of the orbits: that his gyri, and sulci, are as a

MAN AND THE MONKEY

rule, less symmetrically disposed, and present a greater number of secondary plications. But it is also clear that, none of these differences constitute a sharp demarcation between the man's and the ape's brain."

But there is one point here that never seems to have struck Professor Huxley, at least I have seen no reference to it, and it is strange that it should have escaped the notice of so powerful, and sagacious a mind, namely, that the closer you press and prove similarity between the respective organs of the brain of man, and the brain of the monkey, the more fatal is it to the proposition that he wishes to establish.

For if the resemblances are as close as the Professor contends, how is it that the resultant and living output of the two brains, in activity, power, and accomplishment, are so utterly dissimilar, and as far as the Poles asunder. If the two are so nearly similar in their physiological aspects, one would either have expected a much greater similarity in result, or one must look elsewhere for an explanation. The true explanation probably lies hidden away in the recesses of nature, in the mysterious darkness of some undiscovered and impenetrable law. The vital spark that illuminates the one may be different in its essence from that which illuminates the other, and the distinctive qualities of the matter of each may defy the investigation of the most searching chemical analysis. The potentialities in the brain of man, however similar the cerebral convolutions may appear, may be radically different.

And the Professor goes on to say :—

"Again as respects the question of size, it is established that the difference between the largest and smallest healthy human brain is greater than the difference between the smallest healthy human brain and the largest chimpanzee's or orang's brain!"

But this is hardly a fair way of stating the case. The comparison is so drawn as to minimise the difference in size as much as possible. For the average healthy human brain is three times heavier than the average healthy brain of the highest ape. Moreover, Professor Huxley has to admit that the brain of man presents a greater number of "secondary plications." The question naturally suggests itself are these plications really secondary, I mean in importance?

Again, a great deal is made of embryological resemblances.

The embryo of man, it is asserted, can at a very early period be hardly distinguished from that of other members of the vertebrate kingdom. When the extremities are developed, the feet of lizards, and mammals, the wings and feet of birds, no less than the hands and feet of man, all arise from the same fundamental form.

"It is," says Professor Huxley, "quite in the

later stages of development that the young human being presents marked differences from the young ape, while the latter departs as much from the dog in its developments as man does."

Startling as this last assertion may appear to be, it is demonstrably true.

The idea is that the brain of a human embryo appears at first like that of an invertebrate animal, next like that of a fish, then successively like that of a reptile, bird, mammal, and monkey. The heart goes through the same process. The inference that the evolutionist would draw from these facts is, that man actually begins his existence as an animalcule, and passes successively through the conditions of other animals before he reaches the highest. And the reason why he becomes a man rather than a monkey, is only some slight modifying circumstance. Of course there may be a seeming resemblance, but the diversity nevertheless may be really wide and deep. Bischoff says that the convolutions of the brain of the human fœtus at the end of the seventh month reach about the same stage of development as in a baboon when adult. But if that statement were true a seven months' child would always be born a monkey, and I should imagine that there are few physicians, who would sanction that assertion. Could a single example be produced in which the human embyro stopped at the monkey there might be some plausibility in the supposition. But it is as certain to become a man, as the sun is to rise and set, and it is impossible to infer identity of nature either from external or internal resemblances.

Darwin naturally lays much stress on the similarities between man, and the monkey. But, after all, in external conformation and appearance, is a monkey so very like a man! There are many animals, if not in general conformation, at any rate in facial expression, that more nearly resemble him. The head and facial expression of the highest apes is as unlike and remote from that of man as can well be imagined. The Lemurs, or half monkeys, as the Germans call them, are in facial appearance far more like a man. And who has not seen among sheep, horses, dogs, birds of all kind, and even fishes, expressions of face that frequently remind one of some acquaintance. They all, at any rate, have a more civilised expression.

And how about the dissimilarities? A man can stand upright, a monkey cannot, with the possible exception of the chimpanzee and the gorilla, and whether they can maintain that position without a prop for more than an instant or two is doubtful. And there is more in this matter of standing than we are generally aware of. It is by no means the simple matter it appears. The statue of a man placed upon a pedestal would not be secure of standing half an hour; you are obliged to fix it by bolts or the first shake would throw it over. Yet it may express all the mechanical proportions of a living model. It is not, therefore, the mere centre of gravity that is sufficient. But in the living man the centre of gravity is perpetually shifting, and man is kept in his upright position by a succession of imperceptible, but quick-balancing actions. Now monkeys do not possess this power, or at most in a very imperfect degree.

Again, the monkey is a very poor speaker, probably one of the worst in the whole animal creation. He cannot articulate a word, and his want of capacity in this respect separates him immeasurably from man. His oratory consists in gesticulations and in these he has an ample repertoire.

Max Müller, and other writers, consider this incapacity for speech an impassible barrier between man and the lower animals. But Darwin here seems to make good his case that they press this argument rather too far. Max Müller's argument is, that if you cannot speak, and the whole race from which you spring, has never been able to communicate its thoughts by speech, that it can have nothing to think about, and therefore it cannot think.

There is certainly much to be said for the contention, and probably the thoughts of animals take rather the form of wonder, impression, habit and association, directly connected with their various senses and are not akin to what is called ratiocination. But that they can reason in the sense of connecting cause with effect, up to a certain point there can be little doubt. They can certainly, or many of them can, exercise judgment. Dogs most assuredly can.

No one who has lived with a dog for a day can doubt it. Who has not seen a dog pause, hesitate, and reflect, before he decides on a course of action.

But until animals can speak it must forever be a matter of the purest speculation—not perhaps as to what is passing in their minds or affecting their sensatory organs, for there are other ways than speech of revealing emotions—whether they are capable of connected thought, or of forming abstract conceptions.

The best speakers in the animal kingdom are to be found amongst the birds. Parrots are really marvellous in this. It is strange that Darwin, so full as he is of narrative, and incident, and all that, in any way illustrates animal life, is so very short on this subject. It is hardly an exaggeration to say that some parrots can carry on a connected and coherent conversation. And not only can they speak, which might be attributed to mere mimicking, but they seem to know in some cases what their speech means. I can vouch for two instances which are quite remarkable. A servant girl was charged by her mistress, in the presence of a parrot, with having stolen some spoons; the girl flatly denied it, when the parrot cried out, "That's a lie, you put them in that chest," looking at a box in the corner, and there the spoons were discovered. Another parrot, when ill, crawled on to her mistress's shoulder, and, placing its head on her neck, kept repeating the words, "Poor Polly very ill," "Poor Polly very ill," and then fell dead at her feet. And no doubt these stories could be capped, and corroborated, by others equally wonderful.

The grey parrot is especially celebrated for its wonderful powers of imitation and memory. T. J. Wood, in his "Natural History," gives a good illustration of these qualities in the Grey Parrot.

"There was a parrot belonging to a friend of our family, a Portuguese gentleman. The parrot was familiar with Portuguese as well as English words and phrases. The bird evidently had the power of appreciating the distinction between the two languages, for if it were addressed its reply would always be in the language employed.

"The bird learnt a Portuguese song about itself and its manifold perfections. Saluted in Portuguese, it would answer in the same language, but was never known to confuse the two tongues together."

Their power of imitating all kinds of sounds is astonishing, and their memory is most tenacious.

Next to the parrot the magpie is probably the most garrulous and talkative of birds. Though he cannot speak in the human tongue, in his own language he is most loquacious. Ovid long ago remarked on their loquacity, and gives an account of some Macedonian young ladies who were changed into magpies, and says that they retained their fondness for gabble long after they had lost their woman's form.

> "Nunc quoque in alitibus, facundia prisca remansit,
> Rauca garrulitas, studiumque immane loquendi."

> "And still their tongues would wag, though changed to birds,
> In tiresome clack, and never-ending words."

The fact of the parrot being both in speech and reasoning much nearer, and in the latter quality quite as near to man as the monkey, and yet classed far lower down in the scale of organisation, is a discrepancy which the theory of progressive evolution cannot account for.

The late Duke of Argyle remarks that the fashioning of an implement for a special purpose is absolutely peculiar to man, and he considers this forms an immeasurable gulf between man and the brutes.

Darwin's answer to this objection is, that when man first used flint stones for any purpose, he would have accidentally splintered them, and would then have used the sharp fragments. From this step it would be a small one to break the flints on purpose, and not a very wide step to fashion them rudely. Precisely so, but why did not the monkeys do the same?

Again man is the only animal that is capable of progressive improvement. Darwin's answer to this objection is weak in the extreme. He says that young animals are more easily caught than old ones. And that domestic dogs are descended from wolves and jackals, yet they have progressed in certain moral qualities, such as affection, temper, and general intelligence. It is a moot point whether they have improved in general intelligence; and as regards affection and temper, that is merely a softening of the character they already possessed, by a favourable environment. There is no progression whatever about it.

It is frequently said that historic time is too short for such development. But there are examples from the catacombs of Egypt of animals and plants that lived in that country three thousand years ago; and according to Cuvier they are exactly like the living species. It is strange that this great length of time, should not have produced one new organ or variation, any incipience of an organ, or even the marks of a " conatus " to produce one.

And then Darwin continues in his " Descent of Man " and takes us through many pages, and very fascinating and interesting they are, contrasting, comparing and drawing inferences from the mental and moral qualities of animal and man. No one would deny that all animals have some reasoning and mental powers, and in some classes of organic life they may have reached a high level; they may even have morals or rules of life of their own, which may have some shadowy correspondence to what is known as morality in man. They may even have, so Darwin contends, something akin to the religious feeling. But this is a matter of the wildest conjecture, and if it exists at all, can hardly go beyond a certain awe and wonder at the unknown. But whether this be so or not, whether the mental and moral qualities in the animal creation differ in kind or merely in degree, or are qualities apart and "sui generis" in each organism, it hardly assists Darwin's contention, unless he can go on, and prove that they have possibilities in their nature, which only require time and opportunity to pass them into the human order, either by natural selection or the process of progressive generation.

But there is an answer to all this which to my mind appears absolutely conclusive. Now it cannot be denied—indeed, Darwin does not deny it, he fully admits it—that innumerable species, nay, whole dynasties, have appeared on this earth, have run their course, and have ceased to be, never to return again. Geology tells us this, nay, even history itself. The process is even now in operation. The extinction of the bison of North America, which at no very remote period thundered in lonely majesty and in countless hordes over large areas of the North American continent, is within the knowledge, nay, even the observation, of living men. The Dodo and Great Auk have recently become practically extinct. Now is it likely that nature, if there were further latent potentialities, in all these extinct races, should have snuffed them out before their time, and before they had brought their possibilities to full perfection and fruition! It would be very unlike nature to so

MAN AND THE MONKEY

do. They had their limitations, and they had their day, and this is surely a proof that their stock of improvement was a limited quantity.

How then could a monkey ever have become a man; and if he could where are the transitional forms?

CHAPTER VII

THE LAW OF HYBRIDITY

Before proceeding any further, it is necessary to get a clear understanding of what is generally meant, and what Darwin means by such expressions as groups, families, genus, species, and varieties, the words are used very loosely and sometimes almost interchangeably by various biologists. Are they all purely arbitrary classifications, invented for the sake of convenience and arrangement, or is there any real and vital difference between them, any systematic affinity in the members of one class which cuts it off completely from the members of another.

And this has a vital bearing on Darwin's hypothesis, for if there is no inherent difference at all, and if genus, species, and varieties are terms made use of to distinguish accentuated differences, in their various degrees, it would go a long way to prove, or rather would remove from the path one of the greatest obstacles that stands in the way of Darwin's contention, namely, that all organic life emanated from one source, or from a common centre.

Looking at it roughly the difference between a variation and a species is apparent. No one would call two Englishmen variations of the " genus homo,"

THE LAW OF HYBRIDITY

but they would call, say, an Englishman, a Zulu, and a Mongolian, variations of the same. Or a common red geranium and an ivyleaved, would be considered variations of the same species. Many variations of course are obvious, but some varieties closely resemble two or more different species, and then the distinction becomes more intricate and confused.

Moreover, the question is always arising, whether any given specimen should be classed as a species by itself or a sub-species, or variety.

On page thirty of the " Origin of Species," Darwin says :—

" Nor shall I here discuss the various definitions which have been given of the term species. Not one definition has satisfied all naturalists, yet every naturalist knows vaguely what he means when he speaks of species. Generally the term includes the unknown element of a distinct act of creation. The term ' variety ' is almost equally difficult to define ; but here community of descent is almost universally implied, though it can rarely be proved."

Again on page thirty-six :—

" The term species thus comes to be a mere useless abstraction, implying and assuming a separate act of creation. It is certain that many forms, considered by highly competent judges to be varieties, resemble species so completely in character, that they have been thus ranked by other highly competent judges. But to discuss whether they ought to be called species or varieties, before any definition of these terms has been generally accepted is vainly to beat the air."

But surely a distinct act of creation is anything but a useless abstraction. On the contrary, it supplies the axiomatic background, which in this question of biology is so sorely needed. Just as it is impossible to discuss the properties of a circle, until you define what a circle is, so it is difficult to discuss the question of species, and all that it implies, until you come to some clear understanding as to what species actually means.

Once accept the definition " that a species is a set of living organisms that refuse to intercross with any other set of living organisms," and many other things become plain. But Darwin and other naturalists refuse to pin themselves down to any such limitation, with the inevitable consequence that the discussion of such a question as that of hybridity becomes exceedingly difficult.

Not that it is necessary to make " species " the ultimate classification. Take the case of birds. A heron and a sparrow would not, and could not, interbreed, and therefore are as regards each other true species; but they are both birds nevertheless, and belong to the same " genus " or higher classification, namely, " bird life."

This question of biological nomenclature is of more importance than appears at first sight. It greatly exercised so eminent a naturalist as Linnæus, who

THE LAW OF HYBRIDITY

was the author of the binominal system of naming plants.

There seems no reason in the nature of things why the three terms, "genus," "species," and "varieties," should not be sufficient for all purposes of demarcation; to introduce further words, such as "groups," "families," and "orders," only leads to confusion.

Varieties, speaking generally, are merely abnormal and accentuated deviations from the original stock, the result of various causes, such as physical and climatic conditions, transmission by inheritance, the use and disuse of parts, etc.

And again, in the "Descent of Man," Darwin makes on this subject the following observations :—

"In determining whether two or more allied forms ought to be ranked as species or varieties, naturalists are practically guided by the following considerations, namely, the amount of difference between them, and whether such differences relate to few or many points of structure, and whether they are of physiological importance; but more especially whether they are constant. Constancy of character is what is chiefly sought for by naturalists. Whenever it can be shown or rendered probable that forms in question have remained distinct for a long period, that becomes an argument of much weight in favour of treating them as species. Even a slight degree of sterility between any two forms, when first crossed or in their offspring, is generally considered a decisive test of their specific distinctness."

What does this last sentence point to, but to the rigidity of species, and multiplicity, as against simplicity of origin?

But the preceding classification can hardly be called a definition, as it lays down no law and gives no idea or well-cut line of demarcation. And it is incumbent on Darwin to tell us what he means by species, before he proceeds to state that he no longer believes in the stability of species, and that species are not immutable. He frequently uses the words species, subspecies, and variety, in different senses and interchangeably, according as it suits the purposes of his argument to do so.

For instance, he calls the various breeds of dogs and sheep species. But it was common knowledge long before Darwin existed, that various breeds of dogs and various breeds of sheep would intercross. The proper word for these breeds is surely not "species," but "varieties." If he could prove that dogs and sheep would interbreed, or even pigeons or barn-door fowls, there might be something in his contention. But so stern is Nature's law against any intermixture of this sort, that even such near kinsmen as the horse and the ass, as I have before remarked, which both belong to the Order "Equidæ," though themselves capable of a first cross, have yet their offspring, the mule, cursed with sterility.

There is a natural repugnance to union between different species, and in a state of nature this can rarely be overcome. Moreover, the hybrid offspring

THE LAW OF HYBRIDITY 115

is nearly always—probably always if the true circumstances of the case were known—incapable of propagating its own kind, without union with one of the original species by which it was produced, and this inability to continue the mixed race has been generally regarded amongst naturalists, as the best characteristic of species. Occasionally, but rarely, hybrid races do propagate their kind; but there is always a strong tendency to revert to the original stock, and ere long the hybrid race runs out, and were it not for the forcing and fostering hand of man, hybridity would be a thing unknown. Nature has placed strong and fast barriers round species, so that their identity should be preserved, and their identity is kept distinct from century to century. It is idle to suppose that the laws of hybridity will account for any radical transmutation of species as Darwin's hypothesis supposes.

The great law of hybridity is absolutely fatal to any such development, and geology abounds with facts and evidence in support of it. You may search through the whole geological record, and all the archives of geology, in vain for facts that show anything like a passage of one species, genus, or family into another. Indeed, so inflexible is the rule that when pollen from a plant of one family is placed on the stigma of a plant of a distinct family, it exerts no more influence than does so much more inorganic dust.

The need for clearness of definition could not be better illustrated than by the discussion of the law of hybridity, and the want of it lands Darwin in many contradictions—some real and some apparent. He himself admits that " it is difficult to discuss the question of species and all that it implies, until you come to some clear understanding of what ' species ' actually means."

He never does come to a clear understanding, but goes on to discuss it nevertheless, at the cost of much confusion to himself, and of considerable bewilderment to the reader. The whole of this question of hybridity is delicate, dangerous, and obscure, and I have no intention of rushing in where specialists fear to tread. Darwin himself can hardly see his way through the tangled jungle of conflicting, doubtful, and inexhaustive evidence. I only refer to it here, as it shows Darwin at his weakest, and discloses more than any other chapter in the book, the extreme lengths of advocacy to which he will go, to break down, if possible, the barrier of species, and substantiate the fertility of hybrids. His object is apparent. Every chapter in the " Origin " is a strenuous endeavour on his part to establish greater intercommunity in nature, and thereby let in and justify the operation of his law of Natural Selection. But even if he were successful in so doing, it merely proves that Sexual Selection, plus selection by man, are the true instruments in effecting it, and not Natural Selection at all.

But from the general obscurity on the subject some points do seem to emerge into practical certainty.

THE LAW OF HYBRIDITY 117

Species,—if one allows Darwin's somewhat loose description of it to stand,—will sometimes interbreed, though they must be nearly allied; and when this crossing does occur, it is generally under the protection of domestication. Varieties will, of course, frequently, if not always, intermingle, the success and fertility of their offspring as a rule depending on the closeness of their alliance and the proximity of the common ancestor. Hybrids of animals are rarely fertile:—

"Hardly any cases have been ascertained with certainty of hybrids from two distinct species of animals being perfectly fertile."

As regards the sterility of plants when crossed, and of their hybrid offspring, the evidence is very conflicting, partly owing to the want of any great scientific precision in the experiments, and on account of their success and persistence so largely depending on artificial fostering and protection. But, whatever the exceptions, in all classes of organisms there is always a tendency of reversion to type, and it is idle to suppose that the laws of hybridity will account for any radical mutation. To accomplish this, it would need as strong a tendency in nature to a union of species, and genera, as now exists against it.

But to turn for a moment to the actual evidence on this question of hybridism and sterility. Of what does it actually consist, and how does Darwin handle it? The opinion of naturalists is divided and uncertain, and their experiments are chiefly confined to plant life.

Kölreuter, and Gärtner, whom Darwin himself refers to as "two conscientious and admirable observers who devoted their lives to the subject," are both of them of the opinion that species and their hybrid offspring when first crossed are sterile. Kölreuter makes the rule universal; but then he cuts the knot, for in ten cases in which he found two forms, considered by most authors as distinct species, quite fertile together, he ranks them as varieties.

Gärtner was enabled to rear some hybrids, for six or seven, and in one case for ten generations; yet he asserts positively that their fertility never increases, but generally decreases greatly and suddenly.

Now the way Darwin answers this is characteristic of a great deal of his reasoning. Instead of admitting at once that this is strong evidence against his contention, he explains the difficulty in this way.

"With respect to the decrease, it may first be noticed that when any deviation in structure or constitution is common to both parents, this is often transmitted in an augmented degree to the offspring: and both sexual elements in hybrid plants are already affected in some degree. But I believe that their fertility has been diminished in nearly all these cases by an independent cause, namely, by too close interbreeding."

THE LAW OF HYBRIDITY 119

But how does that help him! Whatever the cause of it, it is part of the method by which nature works out her beneficent design, and puts her ban on intercrossing, and illicit intercourse in nature. If there is any truth in Darwin's statement that sterility is due to too close interbreeding, why does not it act in the same way on the pure species as well as on the hybrids?

It will be noticed that the very few instances of intercrossing that Darwin is enabled to produce, chiefly refer to plant life and are not verified with any great scientific precision, and it is quite possible, that so low down in the scale of organic life, nature may be slightly more lax and allow a somewhat greater latitude, as promiscuous interbreeding would not be nearly so confounding and disastrous in its results as in the higher families, but one may be pretty certain that even if among plants species do sometimes intercross they are closely allied and the common ancestor is not remote.

Darwin lays great stress on the Hon. W. Herbert's experiments and says:—

" Of his many important statements I will here give only a single one as an example, namely, ' that every ovale in a pod of *Crinum capense* fertilised by *C. revolutum* produced a plant, which I never saw to occur in a case of nature's fecundation.'

" So that here we have perfect or even more than commonly perfect fertility in a first cross between distinct species."

But Darwin fails to state that these two plants both belong to the order *Amaryllidæ*.

As regards the transmutation of animals, he practically abandons the case; for he says:—

"Although I know of hardly any thoroughly well authenticated cases of perfectly fertile hybrid animals, I have reason to believe, etc."

And again:—

"This is clearly shown by hybrids never having been raised between the species in distinct families, and on the other hand by very closely allied species generally uniting with facility."

Of hybrid animals he can give no authentic illustration; and on the strength of this Darwin has the boldness to assert that he has discovered that species are not immutable. Even if it could be proved up to the hilt that some few species low down in the scale of organisation do sometimes intercross, and that occasionally owing either to some freak, or abnormal action of nature, or to the forcing, and fostering hand of man, their hybrid offspring can perpetuate their kind and continue for a time, it would only prove an insignificant exception to a universal rule, that nature has her limits and very strict limits too, to any sort of passage, between not merely a few, but innumerable families of organic life.

He closes the argument in the following way:—

"We must, therefore, either give up the belief

THE LAW OF HYBRIDITY 121

in the universal sterility of species when crossed or we must look at this sterility in animals, not as an indelible characteristic; but as one capable of being removed by domestication."

This is a very negative and hardly a fair way of stating his case, if he means it to be worth anything at all as an argument in favour of the mutability of species. The sterility in hybrids, may not be a universal and indelible characteristic, there may be a few forced and exceptional instances here and there, but that in no way seriously affects the great general proposition and universal law, that species breed true and will never intermingle.

He then asks the following question :—

"Now do those complex and singular rules indicate that species have been endowed with sterility simply to prevent their becoming confounded in nature. I think not!"

Here one would imagine most people would disagree with Darwin and think quite differently. The law is obvious and its intention apparent, for if there were no restrictions on promiscuous interbreeding the disorganisation, and disentegration of animal life would soon be complete, and there would meet us at every turn monstrosities and eccentricities that would shock the imagination of an opium eater.

It will be observed that nearly all the instances of hybrids and their fertility are the result of domestication. Darwin's knowledge of domestic animals was great, and he is nowhere more at home, or felicitous, than when discussing them. His speciality was pigeons; he enumerates their varieties, and gives it as his opinion that the Jacobins, the Carriers, the Pouters, the Tumblers, etc., are all descended from the "Columba Livia," or Common Rock Pigeon. If, he tells us—

> "the several breeds are not varieties, they must have descended from at least seven or eight aboriginal species: for it is impossible to make the present domestic breeds from any lesser number; how, for instance, could a pouter be produced by crossing two breeds, unless one of the parent stocks possessed the characteristic enormous crop?"

But how, if this be true, could a pouter be produced from the common rock pigeon, which has no accentuated crop at all?

And then he proceeds to give a few interesting historical details which may be of interest to the reader, and relieve this somewhat dry, technical discussion:—"Pigeons have been watched and tended with the utmost care, and loved by many people. They have been domesticated for thousands of years in many quarters of the world; the earliest known records of pigeons is in the fifth Egyptian dynasty, about 3000 B.C., but Mr Birch informs me that pigeons are given in a bill of fare in the previous dynasty. In the time of the Romans, as we hear from Pliny, immense prices were given for pigeons;

THE LAW OF HYBRIDITY

' nay, they are come to this pass, that they can reckon up their pedigree and race.' Pigeons were much valued by Akber Khan in India, about the year 1600 ; never less than 20,000 pigeons were taken with the Court. ' The monarchs of Iran and Turan sent him some very rare birds,' and, continues the courtly historian, ' His Majesty by crossing the breeds, which method was never practised before, has improved them astonishingly.' About this same period the Dutch were as eager about pigeons as were the old Romans."

Then Darwin asks the question—

"As man can produce, and certainly has produced, a great result by his methodical and unconscious means of selecting, what may not natural selection effect ? "

Of course, man can produce great results. But why ? Man is a free agent, Nature is not. Man can select his species pretty well when, where, and how he pleases. As far as breeding from them goes, he can practically do what he will. His instruments are like clay in the hands of the potter. According to Natural Selection, nature requires time, and an inordinate extension of it, to bring about the smallest constant modification.

And then he proceeds :—

" How fleeting are the wishes and efforts of man ! How short his time ! and consequently how poor will be his results, compared with those accumulated by nature during whole geological periods! Can we wonder then, that nature's productions should be far 'truer' in character than man's productions; that they should be infinitely better adapted to the most complex conditions of life, and should bear the stamp of far higher workmanship."

This is all very good, as a little piece of rhetorical flourish, but it is somewhat out of place in a serious scientific discussion, and is not entirely true. For are man's results so poor? Why Darwin has just been labouring through several pages to show that they are not.

Man can do more by selection in changing the structure, appearance, and habits of an animal in one hundred years, than nature can do in a million. Would nature unaided ever have produced a horse with the speed of an "Eclipse" or an "Ormonde"?

Could nature with unlimited time at her disposal ever make a watch, yet man can make one in a few days! And he does it by selection precisely in the same way that he selects his animals for mating. He selects the brass, the steel, and the glass and brings them together, and a watch is the result, indeed, it would not be beyond the resources of mechanical contrivance, as Paley has pointed out, to make a watch that would reproduce itself.

Nature's productions in the particular instance under discussion are not far truer than man's, nor are

THE LAW OF HYBRIDITY 125

they infinitely better adapted to the most complex conditions of life.

But even if Darwin could make out a far better case for hybridisation, and its ultimate fertility, than he actually can ; and if he could prove, as he seems to think possible, that most of the barriers between species could be largely broken down by domestication ; how does that advance his theory of Natural Selection ? So far from assisting it, it is inimical to it, and in conflict with it, and for this reason :—

His primary law lays it down again and again, in language that cannot be mistaken, that Natural Selection

"leads to the improvement of *each creature* in relation to its organic and inorganic conditions of life."

" It will never produce in a being any structure more injurious than beneficial, for Natural Selection acts solely by and for the good of each ! "

And again :—

" We may feel assured that any variation in the least degree injurious would be rapidly destroyed."

And yet he admits that hybridisation has a disintegrating and injurious effect on the whole system, more especially on the organs of reproduction.

Both the above propositions cannot possibly be true ; the one undermines the other, and is in direct antagonism to it.

Darwin seems aware of this discrepancy, but is

somewhat shy of it. He makes for it the following apology:—" I am convinced that the struggle between Natural Selection on the one hand and the tendency to reversion and variability on the other, will in the course of time cease. I see no reason to doubt it." But why does he see no reason to doubt it? He does not say. And to see " no reason to doubt " that an obstacle may not ultimately be removed, is not to remove it; and to remove it he must, before his theory gets a chance of even starting on its journey at all.

CHAPTER VIII

TRANSITIONAL VARIETIES, AND THE GEOLOGICAL RECORD

DARWIN opens Chapter VI. of the "Origin of Species" with the following sentence :—

"Long before the reader has arrived at this part of my work, a crowd of difficulties will have occurred to him. Some of them are so serious that to this day I can hardly reflect on them without being in some degree staggered, but to the best of my judgment the greater number are only apparent, and those that are real are not, I think, fatal to the theory."

The difficulties are serious enough to stagger not only Darwin, but humanity itself, and indeed whoever reads the "Origin" with the power of consecutive reasoning at all. He raises many more difficulties than he is able, not only to solve, but either to circumvent or overthrow. He sees the billows ahead, and no one realises their power more than himself. By great subtlety and ingenuity of reasoning he gets through some of them, but they remain really untouched, precisely as the wave does by the diver that goes through it. All through Chapter VI. his style is labyrinthine and verbose, his reasoning very difficult to follow, and where it has any evidential value, it is a mere drop in the bucket to what one would have expected. There is a great deal too much of the "ifs" and "ands" style of argument. Moreover, his tone is apologetic, and hesitating throughout; there is hardly anywhere a note of triumphant vindication. One frequently meets with sentences such as this :—

> "This difficulty for a long time quite confounded me. But I think it can be in a large part explained."

Surely the "onus" is on Darwin, not merely to get rid of difficulties but to establish his theory. For instance, if a miracle is a difficulty in the path of Christianity, you go no way to prove the truth of Christianity by getting the miracle out of the way. To clear a piece of land of obstacles is not to make a road. And nearly the whole of Darwin's time is taken up in the "Origin" in grappling with obstacles that are not merely immovable but unshakable.

Now one of the most formidable dragons that stand in the path of Darwin's theory, that he must slay and overcome before he can make any headway at all is this : "Why, if species had descended by fine gradations from other species, do we not everywhere see innumerable transitional forms ? Why is not all nature in confusion, instead of the species being as we see them, well defined ? "

In the first place, without illimitable time at his

TRANSITIONAL VARIETIES

disposal, Darwin's theory of "Natural Selection" collapses at once, and he himself admits it. He is very anxious on the question of time, even the time allowed for the formation of the various geological strata, which taken together amount to many millions of years, is not sufficient. So to get over the difficulty Darwin suggests, though with some slight warrant it is true for his suggestion—the whole question is, I believe, still *sub judice* in the geological world—that immense periods of time must have elapsed between the close of one geological formation and the commencement of another. But is this illimitable extension of time necessary for Nature's operations, and is Nature willing to concede it? Relatively speaking Nature requires very little time to reveal the hidden potentialities in any organism. Who could believe that the tiny ovule or seed from which man starts, could in the short space of twenty-one years be converted into a senior wrangler, capable of understanding and appreciating some of the most advanced problems of mathematics.

Darwin himself is doubtful, whether Nature is willing to extend him all the time he requires. For on page two hundred and sixty-eight of the "Origin" he says:—

"Here we encounter a formidable objection, for it seems doubtful whether the earth, in a fit state for the habitation of living creatures, has lasted long enough. Sir W. Thompson concludes that the consolidation of the crust can hardly have occurred less than twenty, or more than four hundred million years ago. These very wide limits show how doubtful the data are, and other elements may hereafter have to be introduced into the problem."

One would think that there must be something very doubtful, and wanting, in a theory that requires more than twenty million years as a field of operations upon which to work.

Now how does Darwin fill up this void, and supply and account for the absence, of these expected and infinite gradations ! He says :—

" As Natural Selection acts solely by the preservation of profitable modifications, each new form will tend in a fully stocked country to take the place of, and finally to exterminate, its own less improved parent forms with which it comes into competition. Thus extinction and natural selection go hand in hand. Hence, if we look at each species as descended from some unknown form, both the parent and all the transitional varieties will generally have been exterminated by the very process of the formation and perfection of the new form."

But this explanation is more ingenious than convincing.

What Darwin means is this, that in every species a time arrives when in a certain number of the class a beneficial variation appears, which gives those members who are fortunate enough to possess it, an advantage over those that do not. Those possessed of this advantage do not deliberately destroy those without, but those without it, are handicapped in the struggle for existence, by the want of this advantage, and tend finally to disappear. But this is a slow process, and in a species comprising millions of units, a certain number at any rate would live on and be contemporaneous from the lowest, to the highest, step of the ladder of gradation, and it is almost a certainty that if this principle really operated through the whole field of organic life, that there would be many living representatives of infinite grades of variation. But these are rarely found. Species remain constant, and are for ever well defined. Let me illustrate what I mean.

Man is historically known to have existed for at least five thousand years, and all evidence goes to prove that he was practically the same being five thousand years ago, that he is now, structurally, organically, functionally, and physiologically. No variation, or even incipient variation, of a permanent kind has anywhere been observed. The Chinaman, the Hindoo, and the Negro, all down this long period have remained the same. Of course individuals vary, as they do now, and the appearance of these races may have changed, but whatever changes have taken place, are due either to the environment, to physical conditions, transmission by inheritance, or sexual intercourse. But there has never been any differentiating alteration, to indicate that the race is taking a new departure. But supposing that there had been, surely there would be innumerable instances of these variant members living at the same time, and all down the line of historic knowledge; but this is not the case, and there is no getting away from the fact.

Darwin, I suppose, would say: "Oh! five thousand years goes for nothing, it is not nearly long enough to make even the commencement of a variation." But the question arises, has man been for so lengthy a period an inhabitant of this earth? If he has, how is it that there are no well-authenticated instances of his fossil remains beyond the alluvial period, for his bones have the same chemical composition as the bones of other animals, and therefore are no more liable to decay. The answer, I suppose, to this is, that though man has not been so discovered, his weapons and tools have, such as stone implements. These stone tools, so the geologist tells us, have been found in many places in England and France. There is still a certain amount of pardonable scepticism attaching to these discoveries, as broken fragments of stone very frequently take the form of fashioned articles. Take the wonderful geometrical figures formed by the snow-flakes; if they had been made of enduring material and discovered in some palæolithic gravel, man would at once have set them down as the works of man, but man would have been wrong in so doing.

TRANSITIONAL VARIETIES 133

Darwin would be the first to deny that a variety of living organisms so diverse as sheep, pigs, goats, lions, and tigers sprang immediately from the parent protoplasm of all life. If he were to concede that, his theory of Natural Selection would be unmeaning. The only alternative, according to Darwin, is that the original protoplastic progenitor gave birth to its own kind, and that by the application of the theory of Natural Selection all down the ages, its offspring assumed the variety of forms that they now possess. But it is difficult to see how, at the outset, this is consistent with Darwin's "dictum" that "Natural Selection" acts solely for the preservation of profitable modification.

But the witness of the living is not so powerful, against Darwin's theory, as the witness of the dead. Let us turn to the geological record, and see what it has to reveal.

" But as by this theory innumerable transitional forms must have existed, why do we not find them embedded in countless numbers in the crust of the earth. I will only state that I believe the answer mainly lies in the record being incomparably less perfect than is generally supposed. The crust of the earth is a vast museum, but the natural collections have been imperfectly made, and only at long intervals of time."

And again in the chapter on the Imperfection of the Geological Record, he says :—

"Why, then, is not every geological formation, and every stratum, full of such intermediate links? Geology assuredly does not reveal any such finely graduated organic chain; and this, perhaps, is the most obvious and serious objection which can be urged against the theory. The explanation is, as I believe, in the extreme imperfection of the geological record."

All through this argument, Darwin and the geological record, remind one very much of the story of Balak and Balaam. Darwin entreats the geological record to give him its support, but the record can only answer with recorded facts, or what the Lord has put in its mouth. I called you, says Darwin, as a witness to establish my case, but you have rather discredited it altogether. Reveal some more intermediate species, or my cause is a lost one! But the record is mute, and the little it does say, is so faulty, weak, and inadequate that it had better have kept silence altogether. So Darwin begins belabouring the geological museum much as Balaam belaboured his ass.

"Now let us turn to our richest geological museums and what a paltry display we behold! That our collections are imperfect is admitted by every one. Only a small part of the surface of the earth has been geologically explored."

But this last sentence is useless as evidence. It is idle for a defendant to say there are many more witnesses to my character, but I am unable to produce them. Moreover, he states on page two hundred and sixty-five of the "Origin" "that negative evidence is worthless, as experience has often shown." Not that negative evidence is always by any means worthless, on the contrary it is very valuable. That a centaur has never been discovered, is strong presumptive evidence that it never will be. It is one of the strong points made by men of science against the Gospel miracles, that since the commencement of the Christian era, no well-authenticated instance of a miracle has ever been produced. It is only positive palæontological evidence, says Darwin, that may be implicitly trusted. And what does this positive palæontological evidence come to, even on Darwin's own showing. Why, a mere nothing. The evidence is fragmentary to a degree, and yet Darwin himself asserts :—

"That the number of intermediate and transitional links, between all living and extinct species, must have been inconceivably great."

Indeed so fragmentary is the evidence, that Darwin omits to give any, but wanders off in his chapter on the Imperfection of the Geological Record, with a somewhat irrelevant and rather remote discussion on the construction of the human eye, and on the immense period of time it takes to make a geological formation. The real truth of the matter is that neither alive, nor dead, are there any intermediate forms available worthy of the name, which there unquestionably would have been, had Darwin's theory been sound.

The absence of these intermediate forms in fossil remains is partly accounted for in this way. The imperfection of the geological record, we are told, largely results from another and more important cause than any of the foregoing; namely, from general formations being separated from each other by immense intervals of time. This doctrine has been emphatically admitted, by many geologists, and palæontologists, who like E. Forbes, entirely disbelieve in the change of species.

But some change in the earth's surface must be always and for ever in operation. If a structure is not in process of formation, it must be in process of destruction. There is no standing still. No portion of the earth's surface is precisely the same to-day as it was yesterday; climatic, chemical, and alluvial action are always at work, and the piling up of one formation must, be the denudation of another.

For this reason it is difficult to see, why the fact of a fossil remains of organic life being found in any given stratum, formation, or period, is itself of necessity a true index to the age of that fossil or of the date at which it flourishes on the earth. Of course this would be so, if all the strata and formations were laid in horizontal lines one above the other, but this is by no means always the case.

On the contrary they seem rather to take the form

TRANSITIONAL VARIETIES 137

of segments of a circle laid one within the other, with their ends or "outcrop" protruding on the surface of the earth, and sometimes lying, side by side, with recent alluvial deposit. Now if the fossil were found in the extreme dip of the segment, of course that would be a certain indication of its age, being contemporaneous with that of the formation in which it was found. But if it were found in the "outcrop," I take it that would still be classed by naturalists as contemporaneous in time with the formation. But is that of necessity the case? And if it is not, then the mere fact of its being found in a particular formation is no true index as to its age.

If you were to ask many of Darwin's disciples, or men who wish to be taken as such, and to be thought "well up in their Darwin," though probably their real knowledge of his meaning and writings is second hand; where are the intermediate forms? they would point to this, and that instance, in the various museums of the world, and assert that they were to be found in abundance. In the first place, abundance is a relative word and the theory is immensity itself: for it cannot be too thoroughly ingrained in the mind of any and every reader that Darwin's hypothesis has to account for the procession of the whole of organic life which covers a period of something between 20,000,000 and 60,000,000 million of years. Now I ask the reader to picture in his mind the data necessary to establish with any plausible show of evidential truth such an hypothesis as that! The necessary evidence is unattained, and one may say with certainty quite unattainable.

It is useless to contrast the evidence, with evidence necessary for mathematics, for the two sciences lie in different planes, and are occupied in quite a different sphere of action. The one follows the deductive process of reasoning, the other the inductive. And all inductive sciences are built up of facts, precisely as a house is built up of bricks.

But let us conclude for a moment that there are several, nay many if you will, of fossil remains that have the semblance of intermediate links.

In the first place you have to prove that these intermediate links are really true links, and not things *sui generis* or species apart, having a progenitor, however remote, peculiarly their own. And this is a very difficult thing to do. Sir J. Lubbock has remarked that " every species is a link between other allied forms." But here he begs the whole question. Is it! and if so why so? Surely it is useless to seek for the missing link, that will bind the man and the monkey together, for however great the similarity, that this intermediary creature if discovered might possess, you could never prove that it had not a line of descent of its own. Neither would mere resemblance assist one. Darwin himself is emphatic on this point: for he says :—

" For animals belonging to two distinct lines of descent, may have become adapted to similar conditions and thus have assumed a close external resemblance; but such resemblance will not reveal—will rather tend to conceal their blood-relationship."

A great deal of Darwin's argument in his chapter on Transitional varieties hinges on the meaning given to the word "link." Much confusion arises from the want of clear and precise definition of important words all through the "Origin of Species." Take for instance such words as Selection, Link, Species, and Variety. They are all used in uncertain and different senses. On page two hundred and eighty-three Darwin refers to Professor Owen's discoveries and says :—

"In the writings of Professor Owen we continually meet with the expression of generalised forms, synthetic types: and these terms imply that such forms are in fact intermediate or connecting links. Cuvier ranked the ruminants and pachyderms as two of the most distinct orders of mammals: but so many fossil links have been disembowelled that Owen has had to alter the whole classification. . . . No one will deny that the Hipparion is intermediate between the existing horse and certain older ungulate forms."

As a matter of fact if Darwin's theory of Natural Selection—that is infinite gradation through all organic life produced by almost limitless time—were really true, such words as "orders" and "links" would be altogether unnecessary. No such thing as a link could exist. Every living thing, would imperceptibly shade off into every other living thing, like hues on a dove's neck, that are incapable of definition or outline.

The necessity of the word "link" can only arise when you admit that an infinite number of species, trace their descent from the first to their own peculiar progenitor, that is a progenitor that had a separate creation.

What animals could be much more unlike than a dachshund, a greyhound, and a St Bernard dog! They are all dogs, and belong to the same family. They could not properly be called links at all. They are mere varieties of the same species.

Again turn to the genus "Equus." The type species is the "Equus caballus." But since Darwin wrote, a genuine wild species of horse has been discovered by a gentleman named Prezevalsky, in the mountains of central Asia. It differs in some respects from the Equus Caballus, especially about the mane and tail. And if Darwin were alive, he would certainly call this horse a link or intermediary between the Equus Caballus and the Hipparion. But all these three animals belong to the order "equus" and are no more real links than are a "dachshund," a greyhound, or a St Bernard.

Indeed, whether you insist on a common progenitor for all living things, or admit innumerable stocks of descent, it is difficult to see how a link proper can arise, except by interbreeding.

TRANSITIONAL VARIETIES 141

Darwin himself admits the difficulty, about the uncertain use of the words species, orders, families, and genera. For he says :—

" Finally with respect to the comparative value of the various groups of species, such as orders, sub-orders, families, sub-families, and genera, they seem to be, at least at present, almost arbitrary. Several of the best botanists, such as Mr Bentham and others, have strongly insisted on their arbitrary value."

But be these things as they may, the "infinite gradations" so essential to the hypothesis, have yet to be discovered. The living and the dead alike refuse to reveal them. A distinguished naturalist (Deshayes) has declared that "he has discovered in surveying the entire series of fossil animal remains, five great groups, so completely independent that no species whatever is found in more than one of them."

Each great group was entirely distinct from that which preceded it, though each group was exactly adapted to the climate and food provided.

Moreover, let any man look for himself through any of the geological museums, and he will see the same old specimens eternally. The gastropods, the cephalopods, the brachiopods, the decapods, the ammonites, etc., all as distinct as ever they can be with no, or hardly any intermediary varieties. They meet the eye again and again, with the same invariable monotony, as the Jebusites, the Perizzites, and the Amorites do, in the book of Deuteronomy.

But how does Darwin sum up the whole matter, and what answer has he to make. He finds it impossible to prove that black is white, so he admits the difficulty, but denies its overwhelming objection and passes on.

He says :—

"He who rejects this view of the imperfection of the geological record, will rightly reject the whole theory. For he may ask in vain where are the numberless transitional links which must formerly have connected the closely allied or representative species, found in the successive stages of the same great formation."

Darwin simply infers that if the geological record were fully explored, the evidence would be in his favour. But what right has he to draw that inference? All the evidence that the geological record does reveal, and it is considerable, tells dead against his contention.

Let me illustrate this by taking one system only, namely the Silurian; what story does this tell us, and what fossils does it reveal of the invertebrate class? It reveals about six different species, as distinct and well marked species as could well be imagined, but few if any graduated varieties or anything approaching them are forthcoming. First of all there is a trilobite, so called because the shield

TRANSITIONAL VARIETIES 143

covering their backs is divided into three lobes. Next there is a fossil very like a shrimp, a third one of the oyster class, the fourth a gastropod, and then a cephalopod. And these well marked distinctions run through—whenever and wherever fossil remains are found—each successive geological formation. And the record of the living tells the same story as the record of the dead.

And in his recapitulation, at the end of the work, sums up the whole argument thus :—

> "On this doctrine of the extermination of an infinitude of connecting links, between the living and extinct inhabitants of the world, and at each successive period between the extinct and still older species, why is not every geological formation charged with such links? Why does not every collection of fossil remains afford plain evidence of the gradation, and mutation, of the forms of life? Although geological research has undoubtedly revealed the former existence of many links, bringing numerous forms of life much closer together, it does not yield the many infinitely fine gradations between past and present species required on the theory."

(One might add nor even approximately fine gradation.)

> "And this is the most obvious of the many objections which may be urged against it. Why again do whole groups of allied species appear, though this appearance is often false, to have

come in suddenly on the successive geological stages? Although we now know that organic beings appeared on this globe, at a period incalculably remote, long before the lowest bed of the Cambrian system was deposited, why do we not find beneath this system great piles of strata stored with the remains of the progenitors of the Cambrian fossils? For on the theory, such strata must somewhere have been deposited, at these ancient and utterly unknown epochs of the world's history."

I will conclude this chapter by quoting a few instances of apparent contradictions.

On page one hundred and ten of the "Origin of Species" we find :—

"As 'vegetable repetition,' to use Professor Owen's expression, is a sign of low organisation, the foregoing statements accord with the common opinion of naturalists, that beings which stand low in the scale of nature are more variable than those which are higher."

I do not know what naturalists are referred to, but it certainly was not the opinion of Sir Charles Lyell, who Darwin frequently quotes, for he says, that subsequent researches seem to show that this greater duration of the specific form in the class mollusca is dependent on a still more general law, namely, that the lower the grade of animals, or the greater the simplicity of their structure, the more

TRANSITIONAL VARIETIES 145

persistent are they in general in other specific characters throughout vast periods of time.

But on page two hundred and seventy-two we find :—

"There is some reason to believe that organisms high in the scale, change more quickly than those which are low: though there are exceptions to the rule."

Again on page two hundred and ninety-seven—in contrasting life in the Old and New World he says :—

"Notwithstanding this general parellelism in the conditions of the Old and New Worlds how widely different are their living productions."

But on page three hundred and ten :—

"It is indeed a remarkable fact to see so many plants of the same species living on the snowy regions of the Alps or Pyrenees, and in the extreme northern parts of Europe; but it is far more remarkable, that the plants on the White Mountains, in the United States of America, are all the same with those of Labrador, and nearly all the same, as we hear from Asa Gray, with those on the loftiest mountains of Europe. Even as long ago as 1747, such facts led Gmelin to conclude that the same species must have been created at many distinct points."

Again in discussing the single centres of creation :

K

Darwin remarks on page two hundred and ninety-two :—

"No geologist feels any difficulty in Great Britain possessing the same quadrupeds with the rest of Europe for they were no doubt once united. But if the same species can be produced at two separate points, why do we not find a single mammal common to Europe, or Australia, or South America? The conditions of life are really the same, so that a multitude of European animals and plants have become naturalised in America and Australia, and some of the original plants are identically the same at those distant points of the northern and southern hemisphere."

But on page two hundred and ninety-two :—

"Nor can it be pretended that it is an immutable law that marsupials should have been chiefly or solely produced in Australia, or that Edentata, or other American types should have been solely produced in South America, for we know that Europe in ancient times was peopled by numerous marsupials."

These several statements are to my mind very difficult to reconcile.

And not only does Darwin at times contradict himself, but he repeats himself over and over again almost "*ad nauseam.*" Whole paragraphs are almost verbally the same. The whole book would gain by re-arrangement and condensation. It is another piece of evidence of the weakness of Darwin's contention, and cannot be all attributed to the complexity of the material. His style is vastly different in the "Descent of Man" and far pleasanter and easier reading, as the style there is rather narrative and historic than argumentative or controversial.

CHAPTER IX

CENTRES OF CREATION, THE ICE-AGE, AND MEANS OF DISPERSAL

I PROPOSE to discuss in this chapter Darwin's account of three subjects, all intimately connected, single, and multiple centres of creation, means of dispersal, and the great Ice-Age.

One great difficulty or obstacle presents itself, in the chapters in which these questions are discussed, which, like many other obstacles already enumerated, is serious, and a very serious obstacle it is. The fact has to be accounted for that similar and identical species, are found in regions the most remote and dissimilar, and apparently without any possibility of their having been transported from one point of the earth's surface to another. The natural inference of course is, that there must have been multiple centres of creation, and many stocks of descent. This does not suit Darwin's theory at all. He will have none of it: some other explanation must be forthcoming. But whence the necessity for dragging in such an enormous instrument as the ice-age to account for the identity of species to be found at different, and distant places, on the earth's surface? It certainly does not seem in accordance with the law of "least action" and is a very big instrument to employ, to crack so small a nut. But the nut is a hard one, and it is doubtful if even the ice-age is powerful enough to break its shell. Moreover, to drag in the ice-age seems almost unnecessary, for even if one concedes the point, that a single centre, and not multiple centres of creation, is the true explanation, there are other methods than the ice-age, as I will endeavour to show which are equally capable of coping with the difficulty.

But before proceeding to discuss the subject, again I ask why does not Darwin at once admit that there have been, and must have been innumerable " stirps " of descent. It is a far more probable hypothesis than Darwin's own, it at once accounts for the similarities, and dissimilarities to be found in all organic life, it accounts for classes only interbreeding among their kind, one escapes all the difficulties, complexities, and sea of confusion into which his theory inevitably leads one, and which his evidence is totally inadequate and insufficient to support: a theory the obstacles in the way of which even Darwin himself, with all his ingenuity and powers of reasoning, is quite unequal to removing, and which if he could succeed in removing out of his path would hardly bring him any nearer to his goal.

It will be necessary in discussing Chapter XII. of the Origin, to follow Darwin's reasoning very closely, to take him step by step, and to quote him largely, in order to enable me to disclose to the reader, how very uncertain his position is, and how the very facts which he produces as evidence to support his contention, are perhaps in reality the strongest arguments against it.

"In considering the distribution of organic beings over the face of the globe, the first great fact which strikes us is, that neither the similarity nor dissimilarity of the inhabitants of various regions can be wholly accounted for by climatal and other physical conditions. The case of America alone would almost suffice to prove its truth. . . .

"There is hardly a climate or condition in the Old World which cannot be paralleled in the New —at least as closely as the same species require. Notwithstanding this general parallelism in the conditions of the Old and New Worlds, how widely different are their living productions.

And again :—

"In the Southern hemisphere, if we compare large tracts of land in Australia, South Africa, and Western South America, between latitudes 25°, and 35°, we shall find parts extremely similar in all their conditions and yet it would not be possible to point out three faunas and floras more utterly dissimilar."

The object in the two preceding paragraphs is to minimise as much as possible, the power of climate and physical conditions, in bringing

CENTRES OF CREATION 151

about modified variations, and so let in the theory of natural selection as the chief agent in so doing. But Darwin fails to see, or appears to do so, that while endeavouring to buttress up his theory in one direction he is undermining it in another. For if countries separated by immense barriers of sea and hill, produce species that vary in their difference, in the ratio of the separation and distance between them, surely this fact points to different countries having indigenous productions descended from a stock of their own. If you find a marsupial in Australia, and in no other part of the world, the natural inference is that it sprang from a progenitor peculiar to that country and to be found nowhere else.

Physical conditions according to Darwin are not sufficient to account for dissimilarities, but natural selection, that is a power to preserve a change that has already been effected, is. Darwin here merely assumes that climate and physical agencies, are insufficient for the work. But what proof has he for that? Surely he greatly underrates the effect of these agents in bringing about alterations in species. For instance, the temperature in a given area in America may be roughly speaking the same as that of a given area in Europe, but the soil may be dissimilar, or the electricity which is always present somewhere or other, may vary in its action and quantity. It is not the air that makes the climate, but the air acting on the soil. Apart altogether from any operation by natural selection, if a race of any living organism has shifted its original domicile for many thousand years the representatives of that race are not likely to resemble in every particular the original race from which they sprang. To give a quite recent illustration, drawn from the human race. An American whose ancestors have lived many generations in America, is quite distinguishable, to an observant eye, from the Original British stock, and yet the period of his migration is far too short for natural selection to have brought about the alteration or to have come into play at all.

And he proceeds thus :—

" A second great fact which strikes us in one general review is, that barriers of any kind, or obstacles to free migration, are related in a close and important manner to the differences between the productions of various regions. We see this in the great difference in nearly all the terrestrial productions of the New and Old Worlds. We see the same fact in the great difference between the inhabitants of Australia, Africa, and South America, under the same latitude: for these countries are almost as much isolated from each other as is possible. On each continent, moreover, we see the same fact: for on the opposite sides of lofty mountain ranges, of great deserts, and even of large rivers, we find different productions. Turning to the sea, we find the same law. The marine inhabitants of the Eastern and Western shores of South America are very distinct."

CENTRES OF CREATION 153

Surely all this evidence if it points to anything, points to there being various domiciles of origin, and various progenitors, as many as the necessities of each case require. But diversity of origin, and alteration by mere physical conditions, are both ruled out of court as inadmissible or inadequate means of explanation. And Darwin has to fall back on his enchanter's wand "natural selection," and on a very tedious and round-about process of migration.

Take an imaginary case. Supposing the geographical disposition of the surface of the earth were different from what it is. Supposing instead of continents, it consisted of a thousand islands all equi-distant in the sea, with fauna and flora all radically different the one from the other in each; Darwin denying as he does different stocks of descent, and the sufficiency of alteration by mere physical conditions, if he were consistent would have to maintain, that all these fauna, and flora, were originally one, that migration had originally stocked the various islands and that natural selection would account for the rest, that is the innumerable radical divergencies. Which supposition is absurd!

And here I am by no means denying the power of migration. Of course it is the chief instrument by which the earth has been overspread. Everything possessed of organic life, is either capable of moving, or being moved. With the birds of the air, and the fishes of the sea, or at any rate with most of them, there is no difficulty. But when it comes to fauna and flora, the case is somewhat different.

The whole of the Eastern hemisphere, with the exception of the Australian group, is in terrestrial communication and probably at no very remote period the Western hemisphere, was connected with the Eastern, so granted an unlimited period of time, with the single exception of Australia, there is no reason in the nature of things, why all plant and animal life, should not have overspread the whole earth, either by a slow or rapid process of migration. Nor am I here arguing against true species having a single centre of origin. That may or may not be the case. Or whether or not they sprang from a single pair. The issue is a subordinate one. It is highly probable as Darwin says that the whole pigeon tribe owe their existence to a common ancestor. But to assert that a pigeon and a marsupial owe their origin to a common ancestor is highly improbable, there is not a tittle of evidence to support it, and it is as wild a speculation as ever entered the mind of man. And Darwin contends for that, and nothing short of it, or why does he go out of his way, to link together such distinct creations as reptiles, birds, and fishes?

As regards the accidental methods of dispersal which he refers to, they are conceivable and even probable in a minor degree. His experiments as to how long seeds will survive in salt water, are interesting, and would appear at first sight incredible; but he rather overlooks one important fact when he talks about timber drift, and so on; and that is that as a rule when you throw any floatable material off a coast into the sea, even a mile distant from the shore, it will almost inevitably by the action of the tides, return to that shore again, and not make its way to the opposite coast; and this fact places a very considerable limit on the mere jettison method of conveyance.

" We are thus," says Darwin, " brought to the question which has been largely discussed by naturalists, namely, whether species have been created at one or more points of the earth's surface. Undoubtedly there are many cases of extreme difficulty in understanding how the same species could possibly have migrated from some one point to the several distant and isolated points, where now found. Nevertheless, the simplicity of the view that each species was first produced within a single region captivates the mind. He who rejects it rejects the 'vera causa' of ordinary generation, and calls in the agency of a miracle."

Of course this last sentence is sheer nonsense. Why could not the " vera causa " of ordinary generation, operate in two places at once. And why is it a miracle for an event to happen in one place and not in another! Darwin cannot surely contend that it is a miracle for one species to be created, and not a miracle for another!

And on page three hundred and two he says :—

"With organic beings which never intercross, if such exist."

He must be well aware that there are thousands of species which never have and never will intercross, in all the great families of organic life.

And on page three hundred and four:—

"But I do not believe that it will ever be proved that within the recent period most of our continents which now stand quite separate, have been continuously or almost continuously united to each other."

What he means by this I am at a loss to understand. Why, they are all, with the single exception of the Australian group united at this day, or almost united, and always have been, within historic time.

There is one means of dispersal, and a very powerful instrument ready to hand which appears to have overlooked in the general enumeration; or at any rate not given the attention it deserves. I mean the dispersal by man himself. Within historic memory man has been on the earth at least five thousand years, and according to science many millions more. Now as the great continents of the world are all with the exception of the Australasian group practically connected, man could very well have been the agent and probably was in conveying from one district to another, fauna and flora, of every description.

The similarity of many of the species in the

northern portions of North America with those in Northern Europe, even the similarity of the plants in the polar regions, with those on the Alpine heights, which present to Darwin so peculiar a difficulty, might even be accounted for in this way, without any appeal to the great glacial period. For if once a species—to use a vulgarism—" catches on " in any climate, soil, or country, it will overrun within a very short time any country to which it has attached itself. Take the case of rabbits in Australia, or of many of the cereal crops which will flourish almost anywhere, of the European rat, which has almost exterminated the New Zealand rat, in its own home, and many other instances too numerous to mention. Man may have been the means of dispersal by accident, or design, but the result is the same.

But there are certain living organisms, both marine and terrestrial, both fauna, and flora, whose presence cannot be accounted for on certain parts of the earth surface, by any of the various means of migration hitherto alluded to, and we have to look elsewhere, and find another explanation for the difficulty. Man himself could not have effected it, nor is it probable in many cases that the living organisms themselves were volunteers in the matter. For the Pleistocene deposits clearly prove by their fossils both fauna, and flora, that plants and animals once ranged over central Europe that are now strangers to it. What brought so far south such animals so essentially arctic as the mammoth, the reindeer, the musk sheep, and the arctic fox. And not only were living organisms affected, and localised in an inexplicable way, but inorganic matter was affected in a manner more inexplicable still.

How was it that all over Northern Europe, and the northern part of North America, solid rocks covering immense areas, and reaching immense distances in a southerly direction, are all characterised by a smooth, polished, and striated surface!

What account could be given of those loose rocks, called by geologists " erratics," discovered in quite unexpected places, and detached from the soil on which they rest!

Sometimes they are as large as a cottage, and are found pitched, apparently haphazard, on the mountain sides.

Well, most geologists and men of science, have long ago agreed, that these phenomena could only be accounted for, by a great Ice-age called the glacial period.

" The identity," says Darwin, " of many plants and animals, on mountain sides, separated from each other by hundreds of miles of low-lands where Alpine species could not possibly exist, is one of the most striking cases known of the same species living at distant points, without the apparent possibility of their having migrated from one point to the other. It is indeed a remarkable fact to see so many plants of the same species living on the snowy regions of the Alps or Pyrenees,

CENTRES OF CREATION 159

and in the extreme northern parts of Europe, but it is far more remarkable that the plants on the White Mountains, in the United States of America, are all the same with those of Labrador, and nearly all the same as we hear from Asa Grey, with those on the loftiest mountains of Europe. Even as long ago as 1747, such facts led Gmelin to conclude that the same species must have been independently created at many distinct points, and we might have remained in this same belief, had not Agassiz, and others, called vivid attention to the glacial period, which as we shall immediately see, affords a simple explanation of these facts. We have evidence of almost every conceivable kind, organic and inorganic, that within a very recent geological period, central Europe and North America suffered under an arctic climate. The ruins of a house burnt by fire do not tell their tale more plainly than do the mountains of Scotland and Wales, with their scored flanks, polished surfaces, and perched boulders, of the icy stream with which their valleys were lately filled. So greatly has the climate of Europe changed, that in Northern Italy, gigantic moraines, left by old glaciers, are now clothed by the vine and the maize. Throughout a large part of the United States, erratic boulders, and scored rocks, plainly reveal a former cold period.

" The former influence of the glacial climate on the distribution of the inhabitants of Europe, as explained by Edward Forbes, is substantially as follows. As the cold came on, and as each more southern zone became fitted for the inhabitants of the north, these would take the place of the former inhabitants of the temperate regions. The latter, at the same time would travel further and further southward, unless they were stopped by barriers, in which case they would perish. The mountains would become covered with snow and ice, and their former Alpine inhabitants would descend to the plains.

"By the time that the cold had reached its maximum, we should have an arctic fauna and flora, covering the central parts of Europe, as far south as the Alps and Pyrenees, and even stretching into Spain. The now temperate regions of the United States would likewise be covered by arctic plants and animals, and they would be nearly the same with those of Europe: for the present circumpolar inhabitants, which we suppose to have everywhere travelled southward are remarkably uniform round the world."

The theory of this great glacial period is an imposing, and beautiful one, but the evidence in support of it is not altogether convincing to an unscientific mind, though it has the air of high probability. The evidence, and the only evidence as far as can be ascertained, is as follows: All over the northern parts of both hemispheres the solid rocks were found to present a characteristic polished and striated surface, and this peculiar worn surface is never absent. The groovings and "striae,"

CENTRES OF CREATION 161

do not occur at random but always run in a determinate direction, and by following the directions of these rock-striae, so say the geologists, we can trace the march of the ice across the land and determine its limits. The second piece of evidence is the boulder clay or "Till," the matter pushed along at the bottom of the ice, during its progression. And the third piece of evidence, is the existence of great erratics, or boulders, which are found all over the world, and cannot otherwise be accounted for.

The evidence it will be observed is rather of a negative character. As no other agent can account for these phenomena, then the Ice-age must. All geologists, botanists, and naturalists, are fond of the Ice-age. Whenever they experience anything unaccountable, then the Ice-age must have done it. It is to them a veritable "*deus ex machina*," and is ever at hand to explain the otherwise inexplicable.

But granted that this great Glacial Period, did exist and there is very little reason to doubt it, its operations were far-reaching, and its power though slow-moving was tremendous. For listen!

"The whole of Northern Europe was buried under one vast expanse of snow and ice. The ice sheet was thickest in north and west, in many places not improbably between 6000 and 7000 feet thick. It worked its way southward from the whole circumference of the Northern Pole. In North America its southern limits are well defined by great mounds which begin on the coast

L

of Massachusetts, and run across the continent for more than 3000 miles, and form what the American geologists call the great 'terminal moraine.'"

In Europe it pushed its way eastward and southward in all directions, through Scandinavia and Scotland the Gulf of Bolkura and Germany, reaching as far in one direction as the Alps and Pyrenees, and possibly further still to the shores of the Mediterranean. In the south-west it extended to the Oural range, and there are evidences of its action in the Himalayas and even on the mountains of the Lebanon. According to Dr Hooker, perpetual snow formerly covered its central axis, and fed glaciers which rolled 4000 feet down the valley.

This may be, and doubtless is all very true. But is not the Ice-age, a very big witness for Darwin to summon to account for the fact that a few little plants common to the Polar regions, and the Alps are apparently of the same species, and present a very similar appearance. If a plant could be originally produced, and have a single centre of creation in the Polar regions, why could it not equally well have been evolved on the Alpine heights under approximately similar physical conditions? But Darwin will have none of that, so it is necessary to discover some other method of conveyance. One would naturally think that this great ice journey would have destroyed all plant life in its course. The method of transmission of course is conceivable,

CENTRES OF CREATION   163

but it is a very clumsy and roundabout way of accounting for a difficulty which might easily be explained "*aliunde*." Even man himself might have been the bearer of the seeds, if separate centres of creation are inadmissible. Darwin in this matter seems to affix great weight to the opinion of a certain geologist called " Croll " and takes him as his guide and philosopher in the matter. But Croll's reasoning is rather speculative, than sound, and is open to criticism on more points than one. On page three hundred and fifteen of the " Origin " he says :—

" But now Mr Croll in a series of admirable memoirs, has attempted to show that a glacial condition of climate is the result of various physical causes, brought into operation by an increase in the eccentricity of the earth's orbit. All these causes tend towards the same end; but the most powerful appears to be the indirect influence of the eccentricity of the orbit upon oceanic currents. According to Mr Croll, cold periods regularly occur every ten or fifteen thousand years; and these at long intervals are extremely severe, owing to certain contingencies, of which the most important, as Sir C. Lyell has shown us is the relative position of the land and water. Mr Croll believes that the last great glacial period occurred about 240,000 years ago, and endured with slight alterations of climate for about 160,000 years."

How the long and slow changing process of alteration, in the relative positions of land and water, can bring about, such vast and sudden changes in the earth's temperature, it is difficult to understand. It is a matter very largely of conjecture, and is for the geologists to determine.

But the action of eccentricity of the earth's orbit is somewhat different and its effect on the climate of the earth more easy to follow. To understand it aright we must turn aside for a moment into the field of astronomy. If we imagine the earth as swimming round the sun in a sea of space, the axis of the earth running from the south to the north pole, is not placed vertically in respect of the surface of this imaginary sea. It is inclined and the amount of its inclination varies. At any given moment the axis points to a particular place in the heavens. At the next it does not point there. The shifting from moment, to moment, is infinitesimal, but it occurs. The end of the axis of the earth is describing a very slow circle, and the time it takes to complete it, is no less than 21,000 years. With this slow shifting of the position of the earth's axis, there will be changes in the relative position of the different parts of the earth and of the sun, and consequent changes in the temperature of the former. When Northern Europe is placed in such a position, by the movement of the earth's axis, as to receive the *least* possible amount of heat from the sun, a glacial epoch sets in.

But the criticism, and question, that at once arises is, then why is it that midway between this period

CENTRES OF CREATION 165

of 21,000 years, when Europe is placed in such a position, as to receive the *most* possible amount of heat from the sun, does not the glacial epoch disappear and the warmth of the earth return. How could the glacial epoch last as Mr Croll asserts 160,000 years?

Either Croll is attributing the effect to the wrong cause, or he is egregiously out in his figures.

" But the most important result arrived at by Mr Croll is, that whenever the northern hemisphere passes through a cold period the temperature of the southern period is actually raised."

This naturally would be the case if the theory of the action of the earth's elliptical orbit be correct.

" So conversely it will be with the northern hemisphere whilst the southern passes through a glacial period. This conclusion throws so much light on geographical distribution that I am strongly inclined to trust in it."

Now the theory is this, that alternating glacial periods in the north and south, set up a sort of see-saw action, and toss plant life backward and forward, from one extremity of the earth to the other. That the plants of remote regions get alternately transposed, and that through this action identical species are found in most distant and unexpected localities.

Doubtless the antarctic circle, has great accesses of extreme cold, and is more frigid at one period than another. But I can find no corroboration of Mr Croll's assertion that there are great glacial periods at the southern pole corresponding to those at the northern, either in Lyell's or Geikie's "Elements of Geology."

Even if there were, these glacial periods could not possibly have affected the earth in a similar way, nor could their action have been as far-reaching; as the nearest land of any magnitude is many parallels distant from the southern pole and there is no contiguous, or continuous ground for the ice to travel over.

Another great objection to this explanation is, that the action of ice would be destructive, rather than preservative of all plant life. Darwin's whole object in introducing this chapter on Ice action and the Glacial period is to establish his theory of single centres of creation, and to account for what is apparently an otherwise unaccountable fact, and one which if it cannot be explained "*aliunde*," is an obstacle in the path of his hypothesis, viz. that identical species appear and present themselves, in regions the most remote, the most inaccessible, and intransmissible.

But in the case of many instances given by Darwin there is a far simpler explanation of the conveyance, of plant life at any rate, ready at hand. He quotes Dr Hooker and says that he has shown, that besides many closely allied species, between forty and fifty, of the flowering plants of Terra del

Fuego are common to North America and Europe, enormously remote as these areas in opposite hemispheres are from each other. In the first place it is impossible that ice action from the north could ever have extended so far down, as the extreme limit of the South American continent, and an ice action from the south, would not have brought up with it plants identical with those of the north. The whole of the American continent, north and south, is continuous, and what is there to prevent in the course of many thousand years the seeds of these various flora, being transmitted by the hand of man from one region to another, or by birds, or even in the wool of sheep, and other animals, to say nothing of the ships which in later times are ready instruments of conveyance. There is also nothing to show that the plants could not push themselves down, by the ordinary method of their spreading propagation; and on the mountains of Southern Australia several European species have been discovered.

No Ice-age will account for this fact. They must have either been specifically created there, or some organic or inorganic agency, must have been the bearer of their stock. After enumerating many instances of plant dispersal Darwin remarks " that some few analogous facts could be given in regard to terrestrial animals." In marine productions similar cases likewise occur: as an example I may quote a statement by the highest authority, Professor Dana, that it is certainly a wonderful fact "that

New Zealand should have a closer resemblance in its crustaceæ to Great Britain its antipode, than to any other part of the world." Sir J. Richardson, also, speaks of the *reappearance* on the shores of New Zealand, Tasmania, etc., of northern forms of fish.

Now the members of the crustacean class, are commonly known as Crabs, Lobsters, Shrimps, Barnacles, and so on, which could all very easily have been conveyed by ships, barnacles especially as they will adhere to almost anything. It will be observed that Sir J. Richardson speaks of the reappearance; but reappearance since when? Australia and New Zealand have only quite recently been discovered. For if he means reappearance in the last fifty or a hundred years, then direct transportation by shipping of these various crustaceæ is a far more probable solution of their presence in those waters, than any other.

But the greatest obstacle in the way of dispersal has yet to be accounted for. The matter is rather slurred over, and all manner of shifts are resorted to, to discover a satisfactory solution: I refer to the localisation of the various fresh-water productions of plants and fishes.

" As lakes and river-systems are separated from each other by barriers of land, it might have been thought that fresh-water productions would not have ranged widely within the same country, and as the sea is a still more formidable barrier, that

CENTRES OF CREATION 169

they would never have extended to different countries. But the case is exactly the reverse. Not only have many fresh-water species, belonging to different classes, an enormous range, but allied species prevail in a remarkable manner throughout the world."

Fish present the greatest difficulty, for it was formerly believed that the same fresh-water species never existed on two continents distant from each other. Now what answer has Darwin to make to this objection! It appears that the species of one genus, has the power of crossing by some unknown means, considerable spaces of open ocean: that there is one species common to New Zealand and to the Auckland Islands, separated by a distance of about two hundred and thirty miles. But Darwin produces no evidence in support of this assertion; and the probability is that this species is indigenous to both New Zealand and the Auckland Islands. So he has to fall back on such expedients as fish being transported by whirlwinds, and the statements of such naturalists as Andubon with very elastic imagination, that the seeds of a certain water lily were found in a heron's stomach, and that as this bird flew from place to place the contents of its stomach might have stocked different ponds.

One hesitates to accuse so great a man as Darwin, as stating the thing which is not, or even of being guilty of a "terminological inexactitude." But he has some hard sayings. If he were alive, one would like to put this question to him, but as he has gone, or the mortal part of him, let us put the question to the shade of the great man, as it paces the Elysian Fields.

Do you believe now, or did you believe when in the flesh on the single authority of the Old Testament, that Elijah was taken up into heaven in a chariot of fire? His answer would probably be in the negative. Well that being the case, why should I, or another, be asked to believe that flounders were flung from one continent to another by the tail of some erratic tornado. The latter statement seems incredible and less worthy of acceptance than the former. The former statement has at least the merit of a high degree of pictorial imagination.

Andubon it must be remembered is a rather questionable witness. He was an American. Rightly or wrongly he was distrusted by his contemporary fellow naturalists, and was accused of being possessed in a rather marked degree, of a trait peculiarly American, of having an imagination so elastic that it was susceptible of almost unlimited elongation, of a craving for beating the record and of going one better than anybody else. Andubon at times heard sounds and saw sights, which were hidden from the senses of ordinary men.

Waterton most assuredly distrusted him, and contradicts him again and again. For instance Andubon gives a most marvellous account of the fight of an eagle and a vulture in the air ; and this is Waterton's observation upon it.

"I have never read anything in the annals of ornithology that bears any similarity to this aquila-vulturian exhibition progressing through the vault of heaven. Verily, 'there is a freshness in it.' When we reflect that Mr Andubon is an American, that he has lived the best part of his life in America, that the two birds themselves were American, and that this wonderful encounter took place in America, we English marvel much, that Mr Andubon did not allow the Press of his own country to have the honour to impart to the world so astonishing an adventure."

It is strange to say the least of it, that Andubon was the only human being ever privileged to see the "frigate" bird, which has all its four toes webbed, alight on the surface of the ocean. So Andubon's observations are not of the highest value. A great king once said "Put not your trust in princes" he might very well have added, nor in scientific witnesses either. There is a story that used to go the round of the Law Courts, of the remark of a celebrated counsel, that you might divide liars into three classes, "liars !—*liars !!* and—scientific witnesses," and there is a "scintilla" of truth in the observation. Even the accuracy of Professor Ray Lankester is hardly above suspicion, for in the "Origin of Species," he gives a rather unsatisfactory and inconclusive answer, to a question put to him by Darwin. In discussing the subject whether or not longevity was an advantage to a species, he makes the somewhat enigmatical reply:—

> "That longevity is generally related to the standard of each species in the scale of organisation, as well as to the amount of expenditure in reproduction and in general activity."

I suppose by that he means, that the higher up in the scale the species is, the greater is its chance of duration.

"Generally," is rather a wide word, and needs in this instance very considerable qualification. Trees can hardly be called high up in the scale of organisation, and yet what living organism has a longer life than the oak and the yew! Frogs and toads are notoriously long lived, especially when subjected to geological confinement. So are the pike among fishes, the parrot among birds, and the tortoise among reptiles. The ancients were of opinion that the raven lived to an extreme old age. It is certainly difficult to prove its longevity as the bird roams from place to place, beyond the reach of man. Ovid tells of a remarkable old raven which attained the age of 900 years—"*novem scecula passæ.*"

Darwin sums up the whole of this part of the case in his usual way. It wears an air of apology throughout, as most of his summaries do, which

CENTRES OF CREATION 173

have any bearing on the evidential value of his hypothesis. He says :—

"In these chapters I have endeavoured to show, that if we make due allowance for our ignorance of the full effect of changes of climate and the level of the land, which have certainly occurred within the recent period, and of other changes which have probably occurred—if we remember how ignorant we are with respect to the many means of occasional transport—if we bear in mind, and this is a very important consideration how often a species may have ranged continuously over a wide area, and then have become extinct—the difficulty is not insuperable in believing that all the individuals of the same species, wherever found are descended from common parents."

But it is not a question whether the difficulty in believing in a single common ancestor is insuperable or not, but whether there is a sufficient amount of evidence to make it credible. Unfortunately this evidence is again unsatisfactory and by no means exhaustive.

CHAPTER X

NATURA NON FACIT SALTUM

It is a favourite maxim with Darwin, and one which he is frequently quoting, that nature does nothing by leaps and bounds, or in a hurry. That her progress, is orderly, silent and methodical, that nature abhors violence, and sudden convulsions, as much as she abhors a vacuum. Of course there is a sense and a very deep one in which the saying is strictly true. Every act and operation, however sudden and violent it may appear, has been led up to and foreordained from all eternity. If I suddenly jump off my chair the action though relatively sudden has been ordained from the first. Or again, what can be more sudden and violent than a clap of thunder, but nature has been working up from the beginning to every single atmospheric explosion. Of course in that sense nothing is sudden. But regarded relatively to the effect on the object affected, there have been many terrible and violent convulsions in nature, which must have affected the whole geographical formation of the earth, and every species that inhabited it. And when we have to deal with 60,000,000 years, what catastrophes may not have happened in the interval, any one of which might be

NATURA NON FACIT SALTUM

sufficient in itself to shatter to pieces, and scatter to the winds Darwin's theory of orderly evolution and progressive but silent development. Darwin entirely ignores throughout the "Origin of Species" and "The Descent of Man" the possibilities of disturbance, destruction and recreation by the great agency of fire. The Ice-age he cannot ignore, though he dislikes it, is evidently shy of it and would fain be rid of it if he could; but as he cannot be rid of it, he wisely puts a bit in its mouth, and utilises it to his own advantage. The reason is obvious, as it must have destroyed or largely minimised all life which was subject to its operations, and given an entirely new direction and setting, to the many organic species that it affected. Indeed, the action of fire, and the action of ice alone, are quite capable of twisting the theory of Natural Selection out of all recognition. They either of them might destroy in an hour the slowly working operation of centuries. Supposing the temperature of the torrid regions of the earth, was suddenly transferred to the temperate, the effect on species in a few years time would do more to alter their characteristics, and modify their variations, than whole epochs of the almost imperceptible method of natural selection. The idea is not inconceivable or improbable, indeed on Darwin's own showing, it has happened and may happen over and over again.

That very sudden operations do take place in nature, sudden I mean as regards the species affected, both from without, and from within, is certain.

Pestilence, famine, and possibly even the sword, are all occasional and periodic agents, in bringing about a change that may alter the whole character and destinies of any given species. Take the migration of birds, and the sudden shifting of many classes of fish from one locality to another, or the case of the voles in Norway which multiply in countless numbers, and then commence a march towards the sea, and all perish in its waters.

"On the theory of natural selection" (Origin of Species) "we can clearly understand the full meaning of that old canon in natural history 'Natura non facit saltum.' This canon, if we look to the present inhabitants alone of the world is not strictly correct; but, if we include all those of past times, whether known or unknown, it must on this theory be strictly true."

But why must it be strictly true? This is, one of Darwin's quiet assertions, which requires further verification.

And he continues :—

"It is generally acknowledged that all organic beings have been formed on two great laws—Unity of Type, and the Conditions of existence. By Unity of Type is meant that fundamental agreement in structure which we see in organic beings of the same class, and which is quite independent of their habits of life. On my theory, unity of type is explained by unity of descent."

NATURA NON FACIT SALTUM

Unquestionably there is in all natures a true unity of type, but unity of descent is by no means a necessary *sequitur*, as Darwin would have us believe. Unity of type may be entirely due to other causes. He is compelled to stop short as far as evidence goes at three or four stocks of descent. Have the representatives of those stocks, nothing in common, and no fundamental agreement in their structure and conformation ? If that is so, then in these cases at any rate the resemblance cannot be due to unity of descent.

> " For natural selection acts by either now adapting the varying parts of each being to its organic and inorganic conditions of life ; or having adapted them during past periods of time : The adaptation being aided in many cases by the increased use or disuse of parts, being affected by the direct action of the external conditions of life, and subjected in all cases to the several laws of growth and variation."

This surely is putting the cart before the horse. For the disuse of parts, external conditions, and the laws of growth and variation are the primary, and not the subordinate agents in the matter.

But since Darwin wrote, an attack has come from another and quite unexpected quarter. I mean from the disciples of Mendel who point out the fact that within human experience variations take place in species which are not influenced by the slow-moving

178   WHERE DO WE COME FROM?

forces of absolute necessity. There are they say sudden mutations the need for which is not impressed on an animal or plant by the presence of its surroundings but which may be due to other causes and perhaps explained by the laws of heredity. Their theory of course, has yet to be proved, but it is far more capable of positive proof and verification than is Darwin's theory of Natural Selection.

These sudden and abrupt variations and developments the revelation of hitherto unsuspected laws, are experienced even in the rigid region of mathematics.

That they do occur even here, has been clearly proved by that extraordinary machine called the calculating machine invented by Professor Babbage. Professor Babbage was a great mathematician, a somewhat eccentric philosopher, and mystic into the bargain, as the following quotations from his writings amply prove. The machine is adapted to perform the most complicated calculations with absolute certainty. It is moved by a wheel and prints a series of natural numbers 1, 2, 3, 4, 5, each succeeding its antecedent by unity. The following account is taken from the ninth Bridgewater treatise, written by Professor Babbage himself.

"Now reader, let me ask you, how long you will have counted before you are firmly convinced that the engine supposing its adjustments to remain unaltered, will continue, whilst its motion is maintained to produce the same series of natural numbers. Some minds, are perhaps so constituted that, after passing the first hundred terms, they will be satisfied that they are acquainted with the law. After seeing five hundred terms, few will doubt, and after the fifty-thousandth term, the propensity to believe that the succeeding term will be fifty thousand and one will be almost irresistible. That term will be fifty thousand and one: the same regular succession will continue: the five-millionth and the fifty-millionth will appear in their expected order, and one unbroken chain of numbers will appear before you, from one up to one hundred millions. True to the vast induction, which has thus been made, the next succeeding term will be one hundred million and one: but after that, the next number presented by the rim of the wheel, instead of being one hundred million and two, is one hundred million, *ten thousand* and two.

"The law which seemed to govern the series fails at the one hundred million and second term. That term is larger than we expected by ten thousand. The next term is larger than we anticipated by thirty thousand.

"If we still continue to observe the numbers as presented by the wheel, we shall find that for a hundred or even a thousand terms, they continue to follow the law relating to the triangular numbers: but after watching them for twenty-seven hundred and sixty-one terms, we find that this law fails in the case of the twenty-seven hundred and sixty-second term. If we continue to observe, another law then comes into action. This will continue through fourteen hundred and thirty terms, when another law is again introduced, which extends over nine hundred and fifty terms, and this too, like all its predecessors, fails and gives place to other laws, which appear at different intervals. It is also possible so to arrange the engine, that at any periods however remote, the first law shall be interrupted for one or more times, and be superseded by other laws, after which the original law shall be again produced, and no other deviation shall ever take place.

" Now it must be remarked that the law that each number presented by the machine is greater by unity than the preceding number, which law the observer had deduced from an induction of a hundred million instances, was not the true law, that regulated its action : and that the occurrence of the number one hundred million ten thousand and two was as necessary a consequence of the original adjustment as was the regular succession of any one of the intermediate numbers to its immediate antecedent."

This is a very remarkable instance in the mathematical field of an apparent miracle.

Professor Babbage was a strange mixture of the mathematician, and the mystic, and we are indebted to him for the first moral application of the mechanical principle—

" The air is one vast library, on whose pages are for ever written all that man has ever said or

NATURA NON FACIT SALTUM 181

woman whispered. Not a word has ever escaped from mortal lips, whether for the defence of virtue or the perversion of the truth, not a cry of agony has ever been uttered by the oppressed, not a mandate of cruelty by the oppressor, not a false and flattering word by the deceiver but it is registered indelibly upon the atmosphere we breathe. And could man command the mathematics of superior minds, every particle of air thus set in motion could be traced through all its changes, with as much precision as the astronomer can point out the path of the heavenly bodies. No matter how many storms have raised the atmosphere into wild commotion, and whirled it into countless forms, no matter how many conflicting waves have mixed and crossed one another : the path of each pulsation is definite, and subject to the laws of mathematics."

The learned professor then goes on to draw similar instances of the durability of thought and action from the waters and the solid earth. But possibly here he has allowed his tendency to mysticism to outrun his mathematics when he says that every thought, word, motive, and action of every created thing has an abiding, and eternal effect on the whole universe to its remotest confines. That statement may conceivably be true, but he implies by his various illustrations that all thought, and motion are for ever hereafter reproduced and fixed in their original similitude somewhere in the atmosphere and surrounding space : but the great laws of chemical change, neutralisation, and compensation, which have to be taken into account preclude any such awful possibilities. At any rate let us hope so. These sudden departures moreover, occur over, and over again, in the field of morality and of human life. Take the case of the inrush of some unknown power which seems at times almost to compel alteration and movement in human life, in individuals, institutions, and nations. All at times have their days of Pentecost as well as religious communities. Striking illustrations of this strange movement, to whatever cause we may attribute its origin, are to be found in national and individual life. What was the motive power of those strange and great migrations of the tribes at certain periods of the world's history, from Asia to Europe. Northward, eastward, and southward, and then back again from the north, towards the Italian peninsula and the shores of the Euxine.

Even Gibbon who is generally ready to give a rational explanation, or suggestion of any phenomena even the most unaccountable and unexpected says :—

> "That the cause that produced them lies concealed among the various motives which actuate the conduct of unsettled barbarians."

What the cause later on, towards the close of the eleventh century, of that wonderful movement the Crusades, which affected the whole almost of Western Europe, with an intensity and zeal, which our modern apathy is quite unable to understand. All peoples and all classes seemed to have been consumed with a sort of fire. The proximate cause of this strange conflagration may be attributed to the fiery eloquence and zeal of a Peter the hermit, or the masterful spirit and ambitious designs of an Urban the second, but the "*causa causaas*" lay deeper. They were the firebrands that ignited the material, but the material was there in abundance, only wanting a breath to burst it into a flame. The sceptic and the man of science would answer, Oh! only another instance of superstition, and fanatical power acting on the subject matter of ignorance. But let us remember there were men in those days, and great men too. And why one asks at this particular period of time, and with very little previous preparation or premonition, should this strange adventure captivate the minds and bodies of a whole continent of men, and hurry them from the shores of the Atlantic to the confines of the Moslem World?

And here I cannot refrain from quoting a passage from Gibbon, which shows us in very graphic outline the nature of the feeling that was sweeping over humanity at the time.

"The cold philosophy of modern times is incapable of feeling the impression, that was made on a sinful and fanatic world. At the voice of their pastor, the robber, the incendiary and the homicide, arose by thousands to redeem their souls, by repeating on the infidels the same deeds which they had exercised against their Christian brethren; and the terms of atonement were eagerly embraced by offenders of every rank and denomination. None were pure: none were ex- exempt from the guilt and penalty of sin: and those who were least amendable to the justice of God and the Church were the best entitled to the recompense of their pious courage. If they fell, the spirit of the Latin clergy did not hesitate to adorn their tomb with the crown of martyrdom; and should they survive, they could expect without impatience the delay and increase of their heavenly reward. They offered their blood to the Son of God, who laid down his life for their salvation; they took up the cross, and entered with confidence into the way of the Lord. His providence would watch over their safety: perhaps his visible and miraculous power would smooth the difficulties of their holy enterprise. The cloud and pillar of Jehovah had marched before the Israelites into the promised land. Might not the Christians more reasonably hope that the rivers would open for their passage; that the walls of the strongest cities would fall at the sound of their trumpets; and that the sun would be arrested in his mid- career to allow them time for the destruction of the infidels," and he goes on to add:—" of the chiefs and soldiers who marched to the holy sepulchre, I will dare to affirm that *all* were prompted by the spirit of enthusiasm, the belief of merit, the hope of reward, and the assurance of divine aid. But I am equally persuaded that

NATURA NON FACIT SALTUM

in many it was not the sole, that in some it was not the leading principle of action."

But there is still a more striking illustration in recent years, of a quite unexpected, and stirring, movement taking place in a whole people. It is unnecessary to dilate on it, as the story is well known to all, but I refer to the sudden "*volte face*" on the part of the Japanese people, who wrapped for centuries in the close-fitting cloak, of an antique and Asiatic conservatism, are now only too eager to discard it, and to clothe themselves in any, and every garment of Western civilisation. But to leave nations and to turn to individuals. I suppose all men of any sensibility or character, have experienced at some time in their lives, some touch of this inrush of the spirit. In some men the experience is stronger, in others fainter. But it generally dies down leaving but a faint trace behind, or at all events never ripening into that action, which convulses and then alters the destinies of men. But there are instances where this strange power, whether generated from within, or kindled from without, has so operated on the lives of individuals as to blossom into action so far-reaching and strong, that it has altered the destinies of mankind and affected for long periods the thoughts and actions of the race.

Take the case of Buddha. This inrush of the spirit on his personality is one of the most curious and picturesque occurrences to be found in the history of the world. And the great motions or emotions, call them what you will, that swayed his mind at the time of his conversion, or breaking away from his previous mode of life, have affected if not the destinies, most certainly the belief of millions of the human race. And how did it come about! Well the solution of it given by Edwin Arnold, in his beautiful poem "The Light of Asia," perhaps comes nearest the truth. Here was Prince Buddha, the son of a great Asiatic potentate, the heir of a vast Empire, the idol of his father, in the first bloom of his vigour and youth, surrounded by all the luxury, pomp, and abject servility, only to be found in an Asiatic court. And his conversion was the more wonderful when we remember the sensuous atmosphere of his life. Possessed of every gift that man holds dear and that life has to bestow; why did he break away?

Prince Giddârtha heard the Devas play, and to his ears they sang such words as these:—

> We are the voices of the wandering Wind,
> Which moan for rest, and rest can never find;
> Lo! as the mind is, so is mortal life,
> A moan, a sigh, a sob, a storm, a strife.
>
> Wherefore and whence we are ye cannot know,
> Nor where life springs, nor whither life doth go;
> We are as ye are, ghosts from the inane,
> What pleasure have we of our changeful woe?
>
> What pleasure hast thou of thy changeless bliss?
> Nay, if love lasted, there were joy in this;

But life's way is the wind's way, all these things
Are but brief voices breathed on shifting strings.

O Maya's son! because we roam the earth
Moan we upon these strings: we make no mirth,
So many woes we see in many lands,
So many streaming eyes and wringing hands.

Yet mock we while we wail, for, could they know,
This life they cling to is but empty show;
'Twere all as well to bid a cloud to stand,
Or hold a running river with the hand.

But that thou art to save, thine hour is nigh!
The sad world waileth in its misery.
The blind world stumbleth on its round of pain;
Rise, Maya's child! wake! slumber not again!

We are the voices of the wandering Wind:
Wander thou, too, O Prince, thy rest to find:
Leave love for love of lovers, for woe's sake
Quit state for sorrow, and deliverance make.

So sigh we passing o'er the silver strings,
To thee who know'st not yet of earthly things;
So say we: mocking, as we pass away,
These lovely shadows wherewith thou dost play.

It will be noticed that the promptings, and call that came to Buddha, were conveyed to him through the seductive and subtle influence of the whispering wind. Its dreamy, mysterious, and gentle agency are quite in keeping with the Asiatic character, and the most suitable medium for operating on such a personality as Buddha's. In a very different manner, but still in keeping with the majestic nature of the man, did Moses, the great law-giver and apostle of the unity of God, experience the same promptings upon the top of Sinai.

"And it came to pass on the third day in the morning, that there were thunders and lightnings, and a thick cloud upon the mount, and the voice of trumpet exceeding loud; so that all the people that was in the camp trembled."

A suitable accompaniment to the awful interview that there took place between man and his Maker.

The story of Mohammed's night journey to heaven and his interview with and revelation from the Archangel Gabriel, stands on rather a different footing both of dignity and truth. The man seems to have been an extraordinary mixture, of the sensualist, the enthusiast, and the imposter. But that is no reason why he should be condemned off hand as a mere clever piece of organised hypocrisy. Human nature in its everyday and ordinary manifestations is very complex, and to condemn another because his complexity takes violent turns and directions, is to condemn oneself. We are all of us, or nearly all in the same boat, it is a mere matter of degree. The bedrock of the nature of the sensualist and the saint, are the same, they are both founded on emotion; and why there are so many more sinners than saints, is that the Devil as a rule makes very short work of impatient and emotional natures; and whether any given individuality becomes either one or the other, is largely determined by education, and the pressure and nature of surrounding circumstances in youth. But let no man console himself with this reflection. The one course if persisted in leads to degradation and death; the other to happiness and life. There is truth in the assertion that man is often a hypocrite to himself, and extraordinary as has been the success of fanatic imposters in every age, their self-delusion is still more wonderful. In character Mohammed strongly resembles our own Cromwell, the parallel has often forcibly struck all who have compared their lives. But whether the altered circumstances attendant on the introduction of the respective careers of these three men are fact or fable, or partly one and partly the other, they themselves unquestionably asserted their veracity, and if the magnitude of the results of their actions and teachings is any measure of their divine origin, then they were all of them worthy of divine sponsors, and all of them the servants of some hidden and mysterious power.

I think the above illustrations, taken from the world of nature, of mathematics, and human life, are sufficient to show that nature is no stranger to sudden, nay, violent alterations in almost every field of her activity, and that "*Natura non facit saltum,*" is not the only motto that could suitably be inscribed on her shield.

CHAPTER XI

THE MENTAL AND MORAL QUALITIES OF MAN AND THE ANIMALS

PERHAPS among all the fascinating chapters, and chapters of extraordinary interest, which Darwin's great works on the "Origin of Species" and the "Descent of Man" contain, and they are many, none are more captivating to the mind than those which treat on the mental, and moral, faculties of man and the animals. They can be read with great pleasure, and profit, and altogether apart from any reference or bearing they may possess on Darwin's speculative conjectures on the origin and nature of man.

Darwin himself never loses sight of the end he has in view, namely to establish his theory of natural selection operating on all organic life from the minutest organism up to the brain of a Newton. He claims all organic life for his province, and in all its parts. Nor does he stop short at the mental, moral, and even religious nature of man. His law holds good and prevails right through a man's whole being. He refuses to cry a halt anywhere, and will accept nothing but the whole. And here, whether right or wrong in his whole contention, he is surely consistent.

It must be remembered that matter, and absence of design, are the real foundation stones on which the whole of Darwin's theory of evolution is founded. Things are what they are, not by the express wish or purpose of a designer or Creator, but by the operation of an infinite series of innumerable and fortuitous accidents, by which the similarities, divergencies, and distinctions, in all organic life are accounted for. Darwin nowhere openly asserts this. He was a sensitive man, and was unwilling to wound the sensibilities and prejudices of any member of the race. But disguise it as he will the inference of his reasoning is obvious, and its ultimate goal inevitable.

If there is any truth in Darwin's theory at all it must be applied in its entirety. There are no intermediate halting places. If his law operates on one organism, it must operate on another, if it is true of any given part of an organism, it must be true of the rest. If it applies to a man's legs and arms, it must equally apply to his head and his heart. You cannot cut human nature up into compartments, and make one law prevail in one compartment and another in another. And yet this is what many of Darwin's admirers and supporters are already beginning to do.

"Natural Selection" is a very small and unaccommodating bottle into which to pour the whole nature of a man. And if the whole nature of man will not go into it, then the cooper has not produced the right cask.

Professor Wallace himself is beginning to shake, and to confess his uneasiness and uncertainty, for in his notice in the " Daily Mail " on the centenary of Darwin's birth he says :—

" ' The Descent of Man ' was written to show that his great principle of ' Natural Selection ' served to explain how man had been developed from some lower animal form, which was also the ancestor of the various anthropoid apes and he adduced a large and convincing array of arguments showing that he had actually been so descended.

" In this conclusion the great majority of thinkers to-day are in entire agreement with him ; but in his further contention—that the whole mental, moral, and aesthetic nature of man has also descended to him from the lower animals— a large and increasing number of his admirers do not follow him, there being at least as much positive evidence against as in favour of his contention."

But in this connection Professor Wallace uses the wrong word, " positive evidence." Of positive evidence, there never has been, and never can be any either way, from the very nature of the case. All the evidence that there is, is of an analogous, inferential and circumstantial description.

Darwin maintains throughout the " Descent of Man," that the mental and moral powers of the lower animals, if they have any, differ from those of man only in degree and not in kind. Of course it is impossible to prove this. No one knows what goes on in the minds of animals, they have no powers of speech and therefore no means of communicating their thoughts. Everything concerning their inner life must for ever very largely remain a matter of the purest conjecture.

This much we do know, that alike with man they experience pleasure and pain, they are possessed of the same senses as he is, as they live on the same earth as man, and are subject to the same physical and atmospheric conditions; impressions from the outside affect them as far as their physical nature goes, in a very similar way to that in which they affect man. But if we go beyond this we are treading on very uncertain ground. Too much stress is laid on the distinction between similarity in kind, and in degree. The resultant effect of a difference in degree, may be as great, possibly even greater than a difference in kind. Let me illustrate this by the thermometer. When it stands at thirty degrees centigrade its influence may be beneficial, but if it rose to three hundred it would be destructive of all life, and yet the result would be purely due to a difference in degree only. A difference in degree may be so great that it amounts practically to a difference in kind. Again, the thermometer of all animal life as far as we know can never rise above a certain point on the chart, the point varying, with the various natures of the particular organism; but in man this is not the case; his thermometer is capable of almost indefinite expansion. Man is susceptible of progress, an animal is not. Darwin attempts to show that this is not the case, but here he utterly breaks down. No animal has ever been known to progress, unless a certain improvement in the breed due either to natural causes, or to the result of domestication, or to an adaptability to a given set of physical conditions, can be called progress. It can only attain to the perfection of its peculiar organism and beyond that point, it is unable to advance. But man can progress, and not only that, but if the circumstances are favourable he can progress with extraordinary rapidity. His mental powers like those of some savages may have lain dormant for ages, but at the mere touch of the wand of opportunity, they will burst into their full perfection, like the vegetable creation at the vivifying warmth of the sun.

Take the case of the Maoris of New Zealand; the conformation of the brains of some of them is nearly perfect. The subject matter was all there, ready for fruition. I believe I am right in saying that some of the best speakers in New Zealand are of pure Maori blood. Some of them in their skill at the game of draughts are unsurpassed, and they can beat at that game the best European specialists. Now to excel in draughts, requires a brain of a relatively high order. It is a game of calculation, and to play it well, would tax the powers of a respectable mathematician. In some ways it is a far more difficult

MENTAL AND MORAL QUALITIES 195

game than chess. Chess requires not mathematical, but quite different qualifications, such as patience, attention, and concentrated observation. It is quite a mistake to suppose that chess requires any great effort of memory or calculation. It is no exaggeration to say that the grandson of a pure blooded Maori if he had opportunity, and education, would be quite capable of becoming a senior wrangler, though his recent forebears were island savages. This shows how readily man is capable of improvement, and with what speed he can advance. Is there or has there ever been any sign of such advance, even along the lines of their own nature, in the whole animal creation from the monkey downward! It must be confessed there is none. Though animals in this respect have had far greater opportunities than men: for they have man at the head of them, to suggest, and point out the way.

Again, as far as we know, no animal is capable of abstract reasoning or abstract thought. It has no conception of the meaning of such words as "Why," "Whence," and "Whither." It has no idea how it came into the world, and no idea how it will go out of it. No conception of the meaning of life, and death, of the laws of nature, or of the great Being that created them. It has no power of communicating its wishes or feelings through the organ of speech, to man or to any race other than its own. And more important still, it may be almost positively asserted that it never will possess them. The truth of the matter seems to be that all species and living organisms have, from the cradle of their race, certain powers and capacities inherent in them, varying in quality and differing but limited in quantity, suitable to, and limited to their future life history on earth. These powers may be hidden, and at the outset largely potential to be developed, expanded, and directed, to meet the varying emergencies that arise as the race proceeds, and runs its course towards its zenith. That when the perfection of the species has become constant in the majority of the members that compose it, it may endure for ages if circumstances are favourable in a state of stagnation : it can go no further. But nature abhors persistent stagnation. The law of change is imperative, and as it can go forward no more, it must needs go backward, and decline; and decay sets in, to be followed by final extinction.

Nor will the race of man in all probability be exempt from this great law. His time is not yet, but his race will surely one day be run. There is just one chance of his becoming possessed of a lease in perpetuity. Some hitherto unknown quality may evolve from his brain, differing not merely in quantity, but radically in quality, from any quality he is now possessed of. Some fourth dimension may assert itself. But this of course is highly improbable and contrary to all the teachings of analogy. And if such an extraordinary phenomenon were suddenly to reveal itself, man would cease to be man, and would take

MENTAL AND MORAL QUALITIES 197

on another nature. It would be impossible for man to tolerate by his side a rival or superior in this world. If man's superior really were to appear, what would man do with him! For unless man nipped him in the bud and got rid of him at once, man would find himself in the invidious position towards this superior being, that a sheep now is to a man.

But the resources of man's mental powers are by no means exhausted. His development has not reached its zenith. The qualities and potentialities inherent in his brain, may still be capable of almost unlimited expansion, in degree if not in kind. His brain will improve by accretion and accumulation, and every step of knowledge gained, gives increased acceleration to its advance. But as the potentialities of his brain have their limitations, the race will ultimately reach a point when it can no longer proceed. It too, will experience a long period of stagnation, to be followed by decline, decay, and death.

Darwin endeavours to show that there is no fundamental difference between man and the higher mammals in their mental faculties. But his evidence on this head is weak and faulty in the extreme, and he signally breaks down. Now it is a very significant and remarkable fact that in the two chapters in "The Descent of Man" where Darwin contrasts the mental and moral powers of man and the higher animals, the monkey is almost entirely ignored, though innumerable other animals are called in, in support of Darwin's contention. Why does not

Darwin place the monkey in the witness-box? Surely if his relationship to man is as proximate as the scientists contend, if his brain more nearly resembles the brain of man than that of any other animals, then this question of his mental and moral affinity with the human race, would be the very question on which his evidence would be most valuable. But the monkey is kept in the background. Darwin's omission to place him in the witness-box is significant; he dare not place him there, as he has no evidence to give, and if he opened his mouth every word he uttered would be hostile evidence.

It has always been a mystery why a monkey has been placed next to man in the scale of creation. In no way does he resemble man, beyond a similarity common to all the mammals alike, due to the fact that he lives on the same earth, is possessed of the same senses, and therefore of the same fundamental intuitions. Darwin strains every point, every little story, every incident however trivial to establish some sort of connection between the mental powers of the animals and man. Much of his knowledge on the subject is probably second-hand, and not always above suspicion. For instance, he gives an instance on the sole authority apparently of some antiquated work, of a chimpanzee in a state of nature cracking a nut with a stone. That they can perform that feat under domestication there can be little doubt. Monkeys, as is well known, are extraordinary mimics, and will imitate as far as possible, any action of a man. As for the stories about monkeys, throwing sticks and stones, they have never been properly verified. Monkeys know nothing at all of the art of throwing projectiles. The most they can do is to pick up a nut, stone, or stick and drop it again. If they were to retain a projectile in their hands and whirl it round and round, the projectile might fly a short distance erratically, but would be entirely devoid of direction. The whole race of monkeys are purely arboreal. They live in trees, they build nests, and sleep in trees, all their four-limbs are fashioned for that purpose. The ends of their two fore-arms, are hands, and very soft hands too. The extremities of their after limbs, are a mixture of hands and feet, quite unsuited for terrestrial progression. The extremities of their four limbs are not nearly as well suited for progression on the ground as are those of a squirrel. Monkeys will venture into a rice-field, and some few, by force of circumstances, dwell among the rocks, like the mascots on the rock of Gibraltar. No one seems to be able to offer an explanation as to how the mascots—the only monkeys known to Europe—ever got to Gibraltar at all. Their origin is as mysterious as that of the wild dogs that infest the streets of Constantinople. In captivity, some monkeys can be trained to stand and hobble on their hind legs, but in a state of nature they would not do so if they could avoid it, as the trees are ever at hand for their reception. The whole race of monkeys are as much arboreal creatures, as fish are aquatic.

In this respect, at any rate, they have not much in common with man.

As regards the power of speech, they are as remote from man as any other animal, far more so than the parrot, who is really capable of carrying on something very like a conversation, in any tongue you may teach him.

Certainly a monkey can howl. A single Red monkey in the forests of Demarara, is credited with making a noise like hell let loose, but beyond that his linguistic capacities seem unable to carry him. This is the more remarkable as one would naturally expect, that the being nearest man, would at least approximately approach him in some form of utterance. But the monkey is the worst speaker of all, chatter, grimace, and howl as he may, not one single solitary word can he utter. The jackdaw, the raven, and the parrot can all say something.

Monkeys are covered with hair, unlike man who is smooth. Their timidity is extreme and at the appearance of man they will scamper away amongst the trees, until they reach their topmost elevation.

But as regards their reasoning powers :—for of instinct they have very little when contrasted with some other mammals. In real reasoning power, they are certainly not the superior, probably the inferior, of the bee and the ant, the beaver, the elephant, the parrot, and the dog. Most assuredly the dog could give them points. How again I ask can this be the case, if the monkey ranks second only to man!

MENTAL AND MORAL QUALITIES 201

As regards the close resemblance of the head and facial expression to that of man, for myself I never could see it. A lemur in face far more nearly resembles a man than most true monkeys. A lion if you look him full in the face when in repose, has a much greater likeness to some men.

"The relative position of our features is manifestly the same," says Darwin. Well, naturally they would be. The relative position of the features of all animals are the same. But a monkey has no forehead, no nose beyond a squat indentation hardly worthy of the name, his jaw is differently set, his face is covered with hair, and eyelids are nearly always absent.

So far for the monkey's externals. But now how about his internals, by the scrutiny of which the scientists think they can find the key which will unlock every mystery however deep. Well, in internals, the monkey more nearly resembles those of a donkey than a man, with the possible exception of some of the convolutions of his brain. Even in these convolutions, though in many respects, they are similar in the man and the monkey, yet " *pace* " Professor Huxley, there are differences, and a man's brain weighs three times more than a monkey's. And last, but by no means least, a man is a carnivorous animal, a monkey is not.

Now, if the above description is an accurate one of the ape, I ask any sober-minded person, can he really bring himself to believe, that in the brains of these volatile, eccentric and capricious creatures of the forest, there lie hidden the possibilities, of the mental faculties of a Newton, of the ear of a Beethoven, or of the poetic rhapsodies of an Isaiah, I honestly say I cannot.

If the truth must be told these scientific analysts, like the dyer's hand, get subdued to what they work in. Their living brains are for ever pondering, on the dead brains and stomachs of their comrades in organic life. What wonder then that they become obfuscated, their vision obscured, and their sense of true perspective and proportion distorted, until at last they regard all nature as a "*pot pourri*" and life itself a hum.

I would far sooner put my faith in an outdoor naturalist like Waterton, who lived and wandered many months in great forests of Guiana for the express purpose of studying the monkey tribe, to give one an accurate and reliable account, of the life habits, and nature of the monkey, of his place in creation, of the true inwardness of his existence, and of his probable origin and destiny, than I would in the greatest closet scientist of them all.

Nay, I would sooner trust the old pagan poet, when he says "There was wanting a more perfect animal, and one which could hold dominion over the rest, and so man was born." And, continues the poet, whilst other animals have their vision downward to the earth, man alone looks upward to the skies:—

"Pronaque cum spectant animalia cœtera terram,
Os homini sublime dedit, cœlumque tueri,
Jussit et erectos ad cœlum tolere vultus."

I do not wish for a moment to imply that Darwin himself was a mere bookworm or closet naturalist, or that he was devoid of a very large and intimate first-hand acquaintance with nature. In many directions, particularly in all that concerns plant life, and worms, his knowledge was immediate and unique. His range of information covers an immense field; his reading was enormous, and there is hardly a department of human thought with which he was entirely unacquainted.

But the very fact of Darwin's possessing knowledge in so many directions must have limited it in others, and he was certainly no specialist in all that he dilates upon. Take this case of the monkeys. Nearly all he has to say about them is derived second-hand, and frequently from the writings of others whose assertions are not necessarily unimpeachable. His personal knowledge of monkeys was probably bounded by the circus, the menagerie, and the dissecting room; but their native haunts are the real places to see them in and to draw profitable deductions as to their true habits and character. For the monkey's powers of mimicry are inexhaustible and, under the tuition of man, he could be made to assume airs of knowledge, which are superficial, and imitative, and quite foreign to his real nature.

The dog stands on a somewhat different footing.

He has long lived with man, and knows man as thoroughly as man knows him. He is the only being that loves man, better than he loves himself. We all of us know something of dogs, and it is unnecessary to expatiate on their many virtues. It is with their reasoning powers that I am here solely concerned. It seems impossible to deny them the gift of reason, and reason in a very large degree. They even seem to possess the power of consecutive thought, as the two following stories, perhaps the most remarkable in all the annals of dog stories amply testify. I have no doubt as to their accuracy as many people could corroborate them though I cannot at the moment put my finger on where I saw them. The one of a sheep dog is the more remarkable of the two. Now it is well known that among sheep dogs there are occasionally to be found murderers, that is dogs that destroy and devour by stealth the sheep committed to their charge.

A certain flock of sheep was unaccountably depleted, and the owners if they could divine the cause were unable to detect the offender. Their suspicions were aroused, but on which dog to fix the guilt they had no evidence to assist them. Now one of these dogs invariably slept in a room on the ground floor with a girl of fourteen. The window was closed, but when the child slept the dog pushed it up, slipped out, and night after night secured its victims. It invariably returned clean and free from blood at an hour when it knew the child would still

MENTAL AND MORAL QUALITIES 205

be slumbering. But one night, on its return the child was awake. The dog saw the danger and instantly attacked it, though hitherto they had been the best of friends. The child was only saved by the noise brought about by the confusion, which brought down her father, and the dog was destroyed.

Now for the completion of this nightly transaction, a whole train of reasoning must have passed through the mind of the dog. The determination to slay, the favourable opportunity, the method of effecting an exit, the consciousness of guilt, and a knowledge of the consequences if detected, must have all passed through the brain of the dog, in connected sequence. It would really seem that if one could convey a problem of Euclid to the mind of a dog, it would have little more difficulty in solving it, than have many men.

The next story is that of the dogs of Constantinople. As is well known, they live in packs, each pack elects a leader, and each pack is exceedingly exclusive, any breach of their respective rights is followed by instant war. One pack may never intrude on the territory of another. Water at times in Constantinople is scarce, and the dogs whose territory borders on the water, have an advantage over those whose territory does not. But in dry seasons, the favoured packs, will always allow a neighbouring pack, if headed by its leader and properly accredited, to come down to the water and drink, but when their thirst is slaked they have at once to march back to their own territory. If this concession to the necessities of the race is not the outcome of collective and connected reasoning, it is difficult to say what is.

Darwin gives no such remarkable stories as these. Indeed, the evidence he succeeds in extracting from the dog is far more meagre than it need have been. He does not cross-examine him sufficiently or particularly well: and this is strange as the dog is the most valuable witness he possesses in endeavouring to merge into one the reasoning powers of mammals and man.

Innumerable other animals are passed under review all with the same object of drawing together as closely as possible the mental affinities between man and the mammals. But unlike the animals of Noah's Ark, they refuse to go into the ark of Natural Selection, which Darwin has provided for their reception.

He endeavours to show the underlying unity in, and common conformation of all created things, and argues from that, that they must all have had a common origin. But the whole evidence points rather in the direction, not of a single progenitor, but of all the various species of organic life having separate stocks of descent. Darwin himself is compelled to stop at three or four stocks of descent, for he has only analogy to lead him on to unity, to which he would fain proceed. But do the evolutionists really mean to contend, that the conformation of the representatives of these three or four various stocks,

MENTAL AND MORAL QUALITIES

which they are compelled to admit, have nothing in common. Most assuredly they have, and if the evolutionists admit that, which they are compelled to do, then what becomes of their arguments ? They are hoist on their own petard !

As regards instinct in animals, Darwin is very fond of rudiments and incipiences, but he nowhere attempts to show that instinct is an incipient form of reason and in this surely he is right. Instinct is a thing "*sui generis*" a quality quite apart and distinct from reason, and nearly all animals are endowed with it, even man himself. We all know what we mean when we talk of instinct, but it is a quality not easy to define. It is a kind of inspiration of the sensatory organs a very efficient substitute for reason, conferred on various species for their guidance and preservation. Some instincts are unerring, and far surpass reason as a guide. Take the instance of the instinct of migration in birds. No instance could better serve as an illustration of the difference in kind, between instinct and reason than this. If swallows before one of their migratory periods were to hold a conclave, and to discuss the advisability of migration, and certain scientific swallows were to rise up, and to point out, the madness of the move, how the journey was long, the destiny uncertain, and the dangers on the wing unknown, their reasoning would be right and have much to commend it. But the advice would be wrong, instinct would be the truer guide, as is proved by the result.

Nor is instinct intuition. Intuition is rather the timid daughter of reason. We often hear of a woman's intuition, but it is to be attributed to keen sensibility, quick observation, and a very rapid though unsuspected process of reason itself. Cuvier was probably right, when he asserted as a general proposition that instinct and intelligence stand in an inverse ratio to each other; but Darwin on the authority of a gentleman called Pouchet dissents from this view. But one thing I think may fairly be asserted of it, that it tends to disappear both in men and animals under domestication; and that it is a gift more peculiar to a wild and natural state of life, than a civilised one, whether imposed or acquired.

He then goes on and attempts to show that some animals at any rate have a sort of rudimentary moral sense, some elementary idea at any rate of morality. Animals feel remorse and guilt, of that there can be little doubt, but these two feelings are the result in one case of grief, and in the other of apprehension. It has yet to be shown that any animal ever refrained from this, or that act, on the ground that it was moral, or immoral. Their line of conduct is guided entirely by their senses and they have no idea of self-conscious morality. Innumerable instances are then quoted to exhibit the fidelity of various animals, but their actions in the field of morality at any rate, can all be attributed to love, necessity, or hate; no reasoning or self-conscious power comes into play to regulate, modify, and

MENTAL AND MORAL QUALITIES 209

direct them. So the great and permanent dividing line between man and the rest of organic life, appears to be this, that man is capable of advance and self-improvement and that the rest of creation is not.

The very physical conformation of animals, is an effectual barrier to their intellectual improvement and advance, and these barriers are obviously placed there by nature, for a purpose. The very structure of the throat in animals prevents the possibility of most of them ever even imitating much less learning the human tongue, and for ever will; and it is as well for man that it is so. There is enough talk as it is. And if the Babel of the animal creation were added to that of man, the suffragettes would not be in it, and the burden would be too heavy to be borne.

Truly nature is a wonderful paradox. The old writer of the book of Ecclesiasticus has told us "That all things are double one against another, and He has made nothing imperfect." One of the profoundest truths very beautifully expressed, though one rarely hears the text quoted or referred to, on the platform, in the pulpit, or the press. In the light of it many things become plain, "Predestination" and "Freewill" are no longer irreconcilable.

And man is more wonderful still, fearfully and wonderfully made, how wonderfully, few people even yet either realise or imagine. For man is not a single being, as has hitherto been supposed but two distinct natures and personalities under one skin.

I have not in my mind now, the idea of a man with a dual nature such as Stevenson depicted in that extraordinary novel "Jekyll and Hyde," but I assert that man has a real and distinct duality, a double person, both physiologically and psychologically. That when you see one man or one woman walking about, you really see, though you are not aware of it, two, and not one being, encased in one skin. If one comes to think of it, this must be so, or how else could a man love himself, hate himself, encourage himself, sympathise with himself, agree with himself, if he were merely a single being. If he were a concentrated unity could he endure solitude for an hour! If Robinson Crusoe on his desert island had been one instead of two beings, could he have existed for a day. Surely no! he would have gone raving mad. Nor is this conjecture, wanting in scientific support. All man's organs are in duplicate, from his brain at the top, to his feet at the bottom. They are homologous, and each and all of them have a correlative correspondence, they act in sympathy and are co-equal and co-existent together. I could almost scientifically demonstrate this assertion, by a curious experience of my own. It is not an experience peculiar to myself, for others have experienced it too, and have been at a loss to account for the phenomenon. I have frequently been in a place quite foreign to me, and which I have visited for the first time, and almost in the twinkling of an eye in an instant, the thought flashes through the mind,

"I have seen all this before": not a mere or general resemblance, but everything alike down to the minutest detail of the situation. For a long time I was at a loss to understand the phenomenon, or to apply it to any sort of scientific explanation, till I chanced to meet the late Professor Rolleston and related to him the circumstances. His answer was: "Yes, there is a possible scientific explanation of that, and the only one I can suggest is that when a person is run down in health it occasionally happens, that the two hemispheres of the brain do not act in perfect unison. The one half of the brain sees the surroundings at one instant, and the other half at the next. You see the same surroundings twice over. The second act of observation is an almost instantaneous repetition of the first, and you imagine you have seen the same scene at some distant period before." Now surely if that is the case man must be possessed of a dual personality.

CHAPTER XII

MISCELLANEOUS OBJECTIONS

THERE are several minor objections to Darwin's theory of Natural Selection. I call them minor not because they are of less importance than others, or that the removal of them is less vital to the establishment of his theory than the rest, but because they do not cover so large a field, nor are they so sweeping in the indictment of his proposition.

Let us take four of the most important. (1) The question of instinct. (2) That of electric organs in fish. (3) That of neuter insects. (4) The question of Colour.

Darwin himself sees to the full the difficulties that these four objections raise, and with his usual candour he admits their power, but it cannot be said with the possible exception of the electric fish, that he satisfactorily accounts for, or disposes of any one of them. He rightly declines to give any definition of "instinct," as it is one of those qualities more readily apprehended than defined, but it is nevertheless a great obstacle to the smooth working of his hypothesis. Some instincts are so wonderful, that "natural," or indeed any other principle of selection, appears quite insufficient to account for them.

Take the case of the tumbler pigeon. Why should one pigeon appear incapable of travelling even quite a short distance in the air, without turning many times, head over heels, and another not?

What makes the Formica ant absolutely dependent on its slaves for its existence; and what process of modification by natural selection could ever have produced a sterile female for the purpose?

And again, and most wonderful of all, what makes the hive-bee construct a cell far more suitable for the purpose it serves than anything that the ingenuity of man could devise.

Of course if Darwin really means that there is an accommodating power in nature, that enables every living organism to meet the exigencies of the particular circumstances and environment in which it finds itself, and that this compulsory accommodation has a tendency to bring about alterations and to perpetuate those alterations indefinitely, in one direction or another, then no one would quarrel with him, but why call it Natural Selection, as if Natural Selection were some new and hitherto unknown law; some magician's wand, which on its own merits accounted for the whole.

As regards instinct, the difficulty consists not so much in its progress, but in its origin. What set the top spinning, and why should it spin in one direction rather than another? Darwin sees this difficulty as the following passage clearly shows :—

"No doubt many instincts of very difficult explanation could be opposed to the theory of Natural Selection, cases, in which we cannot see how an instinct could have originated: cases, in which no intermediate gradations are known to exist: cases of instincts of such trifling importance that they could hardly have been acted on by natural selection; cases of instincts almost identically the same in animals so remote in the scale of nature, that we cannot account for their similarity by inheritance from a common progenitor, and consequently must believe that they were independently acquired through natural selection. I will not here enter on these several cases, but will confine myself to one special difficulty, which at first appeared to me insuperable and fatal to my whole theory."

So Darwin gives the majority of them the go-by and passes on.

(2) The electric organs of fishes, offer another case of special difficulty, for it is impossible to conceive by what steps these wonderful organs could have been produced. Certain members of the fish tribe such as the Torpedo, the Ray, and the Eel, develop and discharge a large amount of electricity, some of them being even possessed of a sort of electric battery, situated according to the species of the fish in various parts of their body.

Now how can these organs be accounted for by any process of modification by variation. For if one set of fishes have experienced this peculiar modification why not another ? The difficulty at first sight seems insuperable; but Darwin with the assistance of a certain Dr Radcliffe, surmounts at any rate the " gravamen " of the difficulty, very cleverly and in the following manner. All muscular contraction is, it appears accompanied by an electrical discharge.

" In the electrical apparatus of the torpedo during rest, there would seem to be a charge in every respect like that which is met with in muscle and nerve during rest, and the discharge of the torpedo, instead of being peculiar, may be only another form of the discharge which depends upon the action of muscle and not on nerve."

In other words the electricity of these fishes, is a mere intensification, of the electricity which is discoverable and discharged from nearly all organic bodies.

So far, so good; but there is a subordinate difficulty yet to be accounted for, namely by what graduated steps these organs have been developed, in each several group of fishes, and Darwin's attempted elucidation of this point is by no means satisfactory or conclusive.

The third and most serious difficulty of all, and Darwin fully admits it to be, is found in the case of "neuters." To understand fully the nature of the difficulty and its significance, one of Darwin's primary laws must be borne in mind and one which he reiterates over and over again as of great importance.

"Natural Selection acts only by the preservation and accumulation of small inherited modifications, *each profitable to the preserved being.*"

And again :—

"Natural Selection will never produce in a being any structure more injurious than beneficial to that being, for natural selection acts solely by and for the good of each."

Now it cannot be pretended that to be sexless and a neuter is beneficent to, or for the good, regarded from the natural point of view, of any individual. Surely then these neuters violate one of Darwin's first laws. He sees the danger to his theory and recognises it for he says :—

"It will indeed be thought that I have an overweening confidence in the principle of natural selection, when I do not admit that such wonderful and well-established facts at once annihilate the theory" and "I do not pretend that the facts given in this chapter in any way strengthen my theory, but none of the cases of difficulty to the best of my judgment, annihilate it."

And how does Darwin meet this difficulty. He is compelled to abandon his former proposition, that natural selection acts solely for the benefit of each

MISCELLANEOUS OBJECTIONS 217

individual, and transfer its benign influence to the whole class. For he says :—

"This difficulty though appearing insuperable, is lessened, or as I believe, disappears, when it is remembered it may be applied to the family as well as to the individual, and may thus gain the desired end."

So in the interest and to meet the necessities of this particular case, which cannot otherwise be got over, Darwin has to step down the ladder, and modify his whole proposition.

(4) It may be laid down as a general rule that colour in nature follows the climate, and that the colour of all organic life, reflects very largely the colour of its inorganic surroundings whether on land or sea. For instance, nearly all fishes are for the most part the colour of the water out of which they are taken.

In the polar regions the majority of living things take on the colour of the snow and ice, as the seal, the bear, the white arctic fox, the extinct mammoth, and in a modified way, the reindeer and so forth. To come lower down to the temperate regions of Northern Europe, the colours of the indigenous "fauna" and "flora" are as a rule subdued rather than brilliant to whatever class of colouring they belong.

Again throughout the whole of Northern Africa much of the colouring of the "fauna" takes on the colour of the surrounding sand, as in the case of the lion and the camel. It is not until we arrive at the tropical regions that the more brilliant colours in nature begin to display themselves. And all this seems to point to the fact that colouring is due not to Sexual Selection, or Natural Selection at all, but to the action of light acting on the different chemicals in the various organisms. Darwin does not actually deny this, as a general proposition for he says very little about it, but his fetish, Natural Selection, must in this case, as in every other have its food, so he attributes the brilliant colouring on the plumage of certain birds and on the wings of butterflies to sexual selection, preserved and perpetuated by natural selection. But this action can really at the best be very slight, for organisms, in a wild state whether as regards colouring or what not, soon reach their maximum of perfection. Darwin says he cannot see any purpose of all the display and colouring of the males, if it is not for the purpose of attracting the females. One may as well ask why the sky is blue!

His reasoning here is somewhat on a par with that on the colour of the red and white grouse respectively. He attempts to show that nature by modification has conferred on those birds those particular colours for purposes of protection, and to enable them to take cover in the heather and the snow. But as regards this question of protection, nature strikes the balance pretty evenly between protection, and exposure, and shows no favouritism either one way or the other. Surely the right line of reasoning to pursue is, not that nature gradually conferred on the grouse their particular colours but, that having those particular colours and finding by experience, that in particular localities which happened to be of the same colour as themselves they were more immune from danger than in others, they resorted to those localities in preference to others.

Again take the case of the elongation of the neck of the giraffe. It seems incredible that natural selection through countless ages has been gradually elongating the neck of the giraffe to enable it to browse on rather higher foliage than its fellows. Whence the necessity! Sir George Mivart very pertinently asks the question, "Why are not the necks of other animals elongated as well?" and Darwin cannot answer him. One cannot help sometimes suspecting that Darwin is not merely elongating the neck of the giraffe, but pulling the leg of the public at the same time.

CHAPTER XIII

SEXUAL SELECTION

As nearly two-thirds of " The Descent of Man " is taken up with the question of Sexual Selection and the courtships of insects, birds, mammals and man, it is necessary here to make some passing reference to the subject. But it must never be lost sight of, that Sexual Selection, and Natural Selection, are two distinct things. Sexual selection is one of the prime factors and agents in producing variety and modification in the individuals of any species and of the species itself : natural selection merely fixes and preserves those varieties when produced. The meaning of the term " sexual selection " speaks for itself and the nature of its operation is apparent.

" This form of selection," says Darwin, " depends not on a struggle for existence in relation to other organic beings or to external conditions, but on a struggle between the individual of one sex, generally the males, for the possession of the other sex. Sexual selection is less rigorous than natural selection. Generally the most vigorous males, those which are best fitted for their places in nature, will leave most progeny. But in many cases victory depends not so much on general vigour, as on having special weapons, confined to the male sex. A hornless stag, or a spurless cock, would have a small chance of leaving numerous offspring.

"How low in the scale of nature this law of battle extends I know not! The battle is perhaps severest between the males of polygamous animals."

When animals have their sexes separated, the males necessarily differ from the females in their organs of reproduction, and Darwin calls these organs the "primary sexual characteristics." But the sexes moreover often differ in what are called "secondary sexual characteristics." Secondary sexual characteristics are not necessarily connected with the organs of reproduction, but are merely the physical advantages possessed by the male or female as the case may be, such as strength, courage, general vitality, plumage, colour, power of song in birds, and so forth, which make certain individuals of any given species more reciprocally attractive to each other, than other individuals, and give them an advantage in their courtship over the rest.

And these secondary sexual characteristics according to Darwin, play a very large and important part in the improvement, modification and variation of the species. The rule is that the best and most favoured individuals of a class select and capture, or are captured by, the best females and that this rule running through all organic life tends to the improvement of individuals and species alike.

That is to say: to give three class instances—that in the mammals, the strongest, most courageous, and best equipped males, can always or nearly always secure the females of their choice which are usually the best and most perfect of their sex.

That among birds, selection depends more upon powers of song and other attractions, than on the law of battle. The voices among many of them are the most efficient instruments in securing the most favoured mates.

Among insects, such as butterflies, the beauty of the colouring of the wing of the male is a powerful passport to the preference and favour of the female.

At first sight this reasoning sounds plausible and attractive enough, but it is more than doubtful if it is the whole truth, and the question arises whether Darwin has not carried his generalisations a great deal too far. He makes the choice of the female in many cases, on quite insufficient evidence the governing factor in the situation.

Moreover, if this law invariably held good that the strongest and best equipped male, always or as a rule, secured the strongest and most beautiful female, the species would surely go on, generation after generation, improving until it had advanced out of all recognition. But this is notoriously not the case. Every species soon reaches its limit of perfection and then becomes constant. The Egyptian goose of to-day is precisely the same bird as the Egyptian goose of five thousand years ago. The truth seems

SEXUAL SELECTION 223

to be that Darwin rather overlooks the fact, that all the members of a species in a wild state, when of an age are, as regards strength, fitness, and general vigour, nearly on a complete equality, and there is little in these respects to choose between them. Take ten thousand males of the " passer vulgaris " or common sparrow, they are all alike as peas, and the female would be equally well satisfied with one as with another. The case is quite different under domestication, where there is greater choice, and more inequality, and consequently any species can be altered or improved almost out of recognition. And it is the same under domestication, both with fauna and flora.

Darwin seems to imply, that all the strength of the lion, all the song of the male bird, and all the beauty of the butterfly are conferred on them, and improved upon, generation after generation for the sole purpose of enabling them to secure, and making them attractive to, the female. But surely this is going a little too far, and paying the ladies of the world if it were possible to do so, rather too great a compliment.

One might as well argue that every young blood at Oxford, when he swaggers down the High, adorned with a salmon coloured tie, a variegated waistcoat, with green stockings and his trousers turned up, does so with the express and sole purpose of captivating the ladies. The idea may conceivably enter into his imaginings, but as a rule he so bedecks himself because it is " the thing " and he naturally does not wish to be out of the swim, though no doubt it adds to his satisfaction when in full plumage, he encounters some attractive representative of the opposite sex.

Even Professor Wallace himself, and many others of Darwin's supporters, are beginning to desert Darwin on this question, and to candidly admit that they can no longer follow his reasoning. In a recent article, Professor Russel Wallace makes the following observations on this subject :—

" As to the conclusion on Sexual Selection, there is equal diversity of opinion, two quite distinct phenomena being included under the term. These are :—

"(1) Weapons used in the combat of the males, which being clearly useful to them and to the race have been developed under the law of natural selection, and (2) colours and ornaments in the male sex only, the use of which is not so clear. Here Darwin's contention is that the latter have been developed by the influence of female choice of the most highly ornamental males. The evidence collected by Darwin on this point is so abundant, and so extremely interesting that most students were at first carried away by it : but further consideration showed that direct evidence for any such choice was very scanty, while there was a fully equal amount against it. The fact that these colours and ornaments were almost equally developed in male butterflies, while it

SEXUAL SELECTIONS 225

was almost impossible to postulate an identical æsthetic faculty among the females, together with our increasing knowledge of the various ways in which colour is of use, has led to a very general rejection of the theory of female choice."

Quite so, the choice of the female, and the strength of the male is really quite a minor factor in the matter. The most powerful factors are really, proximity, and opportunity.

" Amongst birds," says Darwin, " the contest is often of a more peaceful character. All those who have attended to the subject, believe that there is the severest rivalry, between the males of many species to attract by singing the females. The rock-thrush of Guiana, birds of paradise, and some others, congregate : and successive males display with the most elaborate care, and show off in the best manner, their gorgeous plumage, they likewise perform strange antics before the females, which, standing by as spectators, at last choose the attractive partner."

But supposing they all fixed their affection on the best tenor among the males, the unfortunate songster would be smothered and it would be a case of love's labour lost.

Why from a sexual point of view the necessity of all this adornment and display ? The courtship must in the first instance have taken place, before countless generations had bestowed on the male bird all these

P

accumulated and auxiliary advantages. And why could not the courtship continue without them!

Moreover what proof is there that birds and insects have the same eye and ear, for colour and sound, as that possessed by man!

But be that as it may, whatever Sexual Selection does or does not effect, it is one of the most powerful rivals that Natural Selection has to encounter.

It is itself one of the primary agents in promoting change and variety in all varieties of organic life, whereas Natural Selection does nothing more than fix and preserve that change when established.

CHAPTER XIV

THE LAW OF EVIDENCE, AND GENERAL OBSERVATIONS

BEFORE bringing this criticism on Darwin's theory to a close, it may not be out of place to make some observations on the law of "Evidence," and on the quality, and quantity, of the evidence required, to substantiate such a theory as that of Natural Selection. And here it must be remembered, that the evidence that may be sufficient to support one proposition, event, or theory, may be quite inadequate to support another. Many people are hopelessly at sea, as to the true meaning and value of evidence. How often does one hear it stated from the pulpit: "You believe the evidence for the ordinary facts of life, why is not similar evidence sufficient in the case of a miracle?" The answer to that is very clearly and convincingly enunciated by Professor Huxley as I will presently endeavour to show. But first: what is evidence? and what do we mean by it?

Evidence then in its most general sense, is a witness which establishes or has a tendency to establish, any given facts or conclusions. There are three sorts of evidence all of which more or less cut into one another, but for purposes of classification, and departmental use, may be distinguished as follows: Mathematical, Moral, and, Legal. The first is employed in pure mathematics, and is testimony and conviction in one, the evidence is useless to a mathematician if it does not end in proof, and proof is the criterion of the value of the evidence, for it must be remembered that pure mathematics are entirely independent of the nature of the objects, and are concerned only with their numerical relations. Their character is logical and rational and they are an extension of logic to a certain order of deduction, which is arrived at, be the process long or short, by a series of evidential steps, knitted together link by link, until the chain is complete.

The second kind of evidence, " moral," is employed in the general affairs of life, and in those reasonings which are employed to convince the understanding in cases not admitting of strict demonstration. It is evidence not amounting of necessity to a mathematical certainty, but merely to a high probability. Legal evidence may be either moral or mathematical, as the nature of the case admits. It is merely evidence restricted and confined within certain limits, to meet the ends of justice, and to safeguard as far as may be the individual incriminated, and for the purpose of obtaining decisions upon the rights and wrongs of litigants. But it is with " moral," that is inferential or circumstantial, evidence with which we are here chiefly concerned. And here it is important to notice how very often people, and whole classes of people, containing among them some very able intellects, fall into great errors, blunders and mistakes, by applying wholesale one class of evidence, such as mathematical, to solve the difficulties and meet the needs of problems which are foreign to their application. Statesmen and politicians are sometimes very great delinquents in this respect, and have not infrequently by their ignorance gone very near to making shipwreck of entire nations. They start a theory, which if it could be treated like mathematics as entirely independent of objects would be sound and convincing enough. The chain of reasoning is complete, and as a theory no flaw or fault can be found in any of its links. But unfortunately they are only too apt to leave out of their reckoning, the cross currents of other conflicting and neutralising theories, which taken by themselves are equally true, such as the surrounding circumstances, the nature of object to which the theory is to be applied, and the worst and greatest error of all, they entirely neglect the human equation.

Mr Gladstone once said in the House of Commons, that—"We are not legislating for the Planet Saturn." He probably never made a profounder or truer observation in his life. What he meant was the very truth I am contending for here, that you cannot drive a mathematical theory, rough-shod, through the human equation. French statesmen are the greatest of all delinquents in this respect. If anything is dear to the French mind it is theoretical completeness, logical sequence, and lucidity of utterance. The " Church is a nuisance,—they say—its existence does not fit in with the human intellect, therefore get rid of it root and branch, whether it is necessary for the good and preservation of the people or not." "Liberty, Fraternity, and Equality" are very beautiful things; in theory, you cannot find a fault with them, therefore "*nolens volens*," bind them round the necks of the people by the strong arm of the law. Very much the same cries are being uttered in England now. Socialism is a Utopia therefore apply it at once; the only objection to it being, that it is impracticable and impossible.

But to turn to evidence as it is regarded in gross so to speak, to evidence as utilised by the individual. To be a really good judge of the value of evidence as applied to the various departments of knowledge, and all the circumstances of life, necessitates a long experience and qualities of mind of a high order. Mathematicians are nearly always good masters of evidence, their very training makes them so, in whatever field of thought or action their testimony may be requisitioned. If they have any versatility of mind at all, they very soon, and very readily, transfer their powers from one field of action to another, and they become as great masters of the value of moral and legal evidence, as they are of mathematical—as witness a Paley and a Salmon in the ethical field—and I believe there are at least four

ON EVIDENCE IN GENERAL 231

judges of the Court of Appeal still living and in office who were in their day Senior Wranglers. But there are vast numbers of people, less gifted perhaps than they, but in their way and in other directions sometimes very highly educated and accomplished, who taken out of the line of ordinary intuitional reasoning, which affect their own avocations and daily necessities, seem to have but the remotest notion as to what constitutes valid evidence, of past events, or future probabilities. How often does one hear people say, when asked a reason for the faith that is in them: " Oh, the parson says so," " the doctor says so," " they say so," " the newspapers say so," and regard that as quite sufficiently conclusive. I have even heard men stand up in a club and boldly affirm, that if you toss a coin up, and it comes down heads a hundred times in succession, that that is powerful evidence to prove that on the hundred and first toss it will come down tails. And there is no convincing these people that they are mistaken.

Again take the case of successful men of business; almost invariably they are good reasoners; they have as a rule an intuitive, and instinctive knowledge of the value of any testimony bearing on the success or otherwise of a given transaction. Indeed, success in almost any practical undertaking, depends very largely on a rapid process of correct reasoning : but take those same men away from their own peculiar field of work, and let them apply their reasoning powers, say to their own state of health. Many of them will flounder hopelessly, and be imposed upon, by the first quack, or plausible advertisement, that they happen to fall in with. They will often attribute their ailments, notwithstanding there is glaring evidence to the contrary, to any reason but the right one.

It must moreover always be remembered, that the greater the magnitude of any theory, and the less knowledge we possess of the phenomena to which it is to be applied, the greater must be the evidence forthcoming to establish it. If I said I had seen a ghost, people would expect from me far more evidence in support of that assertion, than if I had said I had seen a man. It is not necessary to take up the extreme position assumed by Hume: "That it is more probable the evidence is false than the miracle true." That proposition really is not sound, if by that Hume means that no evidence is conclusive to establish an unexpected and hitherto inexperienced occurrence. But the rule holds good, and cannot be too much insisted on, that the more improbable and outside the domain of experience, the occurrence of any given phenomena, the greater is the weight of evidence you require to support it.

The late Professor Huxley, one of the soundest and most logical of the agnostic philosophers, with his usual felicity of illustration puts this exceedingly well. He says in words, or words to this effect: If my friend Jones, who I believe to be an honourable man, and on whose word I can generally rely, were to come and tell me that he saw our friend Brown, riding down the street on horseback, and I knew my friend Brown was capable of, and in the habit of so doing, I should be satisfied with the evidence, and say: "very well that is quite sufficient": but if on the following day he were to come and say, "I saw our friend Brown riding down the street on a zebra," I should begin to wonder whether Jones was not suffering from some temporary aberration, and should require some further testimony, before I placed complete reliance on his statement. But if Jones called again the next day, and said, "I saw our friend Brown, riding down the street on a unicorn," I should think Jones was off his head, and should require a hundred-fold more evidence for that, than for either of his previous assertions. But if he were to return again on the fourth day, and say he saw Brown on a centaur, I should probably give a sigh, and ask for Darwin's "Origin of Species."

But the above law of evidence laid down by Huxley, important though it is, relates rather to the quality than the quantity of the evidence required, owing to the unusual nature of the event evidenced. But the error as regards the quantity of the evidence necessary to establish any given proposition is a much more common one, than the error as to quality. For instance: the evidence required to establish the amount of population in the British Isles, say a hundred years ago, is as nothing compared to that required, to establish the health and physical condition of the units of the population at the same period. A square yard might be sufficient space for the data of the one, a square mile might be necessary to contain the data of the other. It is on the amount of data necessary to establish any given fact, or proposition, that so many people err, and are thereby led into false deductions.

Having said so much as to the nature of the evidence required, let me shortly restate some of Darwin's leading " dicta " and ask the reader to regard them impartially in the light of the evidence adduced.

It would take too long, and is moreover unnecessary to recapitulate here all Darwin's propositions, for the purpose of showing how far they conform to the laws of evidence, so I will confine my attention to four points only.

First of all:—We are dealing with a transaction which has been in continuous operation for at least 60,000,000 years, namely, the alteration and evolution of specific forms of life, all down that long period of time. Well, of course, any evidence in the positive, or mathematical sense, either one way or the other, except that relating to the period of historic time and contemporary observation, is quite out of the question: from the very nature of the case, it must be so.

Secondly:—Any evidence that is forthcoming or adduced in support of the theory of the Struggle for

ON EVIDENCE IN GENERAL 235

Existence, plus Natural Selection, is really not "ad hoc," to the purpose, for which it is required; for it is difficult to see how these two agents, taken either separately or together, can either deflect, or greatly modify the character of a species. What they really do is to limit, regulate, and reduce its numbers. If 100,000 men, on each side are drawn up in battle array, and half of that number perish, and if you repeat that operation, one hundred times over, on a hundred different occasions, the units that remain are specifically the same, though they are numerically less. The control of species by the struggle for existence is so obvious, that no evidence is needed for its corroboration. It certainly is a mystery and must be to many, how a tendency in nature towards preservation of what is worth preserving, can be any indication of a clue to the process by which any organism is evolved. No evidence is required for this assumption. Nature naturally tends to preserve herself.

Thirdly :—Darwin contends for the mutability of species yet he nowhere defines what he means by species. Indeed he positively refuses to define it. This certainly seems a very extraordinary position for a scientific man to take up. I am not here denying that modification by variation does take place of course it does; but does it do so in the manner that Darwin suggests ; and this modification may be due, as Darwin would have it, to some inherent natural law, though it also may be due to the operation of other external factors. But granted that there is evidence for the law, my contention is that it only acts within species, and is never sufficiently prolonged or powerful enough in its operations to convert one species into another.

Fourthly :—This perhaps is the most important point of all. Says Darwin: " It is generally acknowledged that all organic beings have been formed on two great laws, unity of type, and the conditions of existence."

No one would deny this statement, or that there is a fundamental agreement in structure in nearly all organic beings (or that the evidence for it is sufficient and abundant). Now Darwin asserts that unity of type is due to unity of descent, but here the evidence produced is most assuredly deficient and by no means in conformity with the laws of evidence laid down, nor does it even approximately fulfil their requirements. The similarities in nature, he says, are to be accounted for by unity of descent, the dissimilarities by Natural Selection. His argument, and it cannot be too often repeated, is that there must be unity of descent, or the similarities in structure, functions, physiology and so forth cannot otherwise be accounted for. " All living things have much in common, in their chemical composition, their cellular structure, their laws of growth, and their liability to injurious influences." But this by no means of necessity implies unity of descent: it can be readily and very easily accounted for by all organic life

ON EVIDENCE IN GENERAL 237

dwelling on a common earth, living under approximately similar conditions, having to get their living by much the same methods. All organisms must possess organs of circulation, digestion, and reproduction, or without them they could not exist. However many stocks of descent you admit in these respects at any rate they must follow a common outline of resemblance and conformation.

Darwin is himself compelled to stop short and admit three or four lines of descent, though he would fain go on to unity if he could.

Would he contend, that the representatives of these three or four lines of descent, whom he is compelled to assume have not a common origin, *have nothing in their structure, organs and physiology, in common with one another.* He simply could not do so. And if you admit three or four lines of descent then why not three or four millions. Different lines of descent account not merely for the similarities in given organisms, but for the dissimilarities as well, which otherwise have to be accounted for by the roundabout method of Natural Selection.

Which I ask is most probable, a single progenitor or many ? I am not quarrelling with the doctrine of evolution in one sense, no sensible man would, but I am with Darwin's theory of Natural Selection. Man may be, and probably is, the evolutionary resultant of a lower organism, but man I maintain has a " stirps " or stock of descent peculiarly his own, in which lies hidden potentially all his subsequent development, and this of course is vital, not only to man's life history on the earth, but to his place and position in the universe. And so it has been with countless numbers of other families and species, Darwin notwithstanding.

But to apply Huxley's great law, of evidence to Darwin's hypothetical conjecture. What can we know of what took place in the alteration of species during 60,000,000 years, and what data could ever be available to place any theory in the ranks of even approximate certainty? For it must be remembered we are treating of the whole of organic life, all own the line of time.

What does this evidence really amount to, and what value does it possess? One often hears it talked about as overwhelming, convincing, an array of incontrovertible facts and so forth; sometimes by people who have hardly read a line of any of Darwin's work, and sometimes by men of science who consider themselves great authorities on the subject. But if one sifts the matter to the bottom, relatively speaking it comes to very little indeed. " The Origin of Species " is the great work, in which the whole of this theory of Natural Selection is fully set forth and contended for. In it may be found almost the whole deposit of the Darwinian faith. In this work at any rate Darwin is by no means sure of his own position. His tone throughout, nay his confession, is one of uncertainty and apprehension. Over and over again throughout the work he is on

ON EVIDENCE IN GENERAL 239

the verge of throwing up the task as an incredible and impossible one.

How often do we come across such reflections as these :—

"There is much force in the above objections."

"I do not pretend that the facts given in this chapter strengthen my theory, but none of the cases of difficulty to the best of my judgment annihilate it."

"This difficulty, though appearing insuperable, is lessened."

"Geology assuredly does not reveal any such finely graduated organic chain; and this perhaps is the most obvious and serious objection that can be urged against the theory."

And again :—

"Some of the difficulties are so serious, that to this day I can hardly reflect on them without being in some degree staggered."

And these are only a few of such reflections for they abound throughout the work.

The evidence I reassert if sifted to the bottom is really not very great. What Darwin does is to approach the subject from many points, and he uses the same arguments, and the same evidence, over and over again to establish each particular point of his attack; and this makes the evidence appear greater and more conclusive than it really is.

Again nearly all the evidence adduced in the "Origin of Species" is largely available for the alternative hypothesis of the evolution of species from many stocks of descent. Indeed Darwin's idea of Natural Selection is as suited for and would work as well with the one theory as the other, though in a far more restricted area.

As to the array of incontrovertible facts so frequently insisted on, the evidence is as often as not directed towards the establishment of the veracity of the facts themselves, and has no particular reference to or bearing on the naked theory. So when critics talk about the great mass of facts ready, and at hand, to support the theory; these so-called facts, both in the "Origin of Species" and the "Descent of Man," not infrequently resolve themselves into the assertion of various authorities, picked up, and quoted from innumerable works, without any reference to the context, or any allusion to the many arguments, and instances which cut in a quite opposite direction, and can be quoted on the other side. It is as if a person were to say I believe in this or that miracle, how can I doubt it: look at the whole libraries of works that have been written for the very purpose of corroborating it.

Again Darwin fails to see that much of the evidence which supports his theory in one direction, is all the time undermining it in another.

Witness after witness is placed in the box only to be told to come down almost at once, as it is apparent

ON EVIDENCE IN GENERAL 241

from the first that it has very little evidence of any value to impart, what it has is faulty and hesitating, and as often as not more favourable to the other side, than to that of the parties on whose behalf it was called.

One wonders in reading through the "Origin of Species," why these witnesses are called at all, unless it was to prevent them being called by the other side, and experiencing a much severer and more damaging cross-examination.

To show how weak and questionable the evidence of many of Darwin's most important witnesses is, the reader perhaps could not do better than to imagine a scene in a Court of Law, in which Darwin is the cross-examining counsel, and the monkey, the ice-age, the geological record, the neuters, and the hybrids of creation, are some of the witnesses examined.

The evidence of one and all is adverse, and no process of cross-examination can shake it.

But if the reader finds himself disappointed with the nature of the theoretical evidence, he will be amply rewarded in other directions. The whole work throws a light on the hidden workings, and operations of nature, to be found possibly nowhere else. Whatever the value of Darwin's theory may be, his position as a great naturalist remains unshaken. He was not only great as a specialist, but great, if one may borrow a phrase, as a general practitioner. Probably a better informed, better read, and more varied naturalist never existed. The labour be-

Q

stowed, his patience and powers of concentrated observation stand unique, and unrivalled, but those qualities do not entitle him to the rank of a great inventor or discoverer.

Surely Darwin's advocates and admirers do him an ill service when they allow their eulogies on him to transgress the bounds of good sense and moderation. To place him on an eminence equal to that of Sir Isaac Newton, is only to place him on a pedestal from which he will have afterwards to be removed. The following peroration taken from a sort of " Oration funèbre," pronounced over Darwin and his works on the occasion of the centenary of his birth by Professor Wallace is, to say the least of it, extravagant.

" However far our knowledge of nature may advance in the future, it will be by extending still further the pathways which he has opened for us through the luxuriant jungle of the life-world; and the name of Darwin will for ever stand out as the typical example of what the student of nature ought to be. To him, even more completely perhaps than to Newton, may be applied the supreme eulogy of the poet :

" Nature and nature's laws lay hid in night,
God said, ' Let Darwin be,' and all was light."

As a matter of fact as far as any theoretical illumination is concerned there was as much light before Darwin existed as, there is now. Moreover the comparison between the two men

ON EVIDENCE IN GENERAL 243

is not a happy one. The bent of their minds and their intellectual equipment were essentially different. They lived in different spheres of thought, and their work was on a different plane. The one was occupied with the rigid and unbending laws of mathematics, the other with the very plastic inductions of organic life. I ask is it fair to compare Darwin's very doubtful and speculative conjecture, as to the progression of organic life, with the transcendent mathematical genius of a Newton who raised the law of gravitation to the level of a mathematical certainty. So far from discovering even a working hypothesis, Darwin himself did more to destroy and discredit the very theory he suggested than any writer of his day. Whether the egg preceded the hen, or the hen the egg is still a matter of doubt. Scientific men prefer the eggs, the theologians the chickens. But Darwin will not even allow eggs, one egg must go round and do for all. But it is as incredible that all organic life should owe its origin to one egg, as that all inorganic matter should owe its origin to one grain of sand.

Professor Weismann sees no reason to modify in any way his adherence to Darwin's theory of Natural Selection. Professor Weismann's intellect evidently has not experienced the workings of the very law that he admires, nor undergone that modification by variation which it should.

Professor Tyndall's eulogy on Darwin in his celebrated Belfast Address, is almost as extravagant:

"Darwin's vast resources enable him to cope with objections started by himself and others, so as to leave the final impression upon the reader's mind, that if they be not completely answered, they certainly are not fatal. Their negative force being destroyed, you are free to be influenced by the vast positive mass of evidence he is able to bring before you."

But the negative force of the objections is in no way destroyed, on the contrary it is rather increased. And as regards "positive evidence" really Professor Tyndall must be aware there is absolutely none. This assertion moreover seems strange, as a little later on in the same address, he says :—

"The strength of the doctrine of Evolution consists, not in an experimental demonstration for the subject is hardly accessible to this mode of proof."

In other words the positive evidence is not forthcoming. And then continues the Professor :—

"He moves over the subject with the passionless strength of a glacier : and the grinding of the rocks is not always without a counterpart in the logical pulverisation of the objector."

So far from moving over the subject with the passionless strength of a glacier, no one knew better than Darwin himself that he was skating on very thin ice indeed, and not only that but the ice frequently gives way altogether, and he finds himself plunged over and over again, in the chilly waters of discomfiture and disaster.

As a matter of fact Darwin formed a much truer, and more modest estimate of his own hypothetical performance, than any of his would-be advocates and admirers. It must always be borne in mind that neither the theory of "Evolution" nor the "Struggle for Existence" were either of them patented by Darwin. They are self-obvious truisms in their wider and general sense. They could hardly escape the notice of the most ordinary understanding. A boy must see that he is evolved from his parents, the chicken from the egg, and the fruit from the tree, and that everything comes from something in a natural and orderly progression.

The idea of Evolution is as old as the hills and was well known to the ancients, not merely in a haphazard conjectural manner, or as the mere accidental suggestion of some literary philosopher. The whole idea was exploited and well thought out by the Latin poet Lucretius. Lucretius devoted a very long poem the "De naturâ rerum," almost entirely to its elaboration. He puts the theory of Evolution in a nutshell in the following lines :—

> "Quas ob res ubi viderimus nil posse creari
> de nilo, tum quod sequimur jam rectius inde
> perspiciemus, et unde queat res quaeque creari
> et qui quaeque modo fiant opera sine divum."

> "Admit this truth, that nought from nothing springs,
> And all is clear. Developed, then we trace
> Through Nature's boundless realm, the rise of things,
> Their modes, and powers innate : nor need from heaven,
> Some God's descent to rule each rising fact."

This of course is putting the theory in a somewhat negative form, but Lucretius immediately proceeds to develop the positive side of it. It may be observed that the word " creo " was always used by the best Latin writers in the sense " of producing one thing from another," and not in the sense in which we use the word " create " of making something out of nothing.

Lucretius, then goes on to explain and elucidate the atomic theory in language which would have satisfied Dalton himself and which he borrowed from Epicurus, who taught like the modern materialist that the world was formed, not by any divine power, but from a fortuitous concourse of atoms. Moreover he asserted that we are all sprung from celestial seed : the father of all is the same Ether :—

> " All spring from heaven, ethereal, all that live :
> The sire of all is Ether."

From the above passages it can be seen that the ancients were more up to date than is generally imagined, and were quite our equals, in daring, picturesque, and varied conjecture. Where they fell short of us was not in their powers of reason and imagination, but in the instruments, knowledge

ON EVIDENCE IN GENERAL 247

and opportunity, to bring their ideas to a practical test and verify them by experimental demonstration. The sciences of chemistry, and mathematics, and the allied branches of physics, and mechanics, were all still in their infancy. Moreover the ancients were not possessed of either men suitable for the task, nor had they the aid that the moderns possess of swift intercommunication and intercourse.

Roger Bacon, perhaps one of the greatest Englishmen and most learned men that ever lived, a far greater man than his namesake and successor, Francis Bacon, by whom he is somewhat thrown into the shade, made this very complaint.

He boasted, that if he only had the men, the means, and the appliances, he could make conveyances that would go swifter than the fastest horse, and ships that would travel under water; anticipating at any rate the modern motor car and submarine.

And this was assuredly no idle boast, for Roger Bacon was one of the greatest, and most learned men of his day, as his work the " Opus Magus " clearly proves. He was for those days an advanced physicist and mathematician, was the inventor of, or at any rate, one of the inventors of gunpowder, and one of the least showy and most retiring of men.

So Darwin did not originate the idea of evolution, still less that of the struggle for existence, which he himself acknowledges he took straight over from Malthus.

What novel hypothesis can Darwin then justifiably lay claim to? Merely his theory of "Natural Selection."

"Some writers have misapprehended or objected to the term Natural Selection. Some have even *imagined that natural selection induces variability whereas it implies only the preservation of such variations as arise and are beneficial to the being under its conditions of life.*"

In other words nature preserves what is fit to be preserved, and destroys what is only fit for destruction. His style of writing in the "Origin of Species" is significant; it is absolutely different from that in "The Descent of Man." The two books might have been written by two different men. It is impossible to imagine anyone with the literary gifts of a Tyndall or a Huxley producing a work like the "Origin of Species." There is very little method or arrangement in it, and it was obviously and confessedly written in a hurry. This I believe is a recognised thing. There were rivals in the field, and Darwin naturally wished to be beforehand with them in his publication. It is inordinately, and unnecessarily long, and might well have been compressed into at least two-thirds of its size; and this is due to the fact that Darwin repeats himself again and again. Paragraph after paragraph are almost identical in thought and langague; and there are no less than six or seven summaries in the book, which

ON EVIDENCE IN GENERAL 249

are merely recapitulations of what has immediately preceded them.

Professor Wallace himself says of the theory :—

"Some readers may be surprised at the statement that the theory of Darwin is essentially simple, and easily understood. What is meant is, that it needs no special training to understand it : no laboratory work is required, no knowledge of anatomy or physiology. The facts appealed to are throughout, the facts of external nature, which every one has (or ought to have) the opportunity of observing for himself. And the more important principles arising out of these facts are also of the most simple and obvious nature, so much so that the objection is often made that they are self-evident truisms."

But in "The Descent of Man" the controversial part of the subject is kept largely in the background. Darwin is completely at home with every subject he touches upon, and is master of the situation. The style is narrative, descriptive, and historical. He is sure of his ground-work of facts, and quotations, at any rate, with the result that all confusion, and obscurity, almost entirely disappear, and the whole tale is told in the most instructive and fascinating language imaginable.

This difference in style can only be accounted for by the fact, that in the one work Darwin is sure of his position, in the other he is conscious of his weak ness, and of the many dangers that beset his hypothesis : so he covers his retreat by the quiet assertion that this or that objection has been disposed of "Natura locuta, causa finita" or else he makes good his escape in a cloud of verbiage, very much like the heroes in the "Iliad" under the sheltering wings of their respective divinities, when they were on the verge of annihilation.

CHAPTER XV

SOME CLOSING OBSERVATIONS

THERE is one important point, which hitherto has not been touched upon, and to which, as far as I have been able to ascertain, Darwin nowhere alludes, nor does it appear to have suggested itself to his mind.

While admitting, as every one must, that Natural Selection encourages and promotes beneficent variation in species, yet out of this admission two questions arise. Beneficial for what purpose? And beneficial for how long? A change may be entirely beneficial to enable a species to perform its allotted and foreordained life-history on the earth; but the very benefits accruing for that purpose may be at the same time disastrous to its undue prolongation, and a hindrance, rather than the reverse, to a species ever passing into a higher form. All the evidence seems to point rather to this conclusion, than another.

And there is a second point which needs emphasis, and that is Darwin's fixed belief that all life has emanated from a common progenitor. His method of reasoning on this question is somewhat peculiar. " Therefore," he says, " on the principle of Natural

Selection, with divergence of character it does not seem incredible," etc.; so it comes to this, that if you concede the theory of Natural Selection, a common progenitor does not seem incredible. Quite so, and if you concede the idea of creative power, and even if you do not, multiple progenitors, and multiple centres of creation, do not seem incredible either.

The expression, " does not seem incredible," does not bear on it the stamp of even approximate proof, which Darwin has throughout the " Origin of Species " put forth all his strength and exhausted all his ingenuity to establish. And then he proceeds:—" If we admit that, we must likewise admit that all the organic beings that have ever lived on this earth may be descended from one primordial form; but this inference is chiefly grounded on analogy."

So we must accept the preceding " must " on an inference drawn from analogy. If that method of reasoning is not an extraordinary perversion of the use of the syllogism, it is difficult to say what is.

Darwin—if one may say so with respect—is throughout too fond of analogy. It is a perilous guide, and a dangerous weapon in the hands of even the most skilful controversialist, and never more so than when made use of in a scientific discussion.

" Analogy " is usually understood to mean any sort of resemblance affording a ground for argument, which does not amount to a complete induction;

SOME CLOSING OBSERVATIONS 253

and two of Darwin's finest analogies fall somewhat short in this respect, for the one is misleading, and the other, if not exactly misapplied, at least not so well applied as it might have been. Take his celebrated analogy drawn from the Tree :—

"The affinities of all the beings of the same class have sometimes been represented by a great tree. I believe this simile largely speaks the truth. The green and budding twigs may represent existing species, and those produced during former years may represent the long succession of extinct species. At each period all the growing twigs have tried to branch out on all sides, and overtop and kill the surrounding twigs and branches, in the same manner as species, and groups of species, have at all times overmastered other species in the great battle for life. The limbs divided into great branches, and these into lesser and lesser branches, were themselves once, when the tree was young, budding twigs: and this connection of the former and present buds by ramifying branches may well represent the classification of all external and living species in groups, subordinate to groups, of the many twigs which flourished when the tree was a mere bush, only two or three, now grown into great branches, yet survive and bear other branches: so with the species which lived during long past geological periods, very few have left living and modified descendants. From the past growth of the tree, many a limb and branch has decayed and dropped off: and these fallen branches of various sizes may represent those whole orders, families, and genera which have now no living representatives, and which are known to us only in a fossil state.

"As buds give rise to fresh buds, and these, if vigorous, branch out and overtop on all sides many a feeble branch, so by generation I believe it has been with the great Tree of life, which fills with its dead and broken branches the crust of the earth, and covers the surface with its ever-branching and beautiful ramifications."

The analogy would be far truer if it referred to life of man only, or even to a single species. But the analogy is very remote and misleading when contrasted with the whole of organic life. To begin with, the tree when out above the ground is ever and always the same; all it does is to grow in size. It is true that branches succeed branches, twigs twigs, and leaves leaves. But the leaf, say, of the oak is not one year the leaf peculiar to the oak, and the next year the leaf peculiar to the cabbage, and so on, which it would be if the analogy were at all true. For the very object of Darwin's theory is to account for the process by which one species here is converted into another; and for the analogy to be true the tree would have to change its character and the structure and appearance of its branches, twigs, and leaves with the lapse of time. But though parts of the tree perish and fall away, to be renewed

SOME CLOSING OBSERVATIONS 255

again and again, yet the renovation is always the same, and the wood never becomes converted into another and dissimilar material.

But the analogy drawn from "languages," given on page 348 of the "Origin of Species," is far more felicitous :—

> "It may be worth while," says Darwin, "to illustrate this view of classification by taking the case of languages. If we possessed a perfect pedigree of mankind, a genealogical arrangement of the races of man would afford the best classification of the various languages now spoken throughout the world: and if all extinct languages, and all intermediate and slowly changing dialects, were to be included, such an arrangement would be the only possible one. Yet it might be that some ancient languages had altered very little, and had given rise to a few new languages, whilst others had altered much owing to the spreading isolation, and state of civilisation of the several co-descended races, and had thus given rise to many new dialects and languages. The various degrees of difference between the languages of the same stock would have to be expressed by groups subordinate to groups: but the proper or even possible arrangement would still be genealogical, and this would be extremely natural, as it would connect together all languages, extinct and recent, by the closest affinity, and would give the filiation and origin of each tongue."

This is extremely clever and appropriate, and

the analogy would be almost perfect if applied to man's treatment of animals under domestication. In both cases man chooses and rejects, he transfuses and cross-breeds; he retains in both cases, for generations, some classes for his use and benefit, and rejects others. He mixes and retains a variety of animals for a variety of purposes, precisely in the same manner that he mixes and retains, either consciously or unconsciously, some languages and dialects, as they are adapted to this or that climate or race. In both cases he can reject or retain, preserve or destroy, as it suits his convenience and purpose to do so.

The value of an inference from analogy always depends on the ratio of the ascertained resemblances to the ascertained differences. Of course no analogy can ever amount to a perfect induction, but the nearer it approaches it the truer it is. For instance, the leg of a chair to the leg of a man is a very remote analogy, depending merely on their mechanical resemblance. The wing of a bird to the wing of an insect is a nearer one, even if it is not in its structural relations the corresponding organ of the body. To discover a really good analogy is by no means always an easy matter. Many so-called analogies are no true analogies at all. That the human race will perish because the individuals of it perish is not a true induction. Or again, St Paul's celebrated analogy of the seed falling into the ground and dying, to the risen body, is not a perfect one, as the seed is not dead, but very much alive.

The picture that Victor Hugo draws in his celebrated novel, "Notre Dame de Paris," of the book killing the building, would afford a very apt illustration of the way species supersedes and drives out species :—

> "Meanwhile," he says, "what happened to printing? It appropriated to itself the whole life of architecture. In proportion as architecture decreased, the printing-press flourished and grew fat. All the forces of the human mind hitherto expended on buildings henceforward were expended on books. From the sixteenth century the Press increased in proportion as architecture decreased, and finally killed it in the struggle."

And here, on parting with the controversial part of the question, one can hardly refrain from asking—" Why were the 'Origin of Species' and the 'Descent of Man' such favourites with the general public?" They are both of them of course store-houses of information and erudition on the particular subjects of which they treat, and are an abiding and valuable contribution to that field of knowledge. But they are not written with any particular brilliancy of diction, or composition, which is generally necessary to make such works attractive to the public. They seem to reverse the general rule, that the more valuable a work is to the specialist, the less acceptable is it to the general reader.

The answer is probably to be found in the fact that they treat on subjects dearer perhaps than any to the human heart,—the " Why," the " Wherefore," and the " Whither." They affect the whole race of man, and every individual that goes to make up that innumerable multitude.

And when these great subjects are handled by a man pre-eminent for ability in the field on which he dilates, and that man has such startling, novel, and revolutionary doctrines to impart, what wonder that the eyes of all were turned upon him, and devoured with avidity the story he had to unfold.

Hitherto humanity had been taught to believe that man was still an angel, though a fallen one,—capable of reparation and of regaining those kingdoms of bliss which he had forfeited, and which were his just inheritance.

But now all was changed; so far from being the offspring of the angels, man must look for his pedigree to a hairy monstrosity, whose dwelling-place, so far from being that of " setting suns," was to be found in the forest primeval, and in the dark places, and recesses of the earth.

Such a doctrine as that, so startling and so new, was sure to find many adherents, and its teaching was naturally acceptable to fallen man. It was a mistake and somewhat of a discredit to have fallen from an angel, but to have put off the monkey

SOME CLOSING OBSERVATIONS 259

and risen to the man, through one's own unaided exertions was, after all, a credit to humanity, rather than the reverse. And when one remembers that this teaching was accepted, advertised, and illuminated, by two of the most remarkable men of the nineteenth century, namely, Professors Tyndall and Huxley, what wonder that these views caught on, and that the fever has not yet entirely subsided.

And here I will endeavour to answer by anticipation an objection not unlikely to be raised. It may be said that the writer is, by his own confession, no naturalist, and that therefore his criticisms may be safely ignored. There would doubtless be a certain relevancy in the remark, but the stricture can be pressed a great deal too far.

All professions, all arts, and all sciences, have their sanctuaries, and citadels of knowledge, into which the intruder enters at his own peril, and generally to his complete discomfiture. But there are attached to all these departments of learning, large border-lands, and certain broad outlines of thought, and principle, upon which the criticism of the outsider may be as valuable as that of the soldier within the citadel. That "Onlookers see most of the game" is only a half-truth, like many other similar terse and epigrammatic utterances. But it is true in this way. I suppose most men who have ever experienced the drudgery of the early years of any science, or profession, have discovered that the more they get immersed in its detail and intricacies, the more confused they become, and the more, for the time at any rate, do they lose the sense of its general perspective, which the outsider is still roughly enabled to retain: and they are at times surprised and not a little disconcerted to discover that a mere novice who knows nothing of the ropes, puts his finger instantaneously on the spot, and points directly to the true solution.

The reason for that is to be found in the fact that the onlooker, in not seeing the pitfalls that the student does, and, being unhampered by the doubts and fears which the intricacies of learning and its application suggest, goes straight to the point, sees true to the occasion, and for the moment appears the wiser man of the two.

The student is looking through the microscopic end of the telescope, the onlooker through the reverse; and it is not until the former has exhausted the microscopic end of the glass, and returned to the macroscopic again, that his superior knowledge is apparent, and he stands revealed, the master of the situation. The master of any art or science, is the man who can see through both ends of the telescope at once.

There can be little doubt, especially in these days, that the pressure of the Public and the Press, even the opinions of the man in the street, and perhaps the haphazard chatter of irresponsible frivolity, have done much to improve, if not learning itself, at any rate the professional methods of administer-

SOME CLOSING OBSERVATIONS

ing it to the public. The Public prefer, whenever possible, to choose the apples of the tree of knowledge for themselves, and are by no means always disposed to be put off, with the somewhat unripe, indigestible, and often expensive fruit, doled out for their particular consumption.

I suppose that most people past middle age can well remember the time when to question the advice given by the Church, Medicine, and the Law in their respective departments was looked upon as an impertinence, and almost of itself a qualification for Bedlam. Who does not remember the immortal answer of the old solicitor Spenlow in "David Copperfield" to the doubting David, who ventured mildly to differ with his superior, as to the claim of "Doctors Commons" to be a necessary ingredient in the constitution. Mr Spenlow assured David that whatever his opinions might be, it was so. That rightly or wrongly, people liked to have it so, and that a gentleman took things as he found them. This was doubtless a very comfortable doctrine. Gentlemen not only took things as they found them, but left them very much as they found them, and sometimes considerably worse.

No doubt the old Professions were wise in their generation. They were jealous of their preserves, and had a very effectual and ingenious contrivance for keeping off all intruders. They surrounded their various compounds with a barbed wire fence of a very wordy and intricate entanglement, the barbs of which consisted of needlessly difficult and obscure phraseology, largely consisting of decadent Latin and quite unintelligible Norman French. This was hardly fair on the Public, but its efficacy was effectual and undoubted. Before you could pass the fence, you must learn the language, and if you failed to give the password, you were summarily ejected with the remark, that as you did not understand even the vocabulary, you had better leave the subject alone.

Perhaps some critic may reply :—There may have been some force in these arguments when the " Origin of Species " first appeared, but how about subsequent researches and discoveries ? Do not they tend to strengthen and corroborate on all points the Law of Natural Selection ?

But all subsequent discoveries merely prove that Darwin unveiled to mortal eyes the greater inter-relationship and community of nature, and whatever their evidential value may be in support of his hypothesis, that evidence is available within limits for the alternative one herein suggested.

What Darwin really did was this. He substituted the words " Natural Selection " for the word " Change." Nature changes, and tends to preserve whatever is worthy of preservation. Nature rejects, and accepts at her own sweet will ; nature is nature still. And Darwin's law is reduced after all to a thing " in nubibus," a " will-o'-the-wisp," the " unsubstantial fabric of a vision," a " ghost," and nothing more. You hit it, and it abides; you miss it, and it is there all the same. It flits in and out of the " Origin," ever ready to explain the mysteries of the Universe: and in the "Descent of Man" it performs the marriage ceremony over humanity and the ape.

This is your god, oh men of science,—a ghost, and nothing more! Hitherto, whatever else your shortcomings, you have been acquitted by humanity of any leanings towards the world of Shades; but humanity, it appears, was mistaken, and after all ye are even as we, but credulous and unorthodox children of the great mother that gave you birth.

"If Cleopatra's nose had been longer, the shape of the world had been changed," and if the words " Natural Selection" had not been substituted for a shorter one, much searching of heart and uneasiness would have been spared, both in the biological and theological camps.

PART II

THE TREND OF DARWIN'S PHILOSOPHY

AND
CONCLUSION

CHAPTER XVI

DARWIN'S PHILOSOPHY AND REFLECTIONS THEREON

I HAVE endeavoured to follow Darwin to the best of my ability through his two great works, the "Origin of Species" and "The Descent of Man." I have attempted to show where, and why I consider much of his reasoning erroneous, and the conclusions that he arrives at inconclusive, and unsatisfactory. I have taken the salient points of his argument and pointed out where it appears to me that his evidence is inadequate and worthless. But there remains yet another question; what is the philosophy on which Darwin's theory of Natural Selection is founded, or rather what is the philosophy that fits in with this Law of Natural Selection, and indeed is the only one consistent with it? Where does Darwin's teaching lead us to, and how far, if it were true, would it revolutionise and modify man's thoughts as regards ultimate things. I am not concerned here with the inner workings of Darwin's mind, or with that of any man scientific or otherwise. No man knows the spirit of man, but the spirit of man that is in him. And even man himself, knows himself but very imperfectly. As a rule the thoughts of each one of us change from day to day, nay, almost from hour to hour. Our attitude towards everything assumes a very different shape when we are old, enfeebled and disappointed, to what it does when we are young and in robust health. Under one given set of circumstances we are one man under another set, another. Transfer the most self complacent agnostic from his easy chair to a storm at sea and his ideas may possibly undergo a certain amount of softening and modification. If you want to understand realities you must live in realities, and not in books.

It must be remembered moreover that Darwin was no propagandist of this or that creed, of this or that philosophy. He keeps closely to his last, which was the unravelling and interpretation of nature as he saw it, by the best of the light that was in him. And if this law of Natural Selection, conflicted with and overthrew certain preconceived opinions of mankind, that was no concern of his, with that he had nothing to do. For he says :—

"Many instincts are so wonderful that their development will probably appear to the reader, a difficulty sufficient to overthrow my whole theory. I may here premise that I have nothing to do with the origin of the mental powers any more than I have with life itself."

This sentence must be read with considerable modification, for several chapters in the "Descent of Man" are devoted to the origin and growth of man's mental faculties, and an elaborate endeavour to explain them.

But if Darwin's explanation of the origin of life is the true one, then such words as destiny, improvement, and immortality may be as well, at once, struck out of the human vocabulary, they have no longer any meaning for man. For according to Darwin's own showing nature knows no such thing as development in the sense of improvement. And when he comes to this question of improvement he is evidently at a loss and feels, though he does not admit it, the pressure of his own false reasoning. For what is Darwin's idea of development, it is merely numerical increase in a species, and the greater specialisation of parts of the units that compose the organism. And the more highly organised a species is the more it can specialise its different functions, and the more complete is the division of its physiological labours. The acumulation of variations, tendency towards specialisation, is within the scope of natural selection.

So the end and aim of all the operations of nature is to multiply through all eternity various organisms, which when they have reached their numerical zenith, and the specialisation of their parts admits of no further extension, they are ruthlessly succeeded by other organisms, who begin the process of specialisation and multiplication all over again. These in their turn are succeeded by other species more suited to each successive environment, and these operations continue through all eternity, at the dictates of mere chance, without beginning, without meaning, and without end, with no Creator to rejoice in his works, and not even a devil to vary the monotony, or break in upon and pulverise, this kaleidoscopic and never ending repetition of organic adaptation and variability.

If the human race is to pin its faith on such philosophy as that, its future is to say the least of it uninviting. Better let humanity eat and drink to repletion, let it allow no flower of the spring to escape it, let every member of the race seize on immediate gratification, and perish with its own satiety, at least by so doing it will have proved its superiority to these wonderful laws, and will have prevented nature from toying, and trifling any longer, with one of her most cherished specialisations, the brain of man.

It is amazing how two generations of scientific men should have fallen down and worshipped, such a negative idol as that. Better accept the teaching of the monoists, weak and inconclusive as it is, that there is a Creator, but that he is inseparable from his own creation, dissolved in it like sugar in a cup of tea. Monoism is nothing new, it is merely pantheism in solution, and its whole teaching has long ago been expressed by that greatest of all philosophers, Alexander Pope, in a single couplet :—

"Man is but part of one connected whole
Whose body Nature is, and God the soul."

That teaching sounds plausible enough, but one cannot help suspecting it is only half the truth. For if the greater cannot come from the less, then it requires a greater, yes, and a greater person, to make a person, however many intermediate agents may be employed in the operation.

That is looking backward, and looking forward there must be a perfected personal correspondence somewhere in space, to meet and welcome each imperfect earthly personal creation.

Darwin's theory holds out but small hope of a futurity for any living thing, but that there is a future of some sort is at least a high probability, though for how far, and for how long, that future will be conditioned, by man's thoughts and actions here below, it is idle for man to speculate upon. We shall all know something about it sooner or later, but for the moment a veil hides it from our eyes.

Darwin of course teaches directly nothing of the kind, he is dumb on the subject; but the whole of his reasoning leads up to it, and it is difficult to place on it any other construction. Of course no philosophic materialist, or atheist, would assert that there *was* no future for man: all he would assert would be, that there was no evidence to lead one to suppose that there was. Evidence in the sense of mathematical demonstration, from the very nature of the case, there is, and can be none; you cannot expect mathematical evidence in a moral plane. And if the evidence amounted to demonstration, you would be in the region of knowledge, and the kingdoms of hope, and faith would be entirely cut away. No evidence would be needed.

But it is to this question of a future life that I wish to direct my attention. Of course nothing new can be said upon the subject, it has all been said a thousand times before. There is nothing new under the sun, especially on such subjects as these, novelty if there is any can only be found in the manner of its representation. But here I shall avail myself of no mystic sword Excalibur, but shall rely solely, on Darwin's own weapons, Nature, Reason and the Voice of Man.

The whole question is shrouded in mystery, and one ought not to be too curious about such questions as these. Man's true sphere is in relative thought and activity, and that perpetual endeavour to project the mind either backward or forward into the infinite has its dangers, it is hardly conducive to man's happiness, and if persisted in might land him in a madhouse.

But with the vast mass of mankind there is very little fear of their trespassing too far beyond the practical affairs of life. They are occupied day in and day out, with providing for their daily necessities. The trivial round, the common task, leaves them little room or inclination, for merely abstract speculation. There are others who deliberately drive from their minds all such thoughts, they are uncanny, disquieting, and a nuisance. Give us they say pleasure and excitement, and the more of it the better, that is all that we desire.

> "Fill the cup and fill the can
> All the windy ways of man
> Are but dust that rises up
> And is quickly laid again.

But there is another order of mind to whom these questions have an abiding and perennial charm. This order of mind is to be found chiefly among men and women who live much alone, either in their outer or inner life, who never find the correspondence in their fellow men that precisely suits themselves, waifs and strays on the sands of time, who are out of the main current of things, relegated to the backwaters and solitary places of the world.

If the truth were known, it is from these lonely spirits that the greater works of imagination, whether in art, literature, or song, almost invariably proceed.

The following few discursive remarks, on man's past, his present life, and future destiny, may perhaps be entertaining, and possibly instructive to those like minded with the writer. But I propose to discuss them purely from the standpoint of the intellect and nature, without referring at all, excepting incidentally at the close, and then only on its ethical side, to the great question of Revelation and the Christian faith. That is a question that each man must determine for himself, and people of

s

any thought and education do so determine it for themselves, in one way, or another, as they pass along the journey of life.

But before leaving Darwin altogether it must be confessed that in the closing chapter of his book he is not altogether ingenuous, indeed it would be nearer the truth to say that he is extremely disingenuous. For he says:—

> "I see no good reason why the views given in this volume should shock the religious feelings of any one. It is satisfactory as showing how transient such impressions are, to remember that the greatest discovery ever made by man, namely the law of the attraction of gravity was also attacked by Leibnitz as subversive of natural, and inferentially of revealed religion."

Darwin sees no reason why these views should shock the religious feelings of any one! This simply is not credible, Darwin if any man must have seen the conclusion to which all his reasoning points. To put it plainly it is blank materialism. It makes a clean sweep of the whole theological slate. Huxley and Tyndall, interpreted in that way, and seized upon it as a vantage ground from which to attack the theologians.

The theologians regarded it in the same light, for they cried out in their apprehension and fear "O God the heathen are come into thine inheritance, thy holy place have they defiled and made Jerusalem a heap of stones." But they need not have been so desperately perturbed, for the eternal verities are the eternal verities, and no opinions and speculations of mortal man can alter them one whit.

Discover what it will, science will never eradicate religion from the heart of man, it is as essential a part of his being, as are his passions, appetites, and desires. Even the arch-sceptic Voltaire, one of the most versatile, able, and bizarre intelligences that ever trod this earth, was fain to confess, that if there was not a God it was necessary to invent one. This was probably Voltaire's cynical way of confessing to the world his real inner belief. And Voltaire it must be remembered was quite an impossible person. He was conceited, cynical, and irritable to a degree. So far from suffering fools gladly, he could not tolerate any one at all, fool or otherwise, and would probably have preferred the fool, to any one that attempted to rival his pretensions.

Science tells us with a very high degree of plausibility, and probability, that matter and life are eternal, but there is a qualifying factor that must never be lost sight of, that man is tethered to his own intellect, and beyond that he cannot go. And the true value of his own intellect, he is quite incapable of properly appraising. Relatively as regards his surroundings his estimate of it may be true, but as regards absolute, and eternal things, such as time, and space, he may be wrong about it altogether. The laws of mathematics may be true as far as their relationship to man's brain is concerned, but to higher intelligences than man's they may be ridiculously at sea, and misleading.

And what "life" really is in its essence, from the very nature of the case, man can never discover. Even if chemistry could advance so far, as to create a man by chemical manipulation, without the process of ordinary generation, a man so like other men, in all his thoughts, words and actions, that you could not distinguish the one from the other, he would be no nearer in his discovery of the origin and true meaning of life. There is still the fiery sword as there was of old, that keeps the way, not only of the tree of life but of any knowledge of it.

Many great men lived before Agamemnon and many great thinkers lived before Darwin, Tyndall, and Huxley, and many greater than they may live hereafter.

Where then do we come from? This is by no means such an important question as whither are we going. But as the two questions are the extension of the same line backwards and forwards I propose here to discuss them together. The personality of man is made up of two substances matter and life, no one I take it can reasonably deny this. As regards the material part of us the answer is obvious enough. It was answered long ago in the Book of Genesis, and no better answer is ever likely to be forthcoming. "Out of the ground wast thou taken, for dust thou art and unto dust shalt thou return."

So much for the mortal, or material; but how about the immortal or immaterial! Life most assuredly is, and has been coexistent with matter from all eternity. It inhabits for a time a given piece of organism, and when that organism is dissolved or reduced to its primary elements by what we call death, that life must return to the common stock of life again, and can in no wise perish.

But this gives rise to another question. Is life a voluntary and willing agent in matter, or does matter seize hold of life, whenever it finds a favourable opportunity, and so to speak take it prisoner.

But the great question for man is not whether life is immortal, that to my mind goes without saying. But has man a life of identity, and personality of an endurable kind, altogether independent of the particular piece or pieces of organism which in his endless, journey through space and time, he may be compelled temporarily to inhabit. Has man a piece of life peculiarly his own; or rather which is himself, independently of any particular lodgment which it may occupy for a time, and which we call his "Ego" or the "Soul."

It has sometimes been asserted that after death all is a blank. That Nature refuses to give any reply however importunate and persistent man's inquiries become. But is this altogether so, does Nature not enlighten or assist man in this matter at all. There are three very powerful pieces of natural evidence, in support of life, yes and a personal life beyond the grave.

Science tells us, that every particle of the body of man changes every seven years. So at the end of every seven years, a man has an entirely new suit of flesh. In other words the mortal part of man dies every seven years. So that if a man lives to seventy years the mortal part of him has already died ten times in that period: and yet his personality, identity or soul—call it what you will—the name is immaterial—endures. Well if the soul can survive ten gradual mortal extinctions, why should it not survive the last, and most violent extinction of all which is called death!

One cannot help feeling a fallacy here somewhere, though it is difficult precisely to indicate wherein the fallacy lies. But this argument has the support of no less a name than that of Bishop Butler in his " Analogy," and he argues the point with considerable plausibility and power.

A very nice legal question might arise out of this. If a man committed a murder seven years ago, the body with which the man committed that murder, would be a different one altogether from the body he now possesses. Could or ought his present body, to be hung, or incarcerated, for the transgressions of the old body which has already returned to corruption. The point is quite arguable, and will perhaps someday be raised. It would be almost as nice a point as another one. If a man were created by man, without the ordinary process of generation, would that man have any " legal status " or might his fellow men murder, rob, and despoil him at pleasure.

The second clue and answer which Nature affords is really a far more powerful and a better one.

Why has the idea of immortality, the desire of immortality, ever been implanted in the mind of man at all, if there is no answer or correspondence to that feeling beyond the grave! Nature never does anything without a purpose, nature as far as we know never implants a craving, or desire, in any organic life, without at the same time providing its object of fulfilment. A thirsty man craves for water, a hungry man for food, an ambitious man for pride of place and so on. These cravings in any given individual instance, may so to speak miss their mark, but the possibility of their fulfilment exists, and speaking generally the desire whatever it may be, finds its gratification. So it would be strange, to say the least of it, if in this matter of immortality, nature should desert her usual practice and should conspire in so vital and momentous a question to deceive the soul of man. The witness is in itself. The substance of the thing hoped for, is without going any further, the evidence, and the best evidence of the thing not seen.

And thirdly there is the question of conscience. Of course Herbert Spencer, Darwin, and the rest will have it that conscience is a mere growth, initiated and fostered by nature and the social instinct, to enable man to learn his proper place, and retain his equilibrium in the environment in which he finds himself. A growth brought about, and caused by intercourse with his fellows, and at the same time a monitor to warn him not to stray too far afield from the conventions, and limitations, with which nature has hedged him in and safe-guarded him.

This certainly is not the opinion of the majority of the great minds of all ages. If that was so, then why does conscience " make cowards of us all." Why do we all so shrink from the journey to that undiscovered country, from which no traveller returns. Surely the vast mass of men if they really believed in annihilation would not dread it. Nay, to most of them it would be a positive relief; the end of toil and pain. There must be, and is, an immense mass of suffering humanity, suffering in a thousand ways, in mind, as well as in body, to whom immediate and final extinction would be a blessing, rather than a curse. Let any man take the person he considers to be the most favoured and fortunate of his acquaintance; is the joy that that person experiences after the period of early youth has passed away anything so very great as to make life a desirable thing. The pains of life with nearly all, most certainly outweigh the pleasures. And pains, troubles, and discomforts of all sorts, both of mind and body increase rather than diminish as the days go by. Sins and shortcomings multiply and with them the feelings of remorse, and the dread of a future retribution. Friends drop away, if you are fortunate enough to have any, love grows cold, the intellect becomes misty and impaired, and perhaps one interest alone remains, that is the interest in humanity itself.

A man is born let us say into the middle, and professional classes of life, in some respects perhaps the most fortunate of any. What is his time, and what has he to hope for, or rather what as a rule does he actually obtain?

It takes a whole army of mothers, nurses, servants, doctors, pastors, and masters, to bring that man satisfactorily to maturity and steer him safely, if they ever succeed in doing so, through the dangerous period of his early days. Having reached maturity he enters a profession, in which many years of hard and assiduous study are the necessary preliminary to a successful career. When fully launched out, he marries for good or evil, happiness or misery, as the case may be. Up to the age of thirty the merest competency whatever his abilities are, is all he has a right to expect. From thirty to fifty he is making money, if he is one of the fortunate ones and ever makes anything worth speaking of at all. At sixty he is *passé* and placed on the shelf. And what remains? If he has a hobby to kill time with he is fortunate. And the remainder of his time is spent in the exercise of that hobby or in the fulfilment of various little social duties and amenities. And then old age approaches, and is hard upon his heels. And what has old age in store? It may be, and not infrequently is, dignified, and beautiful. But often it more nearly approximates to that terrible picture drawn of it by Juvenal. His satire still rings down the ages.

"Grant me a long span of life, grant me many years, O Jupiter!" This you crave with a firm look of health, and this and nought else when pale with sickness. But see with what endless and grievous troubles a prostituted old age teems! The young have many points of contrast: one is handsomer than another, and he than a third; another again is much sturdier than his neighbour: old men all look the same: limbs and tongues alike palsied! Their relish for wine and food is no more the same, for the palate is now dull. But worse than any physical failure is the loss of mind." And so he goes on. The picture is not exactly a pleasant one, and is too coarse to reproduce in its entirety, but it is frequently only too true.

Death at last knocks at the door and then comes the funeral. A hearse, and a carriage or two, convey the deceased to his last rest. Perhaps some one devoted woman sheds a genuine tear, a male acquaintance or so emits a sob, or a sigh, as much possibly out of apprehension of his own coming dissolution, as for any genuine sympathy for the loss of a friend. "Dust to dust, ashes to ashes" we know the rest, and there lie Brown, Jones, or Robinson, as the case may be, until the judgment day, or until nature shall think fit to clothe them in some fresh chemical combination.

Oh! tragedy in comedy! and comedy in tragedy! Well may the Latin poet exclaim :—

"Sunt lachrymae rerum, et mentem mortalia tangunt."

Well might Shakespeare ask the question :— " Who would these fardels bear ? " But he adds :— " for the dread of something after death : " and if there is no hereafter why the dread ?

All men even the lowest savages, dread and believe in invisible spirits, and the unseen world. They dread the subjective shadows, of objective realities, and this belief is almost universal in uncivilised races. Savages almost invariably believe anything that exhibits power or movement to be endowed with life. It might almost be asserted, that in some ways, the savage realises the unseen world, far more than civilised man. Nearly always with savages the future takes the form of dread. As soon as the faculties of wonder and imagination, together with some power of reasoning, become developed, man would naturally crave to understand what was passing around him, and would speculate vaguely on his own existence. But as ignorance always begets fear, even in civilised man still more so in savages, the savage nature took the direction, of consulting and propitiating the evil rather than of cultivating the good. From the good they reasoned they had nothing to fear, from the evil they had everything to dread. Sir J. Lubbock has observed " it is not too much to say that the horrible dread of unknown evil hangs like a thick cloud over savage life, and embitters every pleasure."

To rid themselves of this dread, they propitiate the evil spirits, and endeavour to buy them off with all sorts of bloodshed and atrocities. And it takes savage life a long time to unlearn this lesson. They have grasped the wrong end of the stick of knowledge. The prophets, and lawgivers of the Hebrews were quite alive to this weakness in human nature, and the evil consequences which followed from it, to the utter degradation of the race, and this is probably why, in the Old Testament, witchcraft and the consulting of familiar spirits, was so stringently forbidden, and put down with so strong a hand.

That wonderful and dramatic story of Saul the son of Kish consulting the witch at Endor, carries with it an abiding lesson for all time. Whose heart has not bled for that rejected and unhappy king! For picture the scene. The enemies of Israel were closing round on all sides, and this was Saul's last day upon earth. The forebodings in his own heart, may have found their counterpart, in the murmuring of the thunder on the neighbouring heights of Gilboa, to be followed on the morrow by the lightning flash of death. And what do we see,

DARWIN'S PHILOSOPHY

the goodliest man in Israel, the Lord's anointed, the hope and chosen of his race, bereft of his royal robes, nay even of his military attire, disguised in the garb of a common peasant, creeping down in the darkness of a Syrian night to the caverns of ignorance, malignity, and greed. The good would not answer him, then the evil must! And Saul said unto the woman whom sawest thou? And the woman said unto Saul, I saw gods ascending out of the earth. And he said unto her, What form is he of? And she said, An old man cometh up; and he is covered with a mantle. And Saul perceived that it was Samuel. The fate of Saul and of his race trembled in the balance. What answer would he,—what answer did he actually receive? "To-morrow shalt thou and thy sons be with me."

The almost invariable answer to, and fate of those, who seek information from illegitimate sources, such as occultists, familiars, Christian scientists and what not.

But there is another and brighter vision, which teaches another lesson, and tells a very different tale. The vision of Jacob when he was left alone, and there wrestled a man with him from the breaking of the day. The position of Saul, and Jacob on these respective occasions had something in common. They were both in one sense alone. It was a crisis in the lives of both of them, they were both of them face to face with their enemies, Saul with the Philistines, and Jacob with his brother. But there is this vital difference between them. Saul sought for aid and enlightenment where it could not, and can never be found : Jacob sought it where it could. If one contrasts the characters of Saul and Jacob, the superiority of Jacob's nature, notwithstanding his craftiness and cunning, is apparent on every page. The one character stands for barbarism, the other for civilisation. But who was this mysterious visitor with whom Jacob wrestled until the breaking of the day ? He is represented in the form of a man, but we are clearly given to understand that he was something more, probably the visible embodiment of wisdom, goodness, and light. Jacob seized the occasion, and did not decline the encounter, for he wrestled until the breaking of the day, and so great was that inner conflict that it affected Jacob's physical nature, for we read that his thigh shrank. But this beneficent being was by no means willing to be taken, or to impart its blessings for nothing. No; knowledge never is. Indeed it endeavoured to make good its escape. "And he said, Let me go, for the day breaketh." But Jacob was resolute and stood firm, "I will not let thee go, except thou bless me." And when the spirit saw that Jacob was not to be denied, it yielded with grace and alacrity and pronounced on him that full and splendid benediction. "Thy name shall be called no more Jacob but Israel —a prince—for as a prince hast thou power with God and with men, and hast prevailed."

These two illustrations clearly demonstrate, that

DARWIN'S PHILOSOPHY

a belief in, and endeavour to learn and to extract benefit, from the unseen spirits whether good or evil, is by no means confined to savage life. The belief in its possibility, is entertained everywhere and in every age, among savages, men of social position, and great intellects alike.

Of course the naturalists would answer that the visions of Saul and Jacob were the outcome of a disordered imagination, the result either of extreme depression, irritability, or anxiety of mind. That the cellular molecules of their brains were in a state of temporary disorganisation, and that the balance and healthy equilibrium of them were for the time being in abeyance. A mere matter of imagination! As if imagination were not every bit as much a part of man's nature, and a much larger and truer part too, than the mere process of any logical formulæ. Besides the retort is obvious, and leaves the materialist exposed, to a very effective "*tu quoque.*"

You cannot expect—and it cannot be too often repeated—mathematical proof in a moral plane, and it is ridiculous to deny the existence of anything, and everything, that cannot be visualised by the physical eye of man. There may be beings as far above man in an ascending scale, as the rungs in Jacob's ladder, which find their limit only in infinity. And not only that but they may be actually materialised bodies. And the trend of modern science is already lending a direct and powerful support to this supposition. The probability is that everything—even a supposed vacuum is a refined form of matter. The atomic theory of Dalton has already been discarded for the Ionic, and the Ionic will ultimately be merged in the infinite divisibility of everything. Everyone's thoughts even, may be a refined form of matter, emanating from the brain, and affecting within their limitations all surrounding matter.

There is certainly, even from the scientific point of view, a good deal to be said for "telepathy." If the thoughts of one being are concentrated strongly and perpetually on the being of another and sympathetic nature at a distance, the transmitted waves of thought may find their correspondence, precisely in the same way as the waves of Marconi's wireless telegraphy. And it must never be forgotten that imagination is the parent of knowledge, and not knowledge of imagination. Knowledge is merely the knowing of the knowable, and imagination the apprehension of the unknown. Nor need faith ever be jealous of knowledge as her domain is the larger of the two, and whatever encroachments knowledge may make, faith has still infinity at her back.

But what did the ancients think about these ultimate things, as individuals, and communities. We can partially at any rate know the thoughts of the greatest among them and of their leading individual exponents. What light do the innumerable peoples of the great Asian continent throw on this problem of the soul. What were their thoughts on the subject, can they give us any light, have they ever produced any great teachers upon it? Of course, in discussing the religions of whole peoples, it must be remembered, and the rule holds good always, and in all countries both in the East and in the West, that the majority of the units which compose these masses, and collectively make the aggregate of them, have no, or very few real thoughts on such subjects at all. The daily cares, the daily work, and the so-called pleasures of life, are enough for them, and occupy their sole attention.

What thoughts had the Persians, Chaldeans, Egyptians, Babylonians, and Hindus, on these matters and the great races of the human family, who lived in what we are apt to consider rightly in one sense, but erroneously in another, the childhood of the world?

But before proceeding, it may be useful to outline the pedigree of the race of man, from the earliest historic times, as approved of by the various authorities on the subject.[1] The first great division of the family of man is into three races, the Yellow Man, the White Man, and the Black Man. It is only with the two former that we are here concerned, and the White Man is the more important of the two. The Whites are generally known as the Caucasian race, and this splits up into two great sections, the first section comprising the "Aryans" embracing also the people of ancient Persia, the ancient Hindus,

[1] The following description of the Akkads, and various races of mankind, is borrowed largely from Mr Robert Anderson, though the account is abridged and the language somewhat altered.

T

the Slavic races, and the Greeks, Italians, Germans, Celts, Anglo-Saxons and so forth: and the second section the "Semitic" or "Shemites" embracing the tribes of Arabia, and Syria, and other settlers in Ethiopia, Abyssinia, Babylonia and Egypt.

There is only one branch of the Yellow race—that is the Mongols or Turanians that need here be referred to — that remarkable people called the Akkads, the history of whom has been recently brought to light by the researches of various Assyriologists, archæologists, and scholars. The light they have thrown on this subject is not mere guesswork, but rests on the sure foundation, of a vast mass of accumulated and ever accumulating knowledge. Indeed it would not be much to say that our knowledge of such great kingdoms, as those of Persia, Chaldea, Babylon, Assyria, and Egypt, many of whom had reached their zenith four thousand years ago, is greater even now, than our knowledge of other kingdoms and peoples, far later down the line of historic time. Now these Akkads were the original founders of the first kingdom of Babylon, and they were essentially a literary people, as is proved by their libraries or inscribed tablets, and cylinders left in their palaces and temples. Moreover their knowledge of science was considerable, they were no mean astronomers, even as judged by a modern standard; they had regular calendars and their division of the year was almost identical with our own. Their cosmogony, or account of the origin of things, was almost identical with that of the Hebrews, or rather the Hebrews borrowed from these Akkads or early Chaldeans, the whole story of the Creation, and many of their philosophic ideas. And it is a remarkable but almost indisputable fact, that the account of the origin of things as given in the book of Genesis really emanated from, and had its origin in the Mongolian, or Yellow race, and not in the Caucasian race at all. At first these early Chaldeans, believed that every object was the abode of a spirit, but as culture spread, and their religious ideas assumed higher forms, their teachers formulated a monotheism. This seems certain from the following inscription on some ancient bricks found at Ur of the Chaldees. They are as follows :—

> In heaven who is supreme?
>   Thou alone art supreme,
> On earth who is supreme?
>   Thou alone art supreme,
> The word is proclaimed in Heaven,
> And the angels bow their faces down.

This seems clearly to show that these very ancient people believed in a Creator, and in a life beyond.

But let us leave the Akkads, a branch of the Mongolian race, and turn to the Persians, who were Caucasians and a branch of the great Aryan family. I refer to the Persians on account of their great teacher Zoroaster. His date seems uncertain, but it was placed by Pliny at 1000 years before Moses. In his great work the "Zend-Avesta" he preached an exalted morality and his philosophic conception, was higher still. God, or Ormuzd, is represented symbolically by fire, or light. His followers the Parsees, were not really fireworshippers, fire was merely the symbol of the great agent behind, though no doubt as is common to nearly all religions, the great mass of its adherents soon forgot the thing symbolised, in the symbol, and worshipped the concrete representation of the abstract idea. Zoroaster taught dualism, a life to come, and a resurrection of the body. The Parsees probably for this very reason hated image-worship precisely as did the Mohammedans and the Jews and as strictly forbade it. Herodotus tells us that this was due to the fact " that they did not believe as the Greeks do that the Gods have the same nature as Man."

Again turn to the Egyptians, a branch of the Semitic race. They certainly believed in a life to come and a resurrection of the body, as their process of embalming clearly proves. The very object of embalming was to preserve the body, until the soul's return when both body and soul would rise again. We are sometimes apt to think that this idea of immortality was the peculiar property of Christianity, but this was certainly not the case, as the three preceding instances clearly prove.

The advanced races of the modern world, are too apt to regard themselves as superior peoples, and far ahead of what they would consider the barbarous representatives of the human family in the twilight of history. But are they really so much their superiors?

In two respects, and two respects only, possibly they are. Modern civilisation knows more than ancient civilisation of the laws and operations of nature, and how to control them. It has at last got nature so to speak into harness, and can drive her almost where it will. And in the preaching and practice of the great law of sympathy and of good will towards men as enforced in the pages of the Gospel, civilisation has made at any rate considerable advance. But in every other respect humanity remains much where it was four thousand years ago. The great minds of those days, were as great as the great minds of these, in all the essential attributes of humanity. The commonality of the various nations, in periods of peace at any rate, were as enlightened, prosperous, and happy, taking them as a whole, as they are to-day. Nothing can more forcibly bring this fact home to the mind than a concrete and vivid illustration. Take the account of the great city of Thebes as it flourished nearly four thousand years ago under the leadership and inspiration of the great Pharaoh, Rameses II.—the Sesostris of the Greeks. The following description of this wonderful city, is borrowed from Mr Robert Anderson a great authority on subjects like these :—

" The renown of Rameses II. is largely due to

the splendour of his capital, Thebes, and to the fact that most of his great works have survived more than thirty-two centuries, and still command unbounded admiration. What have Memphis, Babylon, Ninevah, or even Imperial Rome to show by comparison!

"Memphis though dignified by the neighbourhood of the pyramids, occupied a situation much inferior to that of Thebes, which was built in a great amphitheatre four hundred miles above Cairo, with mountains in the background, and in front the Nile broadened by islands, with long reaches of rushing water. The native name of the city was Apin, or Tapin, ' the city of thrones ' which the Greeks afterwards pronounced Tebai, after their own town of that name. In Homer's time the Egyptian city had long been proverbial for wealth, size, and population—the London, so to speak, of the ancient world.

"The temple to Nu, or Anum-ra was the national shrine of Thebes, and in its present state is one of the grandest structures in the world. No cathedral may compare with it in massive size or cast of construction, being ' among temples what the Great Pyramid is among tombs.' With its surrounding lesser temples it shows by its varied styles and its numberless inscriptions and drawings the history of two thousand years, thus forming an enormous library of Egyptian records. The hall of assembly sixty feet longer than Westminster Hall, would hold the cathedral of Notre Dame within it and is supported by one hundred and thirty-four columns: the gateway is over three hundred and sixty wide, facing the river. On the opposite or western bank is an imposing succession of sepulchres and temples, the chief being the Rameseini, in honour of Rameses himself, with his granite statue lying in broken mass which weighs nearly nine hundred tons. This colossal figure is called ' the greatest monolithic statue in the world.' Not satisfied with his monument in Thebes, Rameses II. had some temples constructed out of a rock near the Second Cataract, one with four colossal figures, ninety feet high, seated in front of a sculptured façade of one hundred feet. The impressive effect of this massive group, when first seen, is said to rival that produced by the Falls of Niagara, or by Mont Blanc.

"The capital of the Nubian or Empire Kings of ancient Egypt was not destined to remain permanently the foremost capital of the world. Who may say how many generations—the capital of the British Empire will maintain its present position? One thing is certain that if the day comes when ' Macaulay's New Zealander ' will be surveying the ruins of St Paul's from a broken arch of London Bridge, London will then show but few traces of such costly architecture, and engineering as are still abundant among the mighty monuments of the Egyptian Thebes."

The above illustration hardly conveys the idea that these ancient peoples, were much behind modern times, in all the essential elements of civilisation.

296   WHERE DO WE COME FROM?

Having reviewed in outline the thoughts on this subject as they appealed to the leading minds among the three great kingdoms of Persia, Chaldea, and Egypt, let us step down in history about a thousand years and consult the views of four other great nationalities, who were largely or nearly contemporaries, though overlapping each other somewhat in point of time, the Hindus, Hebrews, Greeks, and Romans. All the four races, as I will endeavour to show, believed in an immortality or life beyond the grave, in some shape or form, though their views on the subject were all essentially, even radically different.

The most original ideas on immortality proceeded from the Hindus. The religion of Buddha as it is sometimes called, but more truly speaking his philosophy, could only have emanated from the brain of an Asiatic. It is the most original creed in the world. It is a reaction against the indolent and luxurious life of the Hindu, and the reaction takes precisely the form that might have been expected. If ever a moral miracle occurred in this world, it was the appearance of Buddha on the scene of Asiatic life. There is no reason to doubt the generally received outline of his history. Born about the year 620 B.C., of royal parentage, and heir to much of the splendour of the East, at quite an early age and when almost still a youth, he suddenly turned his moral nature right round, abandoned entirely the indulgence of all the appetites and passions so peculiarly alluring to the Asiatic nature, and set himself deliberately in his own person to destroy every vestige of the senses. And this tremendous task he actually succeeded in accomplishing.

Buddha's ethical teaching has many points in common with the ethical teaching of the Gospels, though in some respects far harder and more severe. No man, says Buddha, can secure abiding peace, or bliss, until every trace of self is annihilated. The pleasures of the senses are unsatisfactory, and illusive, the senses therefore must be destroyed.

But after all there is a limit to the complete elimination of self. Even if a man could destroy all thought of self he would by so doing entirely destroy his own personality. And that is precisely, not only the aim, but the end of Buddha's philosophy. It is really a slow process of annihilation. All the essential moral truths of Christianity, are deeply rooted in the nature of things, and do not as is sometimes assumed stand in contradiction to the order and progress of the world. But the same cannot be said of the teachings of Buddha. His teaching may be lofty and sublime, but it is all too lofty and sublime for mortal man. For if a man ever did succeed in treading the eightfold path, and keeping the five rules laid down by Buddha, what has he to hope for and what reward has he to expect! At the cost of all memory, individuality, and activity he sinks at last into a sea of bliss, called Nirvana, a mere drop in an ocean of everlasting repose, and the feeling of bliss that he is to experience for all eternity, is very similar to the sensation that an aspen leaf might feel, when swayed to and fro in the warm embraces of a summer's breeze.

> Never shall yearnings torture him, nor sins
> Stain him, nor ache of earthly joys and woes
> Invade his safe eternal peace : nor deaths
> And lives recur. He goes
> Unto Nirvana. He is one with Life,
> Yet lives not. He is blest, ceasing to be,
> Om, Mani Padme, om! the Dewdrop slips
> Into the shining sea!

Such is the Gospel according to Buddha, which whatever its merits or demerits, is never likely to commend itself to the masculine, energetic, self-assertive, and egotistical natures, of the Western and Northern peoples.

The dominant note in Greek, and Roman literature is that of thought in action, in the Hebrews thought in feeling, in the Buddhist thought in dreams, and in the Anglo-Saxons races thought in practice.

Of course the Greeks and Romans, believed in Gods many and Lords many, but they were really magnified men and women, of a very practical, and mundane description. Their writings are full of them, and of the Elysian fields, the future abode of the blest, or of those who had been sufficiently accommodating in this life, to meet with the approval of their respective divinities. But by the thoughtful men of those days, and the thoughtless alike, they were regarded if with a touch here and there of respect and superstition, generally with amusement, credulity, and contempt. The old Roman Emperor Vespasian, when the touch of mortal illness was upon him, said in jest that " he thought he was becoming a God."

But their writings with few exceptions reveal no conception of the Universe as we now understand it, or of the great laws that underlie its various operations, of the unity of nature, or of the true meaning and destiny of the life of that wonderful being " Man." For the most part their thoughts and imaginings on such matters were those of children rather than men. But there were among them some wonderful exceptions, some really true and great thinkers. Socrates before he drank the cup of hemlock developed the grounds of his immovable conviction of the immortality of the soul; and his greater pupil and disciple, Plato, did the same. Among the Latins Cicero wrote his " De Natura Deorum " wherein he gives an account of the speculations of the ancients concerning a divine being.

But perhaps the most wonderful and fascinating of all the ancient philosophers was Lucretius. His ideas on natural philosophy which he borrowed largely from Epicurus whom he calls the " Glory of the Greeks, who first didst chase the mind's dread darkness with celestial day," were more in accord with those of the moderns, than are those of any ancient writer. He was a poet, philosopher, and naturalist in one. A sort of poetic Huxley of the expiring days of the Roman Commonwealth; but with greater powers of imagination, a fuller nature, and more generosity, and flexibility of thought, than were ever possessed by that latter-day adamantine logician. Lucretius has been called an atheistic philosopher, but whether he believed in the existence of Gods or not is doubtful, but if he did his attitude towards them was very similar to that of the Buddhists towards the Creator. If they did exist, with mankind at any rate they had no dealings, and but little of interest or concern.

> Omnis enim per se divum natura necessest
> immortali ævo summa cum pace fruatur
> semota ab nostris rebus sejunctaque longe
> nam privata dolore omni, privata periclis
> ipsa suis pollens opibus, nil indiga nostri;
> nec bene promeritis capitur nequé tangitur ira.

Far, far from mortals, and their vain concerns,
In peace perpetual dwell th' immortal Gods:
Each self-dependent, and from human wants estranged
There no pain pervades, nor dangers threaten; every
Passion sleeps, vice no revenge, and virtue draws no boon.[1]

He admitted that man had a soul, and discusses very closely its composition, but his account of it would hardly satisfy a modern theologian. He refuted the doctrine of those who thought the soul

[1] Translation by John Mason Good.

merely a resulting harmony of the parts of the body. It was made up of the smallest atoms, and consisted of four substances heat, air, a certain " aura," and a fourth substance to which he gives no name, a sort of fourth dimension, which Lucretius evidently was not equal to coping with. When the soul left the body, it resolved itself into its original elements, and had no enduring personality.

Lucretius is very entertaining, when he discourses on dreams he asserted that they were images, shapes which being separated, like membranes, from the surface of bodies or objects flit hither and thither through the air : and which shapes escape us both when asleep and awake. He suggests that these images are thrown off from the bodies of objects, for we cannot by any possibility he says suppose, that souls escape from Acheron, or that shades of the dead hover about among the living, or that any portion of us can be left after death, when after the body and soul have been disunited, they have suffered dissolution into their respective elements.

One cannot help suspecting that the ideas of many of the modern theosophist, occultists, physicists, etc., and even a good deal of their nomenclature, are borrowed from Lucretius.

Poor Lucretius he lived in a very stirring and interesting epoch, but his thoughts and speculations hardly fell on congenial soil. The minds of men were not ready for them, and if they had been, it must be confessed that they have little practical value. But at any rate he had a system, a scheme of things, and a grasp of the unity of nature, which was wanting in other writers of his day. Many of his ideas and much of his reasoning would meet with the approval of the moderns.

The story of his life, which was not prolonged, for he died at the age of forty-three, was touching and romantic. A Roman citizen, and born about ninety years before the Christian Era, he wrote his poem when the Roman Commonwealth was in considerable disturbance and disorder. He was married to a certain lady called Lucilia with a very jealous disposition. She mistook the wanderings of Lucretius' thoughts on the atomic theory for illicit inclinations in other directions. But all the time poor Lucretius was guilty of nothing worse, than speculating on the very atoms which helped to contribute to his wife's beauty. But Lucilia to bring back Lucretius to his senses, and to a more practical way of evincing his affection, administered to her husband an amatory potion which brought on insanity and he died by his own hand in the forty-fourth year of his age.

The voice of criticism has always awarded Lucretius great praise as a poet. Our own poet Dryden says of him " From the sublime and daring genius of his, it must of necessity come to pass, that his thoughts must be masculine, full of argumentation and that sufficiently warm. From the same fiery temper, proceeds the loftiness of his expression, and the perpetual torrent of his voice, when the barrenness of his subject does not too much retain the quickness of his fancy. For there is no doubt to be made, but that he could have been everywhere as poetical as he is in his descriptions, and in the moral part of his philosophy, if he had not aimed more to instruct in his system of nature than to delight."

And Tennyson later on wrote a fine poem in his honour describing his tragic end.

But the temper of both the Greek and Latin mind was a very temporal one. Their speculations were confined mostly to this life, and their ideas on immortality, were little more than that of enjoyment or misery in the Elysian fields, of the pleasures and pains in an accentuated and magnified form, experienced on earth. And it must be remembered concerning this question of immortality, that the words time, and eternity, to the ancient world, carried with them a very different significance, to what they would to a modern man of science. Time as modern scientists understand it was an idea quite unknown to the ancients and so also were numbers. They dispensed numbers with considerable generosity, and in the matter of enumeration were neither over-particular or pedantic. If they saw a great concourse of people or things, they would put them down at 10,000 or 100,000 as the case might be, without being too curious about the units that constituted the collection.

But if the Greeks and Romans had divine intellects, in the matters of the soul they were children, and in that respect contrast unfavourably with the Hebrews. For the Hebrews had divine souls, though their intellects as exhibited in the Old Testament, if powerful, were rigid, unbending and confined. This no doubt was partly due to the stringency of their Levitical laws. That perpetual devotion to and observance of minute ecclesiastical detail and discipline, always seems to have a sterilising effect on even the finest undertanding. It certainly very largely thwarted the full expansion of the Hebrew mind. But it had its compensations, for being prevented from lateral expansion their natures were forced downwards to the depths, and upward to the heights. Possibly this intellectual compression brought out the full richness of their natures, for the Jews in their literature almost always speak either " de profundis," or " de excelsis." The Jews moreover all through their history, have been the children in one way or another of adversity. " By the waters of Babylon we sat down and wept," may be taken as the abiding expression of the deep sorrows of their race.

In dialectical skill, in oratorical and possibly, historical expression, with the brilliant sword play of the dry light of pure reason, and in the manipulation of the refinement and nicer shades of literary subtlety and thought, the Greeks may have been their superiors, but in the expressions of the deeper emotions of the soul, in its joys and its sorrows, in elevation of thought, in energy and power the

Hebrew literature yields to none. All through the Old Testament from the first page to the last, there is the " thundering reverberation of a mighty spirit " to be found in no other writings in the world. Nothing in English literature, splendid as it is, is in any way comparable to it.

What did this wonderful people think about the soul and its destiny? What they thought about the origin of all life, and of their race, is plainly set forth in the Book of Genesis. But what meaning did they attach to the "soul," and how did they regard its destiny. The word " soul " in our English translation frequently occurs in the Old Testament, but it is used in many and very equivocal senses, and no where has it the precise meaning that a Christian would attach to it. In the Old Testament it is taken for the whole person, both soul and body. It is taken for the life of man " Let the enemy persecute my soul and take it." It is taken for a dead body, " Thou wilt not leave my soul in hell." It is used for desire, love, and inclination. But nowhere do the Hebrews use it in the sense of the " Ego " or of an abiding and enduring personality, independent of the body, and untouched by its dissolution. There are one or two texts to be found in the Old Testament which seem to sanction this meaning: but they occur at rare intervals and when taken in conjunction with their immediate application and surroundings, will hardly bear the strain placed upon them.

U

The celebrated passage in the nineteenth chapter of the Book of Job has been strongly insisted upon, in proof of the fact that the idea of a soul or a life after death was not foreign to the Jewish mind: but Job probably means no more than to express a conviction, that his diseased and corrupt body, would be restored to its former state of health. That it alludes to a resurrection is disproved by the fact that it is quite inconsistent with the design of the poem and the course of the argument, since the belief which it has been supposed to express, as connected with a future state of retribution, would have solved the difficulty on which the whole dispute turns. For if Job was to be compensated in another life for his afflictions in this, then what ground of quarrel had he with his Maker? Moreover the passage, as is generally admitted is wrongly, variously, and inadequately translated.

The authorship, date, and history, of this wonderful book are all alike obscure. There are many reasons for supposing that it was never written by a Jew at all. In the first place the scene of the drama is laid in Arabia. All through the substance, or main body of the poem, the author uses the abstract word to designate the Deity which an Arabian would, and not the concrete Jehovah of the Jews, and the book, cuts through and through the most deeply rooted Jewish prejudices.

So the Book of Job can hardly be relied on as an authority for the convictions and ideas of the Jews on the nature or durability of the soul. There is perhaps only one text in the whole of the Old Testament which clearly enunciates the truth and it is to be found in the Book of Daniel, where it says that "Many that are in the dust of the earth shall arise." But the idea does not find its final consummation until we reach the Christian Era, though prior to that period the resurrection of the body was held by the Pharisees, in contradistinction to the Sadducees, who denied it.

Perhaps one of the most remarkable and unaccountable facts in all history is this silence of the Jews as to a future state. Their emotions were deep, their pride was strong, the belief in their great destiny supreme. They lived so they thought under the immediate and special care, and protection of the Divine Being. Their writings though they never enunciate the doctrine, are saturated through and through, with the idea of immortality. And yet their pedigree, their pride of race, their grandeur and superiority in this world, seemed to obsess their entire natures, to absorb all their thoughts, and to leave them entirely indifferent to speculation as to ultimate things. I repeat it: this fact is almost unaccountable. One would have thought that the many, oft recurring and terrible tribulations both as individuals and a people, to which they were constantly exposed, and which they as constantly experienced, would have caused them to regard pride of place in this world, more lightly, to set less store by it, and to have diverted their thoughts from the possibilities of this life, to the immortal possibilities beyond.

The only reason that suggests itself for the reticence of the Jews on this subject of immortality, which must have suggested itself to their minds, is, that having given the account of the Creation that they did, and having deprived man of the immortality in this world to which according to their own showing he was originally intended, they were precluded or as the lawyers would say 'estopped,' by their own assertion from immediately conferring on him, a higher and a better immortality beyond.

But the Jews were ever, and are in many ways to this day, notwithstanding the rapid and kaleidoscope changes, that are for ever taking place in man, in the mind of man, and in the affairs of man, a people at once peculiar and detached. Not Moses, not David, not Elijah, but Jacob has ever been the true expression of their race. Jacob is the real starting point of their history; and the Jews always revert to their original type. Their history as related in the Old Testament shows how deficient they were in political insight and direction. For of national life and cohesion, for political consistency, and constancy, their history hardly reveals a trace. They were governed alternately and with varying but very dubious success, by prophets and priests, kings and ecclesiastics; but they were ever a stiff-necked people, recalcitrant, and rebellious,

DARWIN'S PHILOSOPHY

alike under them all. With the single exception of Moses they produced no statesman of the first rank, or one who could knead them into a homogeneous and self-governing people. The intellectual gipsies of the world—tribal they were in origin, and tribal they have remained all down the line of their history. They are the only instance in the historical record of a very gifted people, preserving their identity, and the purity of their blood, and racial characteristics, without any country which they can call home to revert to, or any national life at their back.

They have never been a very enterprising people, either in commerce or war. For the preliminary labour that is necessary, for any great developments and undertakings, they have evinced but small aptitude or inclination. The gleaners and harvesters of mankind they have never exhibited any real military spirit. It is true that their whole history as related in the Old Testament, is one long series of internecine and tribal strifes; they will fight for their existence, when fighting is inevitable, as their stubborn defence of Jerusalem against the legionaries of Titus clearly proves. But for great military undertakings and far-reaching conquests, they have never shown any great aptitude. For the sea they had no affection, and have not to this day. It was a Jew who wrote " And there shall be no more sea." The elimination of the sea was a condition precedent to the perfection of the beatific vision. And for agriculture they had as little taste as for the sea. The very elevation of their powers of moral imagination have made any sort of manual labour distasteful to them, and manual labour if possible they invariably avoid.

Then what has preserved the Jews all down the ages, and made them if not as a nation, at any rate as individuals so great a success. Their intellectual powers as a people are high, though they have been probably considerably overrated. In pure intellect alone, they are certainly not the masters of the Greek, the Latin, and Anglo-Saxon peoples. But their intellectual qualities being high, and always supported by an enduring and consistent if somewhat rigid morality, has carried them far and prevented them being merged in the mass of mankind. They are, moreover, a talented people, and in the arts of music, painting, and literature, have when at their best but few equals.

It is doubtful if any alien, ever really fully appreciates or understands the inner workings of the Jewish mind. This air of mystery gives them a certain power. " Omne ignotum pro magnifico." We are always a little afraid of, and apt to exaggerate the value of what we do not thoroughly understand. And who thoroughly understands a Jew or who would thoroughly trust him! The shadow of Jacob's cunning still hovers over the race. It has often been said that no one thoroughly understood Lord Beaconsfield, and consequently no one thoroughly trusted him. Proverbial for their hard dealings, as a rule, they stand by the letter of their bond as interpreted by the light of law, rather than that of equity. Add to this that they have a great capacity for finance, for taking advantage of the situation, for reaping where others have sown, and for appropriating the spoils of victory, and the mystery of their preservation, and success as a people, is largely, if not entirely accounted for. But after all it is not the opinion of this individual or that, of this nation or that, however eminent, that in such matters as these, goes for much, or is of great importance.

The difference in the value of the thoughts of an ordinary or exceptional intelligence, is in questions like these infinitesimal. We must turn to the instincts of humanity as a whole, and they certainly would not endorse the teaching of Darwin, and the materialists, as the last word on the subject of the origin of things or as the true explanation of the formation and transit of organic life across the scene of time.

For what does it amount to: that creation, direction and design, are qualities that have no existence outside the imagination of man: that all phenomena as we now see them, are merely the resultant combination, of a fortuitous concourse of atoms working under, and the reaction of mechanical, chemical, and various other pressures, and evolving out of their capricious and inexhaustible combinations, phenomena so divergent as the feather of a bird, and the brain of a man. For even the very

WHERE DO WE COME FROM?

thoughts and emotions of man are, according to Darwin, merely the refined and intricate outcome of innumerable and infinite adaptations preserved and perpetuated by his law of Natural Selection.

Ask the materialist how he accounts for the construction of such wonderful organ as the human eye, or the feather of a bird, and he will answer:— "matter must have taken on some form, and it may as well have taken on that form as any other."

But that answer is really ridiculous and hardly needs confutation. The feather of a bird is a mechanical wonder, almost a volume might be written on its construction, and yet we are seriously asked to believe that the author and finisher of this exquisitely adapted piece of mechanism is Natural Selection, nothing but a tendency to preserve what is already in existence. If a watchmaker were to show me some very expensive and elaborately constructed timepiece; and one were to ask him who made that, and he were to reply, well, the materials of which that structure is composed must have taken on some form, so they took on the form of the watch you see before you and came together of themselves, one should certainly and rightly think the man a lunatic; and yet that, and nothing short of that, Darwin asks us to believe.

Or take the case of a single organ of organic life —the eye. Now if there is anything in Darwin's theory of Natural Selection at all, it must account for the whole law of optics. But his definition of Natural Selection is so unsubstantial and illusive that it is difficult to ascertain, what it is, or what it effects, for he says on page eighty-two of the "Origin of Species" "What applies to one animal will apply throughout all time to all animals—that is if they vary—for otherwise natural selection can effect nothing." But what, one asks, does it effect if they do vary?

Now the human eye is one of the most marvellous contrivances imaginable, it is made up of coats, and humours, of solids and fluids, of nerves, bloodvessels, and muscles, rivalling the most perfect optical instruments. Yet how few of the eyes either of men or animals fail of vision through any natural defect. A dark plexus of veins and muscles are so situated as to absorb the rays. It is adapted to light, adapted and adaptable to varying distances. For the purpose of seeing near objects the cornea, or outer coat of the eye, is rendered more round and prominent; the crystalline lens underneath is pushed forward; and the axis of vision, as the depth of the eye is called, is elongated. It is adapted to the atmosphere. The eyelid itself is worthy of attention, especially from the point of view of Natural Selection : for it defends the eye, it wipes it, and it closes it in sleep.

Now all these various contrivances and adaptations were brought about according to Darwin by an infinite process of accidental modification, and yet they imply in the producer an intimate acquaintance with the inner laws and finer doctrines of optics and mathematics.

No wonder Mivart shies at Darwin's explanation and refuses to entertain it at all. His answers to Mivart in his chapter on "Objections to the theory of Natural Selection" if they are not absolutely beside the mark, are highly inconclusive and unsatisfactory. Mivart, almost any impartial mind would say, has the best of the argument.

If, says a celebrated Frenchman, we could see through our skin the mechanism of our bodies, if we saw our blood circulating, the tendons pulling, the lungs blowing, the humours filtrating, and all the incomprehensible assemblage of fibres, tubes, pumps, valves, currents, pivots, which sustain an existence at once so frail and presumptuous, we should either jump out of our boots with fright, or be for ever transfixed to the ground.

And yet we are asked to believe that a tendency in nature to preserve what is worth preserving has brought about all these marvellous contrivances.

It has been calculated that the adult man weighs 3,000,000 times as much as the seed from which he sprang: and if you were to set down before this seed, the greatest scientific intellect that ever lived and surrounded him with the most perfect scientific instruments accessible, and if he had no previous experience of the evolutionary result, and you were to ask him if the marvellous physical mechanism of the adult man, to say nothing of his intellectual

DARWIN'S PHILOSOPHY

equipment, could in twenty-five years spring from that seed, he would answer you with a "No" that would make the universe reverberate. But that is what actually takes place in the short space of twenty-five years. Yet Darwin forsooth requires millions of years for his little theory to work at all. 60,000,000 years is with Darwin a very short time. For he says on page two hundred and sixty-eight of the "Origin":—

"Here we encounter a formidable subject for it seems doubtful whether the earth, in a fit state for the habitation of living creatures has lasted long enough. Sir W. Thompson concludes that the consolidation of the crust, can hardly have occurred less than 20, or more than 400 million years ago, but probably not less than 98 or more than 200 million years. These very wide limits show how doubtful the data are: and other elements will have hereafter to be introduced into the problem. Mr Croll estimates that about 60 million years have elapsed since the Cambrian period, but this, judging from the small amount of organic change since the commencement of the glacial epoch, appears a very short time, for the many and great mutations of life, which have certainly occurred since the Cambrian formation: and the previous 140 million years can hardly be considered as sufficient for the development of the varied forms of life which already existed during the Cambrian period."

It is an entirely gratuitous assumption on Darwin's part, that Nature can effect nothing without eternity to work in. But so slow is Darwin's method, that even the ages that it takes to form a geological stratum are not sufficient, so to gain time he has the hardihood to assume, without giving any very heighty reasons for the assumption that great intervals of time elapsed between each successive geological formation.

But to turn aside a moment from the men of science, the nations, and the philosophers, to a few of the great exponents of the humanities, the poets, dramatists, and so forth. Have they any vital information to impart on the subject. As regards most of them it is impossible to arrive at their real inner belief if they possessed any. Apart from the purely ecclesiastical writers, their convictions appear to take the form of a sort of benevolent agnosticism. What were Shakespeare's ideas on immortality. Had he any? As has often been observed little is known of Shakespeare as a man, and possibly even less of his inner convictions. So perfect a mirror of humanity are his writings, and so crowded is the great picture that they reflect, with peoples of all nations kindred and tongues, that there is not even standing room for the great author himself. Here and there he drops a hint :— " We are such stuff as dreams are made of," " Aye but to die and go we know not where, to lie in cold obstruction and to rot " and so forth ; but they afford no real index to Shakespeare's belief, as it is impossible to discriminate the author from his character, though it seems incredible that a mind such as his could ever have found satisfaction in the gospel of annihilation. But if Darwin's theory be true, Shakespeare's views are quite immaterial, his words are nothing more than a fortuitous concourse of letters evolved by the process of Natural Selection. No wonder Darwin wants time if accident set the type of Shakespeare's mental activities.

And what about Lord Byron. His nature was in all probability too wild, unstable, and disordered, to admit of him ever having a fixed or constant opinion on any subject. But his writings are instinct with immortality. If ever there was a great natural poetic genius, surely that genius was Byron. Poetry was his natural language; it flowed straight from his soul and he could hardly speak in any other. It came as naturally to him as song does to a canary. His literary output was enormous. It would cover a thousand large and closely printed pages, and yet through the whole of it you will not find a single line that is laboured, meaningless or obscure. Much of it no doubt is worthless, and wearisome reiteration; but a residuum remains, that would make any name immortal. To what other poet, with the single exception of Shakespeare, alive or dead, native or foreign, could such a tribute faithfully be paid.

And not only is it not obscure, but much of it

is illuminated by the power and beauty of the mind that penned it. But granted that Byron wrote much that was inartistic and irregular, at his best he soars away into the heights and down into the depths where few, either could if they would, or would if they could, dare to follow him. The marvel is that England should be the land of his birth, and the country of his production. The quality of his mind and the bent of his genius, are in many respects rather Hebrew than English.

I am not referring here to Byron's lesser pieces. Beautiful as many of them are, they in no way reveal the full scope, and grandeur of that eagle sweep, which we see in " Childe Harold " and in his dramatic productions such as " Cain," " Heaven and Earth," and many others.

Moreover, with the single exception of Shakespeare, Byron is our only international poet. He is more largely read and appreciated on the Continent than in England. It must be confessed that the English people as a whole, though they have produced many great poets, are sadly wanting in poetic appreciation. The poetry they most admire, is speaking generally a reflection of themselves, and the more tersely and epigrammatically expressed the better. But for the dreams of the visionary, whether lay or ecclesiastic, they have but little inclination. Byron unfortunately nowhere strikes the note of pure and unadulterated joy: it is doubtful if he ever had a happy day in his life. Fire, there is, and beauty there is, and passion in abundance, but the whole of it is to some extent marred by a rather lurid and morbid pessimism. He is for ever kicking against the limitations of his own nature, and against what he considered the cant and hypocrisy of the world; but he dubbed everything cant that did not fit into, and conform with, his own passing moods and inclinations. But for all that he is at his best magnificent, and when the humanities come into their own again, and people become weary of mechanism and dry science, Byron will be again appreciated at his true value and his genius be regarded, as unquestionably it is, as one of the undying glories of the English race. To show how truly great he can really be, the following two quotations sufficiently illustrate; they are taken at haphazard from that extraordinary drama "Cain." They are by no means exceptional, I merely produce them as samples, for passages of equal if not greater beauty abound everywhere in his works.

The following description of the approach of Lucifer, he puts into the mouth of Cain—

> Whom have we here ?—A shape like to the angels,
> Yet of a sterner and a sadder aspect
> Of spiritual essence : why do I quake?
> Why should I fear him more than other spirits,
> Whom I see daily wave their fiery swords
> Before the gates round which I linger oft,
> In twilight's hour, to catch a glimpse of those
> Gardens which are my just inheritance,
> E'er the night closes o'er the inhibited walls

> And the immortal trees which overtop
> The cherubim-defended battlements?
> If I shrink not from these, the fire-armed angels,
> Why should I quail from him whom now approaches?
> Yet he seems mightier far than they, nor less
> Beauteous, and yet not all as beautiful,
> As he hath been, and might be : sorrow seems
> Half of his immortality. And is it
> So? and can ought grieve save humanity?
> He cometh.

And his description of the discovery of death is equally fine—

> I knew not that, yet thought it, since I heard
> Of death : although I know not what it is
> Yet it seems horrible. I have looked out
> In the vast desolate night in search of him ;
> And when I saw gigantic shadows in
> The umbrage of the walls of Eden, chequered
> By the far-flashing of the cherub's swords,
> I watched for what I thought his coming ; for
> With fear rose longing in my heart to know
> What 'twas which shook us all—but nothing came
> And then I turned my weary eyes from off
> Our native and forbidden Paradise,
> Up to the lights above us, in the azure,
> Which are so beautiful ; shall they, too, die?

If that is not true poetry then what is?

And perhaps none of Byron's works more completely reveals his true character, than that extraordinary drama "Cain." In it we see the proud, rebellious, and dissolute, nature of the man, warring with his better and more immortal qualities. It almost seems, as if in this poem Byron were deliberately pitting his evil nature against his good, and that the former, wrestle as it would, could not entirely prevail. Of the description of the approach of Lucifer, quoted above, the great critic Jeffrey has said, that it would shine in the "Paradise Lost." It is surely equal to anything in it, and Byron has this advantage over Milton, that he is softer, and more human. Milton may be splendid and stately, but he is also somewhat hard, formal, and metallic. His poem might be an "Iliad" fought in "space," instead of on the plains of Troy. Like Cologne Cathedral to the eye, his "Paradise Lost," is to the ear too perfect and symmetrical in its proportions, for the proper appreciation of imperfection. Both one and the other need the recoil.

Where among latter day and recent verse, with the great exception of Tennyson, can such lines as those above quoted be matched, or even approached. Certainly not in Browning or another. For whatever else Browning may have been he was not a great poet, if music, lucidity, and rhythm, are necessary ingredients in poetry. His style is too obscure, broken, and difficult. He is rarely lucid, and what is writing without lucidity! Even if the proper appreciation of Browning is given only to the elect, surely it is the business of any writer, and more especially of a poet, to make his meaning intelligible, and not to call on the public to interpret him if they can. There may be diamonds in his mines—so people tell us—but life is short, and

x

possibly they are not worth the working expenses. To throw a pot of paint—as Ruskin has pointed out—in the face of the public, does not make a picture, and to cover a sheet of paper with misfitting and obscure phraseology, *may*, but does not of necessity constitute a poem.

But to turn to science. Some scientific men seem to possess extraordinary and rather perverted views on the Law of Sympathy. Professor Ray Lankester, not many years ago discussed the subject in an address entitled "Man, a rebel against nature." His biology no doubt was sound, but his philosophy is more open to criticism. Man is himself part of nature, and sympathy being one of the highest attributes of man, the sympathy exhibited by man to his fellows is as much a law of Nature as any other. If man had not this unfortunate gift, or rather disease of excessive sympathy, so argued the learned Professor, the human race might rival the lower organism in the health and perfection of the units that compose it. And the inference to be drawn from his utterance was this : why not put out of the way either directly or indirectly the poor, the maimed, the useless, and diseased. If man is nothing more than a brute well then breed him, feed him, kill him, like the beasts of the field. But the better part of humanity revolts against the idea and why, because sympathy is the first rung on the ladder, that separates Man from the organism below him, and if man were to descend from that rung he would by so doing yield up his sovereignty at once, and abandon his own highest prerogative. Even from a selfish point of view it would be a dangerous experiment to breed men like you do beasts for the sake of preserving the health and physical perfection of the race. A triton here and there among the minnows may be all very well, but let the minnows beware, and not advocate their multiplicity to excess.

Let the Professors take heed how they encourage the propagation of that neurotic monstrosity, " the superman," or invite him to rule over them, lest fire come out of this herculean bramble and destroy them and their laboratories.

Let " Messieurs les assassins " commence operations on themselves. There must be many a played out old materialist, who if his theories are correct, can offer but the feeblest apology, for prolonging his stay here any longer. Let him betake himself to the shambles and in his own person put to the test the wisdom and courage of his convictions. No! "*pace*" the learned Professor, "the quality of mercy is not strained."

But humanity owes to science debts that are difficult to repay. It has been largely instrumental, at any rate, in rescuing the body of man from the everlasting bonfire, that the theologians had so ingeniously prepared for it. That shocking idea of physical torture, which made even the dark ages darker than they need have been, and which the genius of Dante did so much to emphasise and promulgate have, thanks largely to its efforts, been finally destroyed.

But the priests being deprived of a man's body still cling tenaciously to his soul. That at any rate is their province, and they will not yield it up without a struggle. If a man's body cannot be damned eternally, at least his soul can. But this idea, more shocking than the first, will not bear inspection for a moment. In the first place it is against all idea of justice whether temporal or eternal : " Can sins of moments earn the rod of everlasting fires " ? Secondly the great law of change has to be reckoned with. Everything in nature from the smallest atom to the largest satellite is changing every instant of time. And even the thoughts, moods, and memory of man, are all subject to the same law. Memory is the storehouse of the conscience and when it is obliterated, which in process of time it inevitably must be, the conscience of man whether good or evil must necessarily disappear with it.

Moreover dare any man honestly assert, that any one man is so much better than another, that this one by whatever means of grace he may attain it merits eternal bliss, and the other eternal damnation. To subscribe to that doctrine is to subscribe to the creed of Calvin in its crudest and most repulsive form.

But this is one of the least of the benefits that science has conferred on mankind. Its theoretical discoveries, and the mechanical appliance resulting from them, great as they are, and which are utilised in every trade, and profession, and in all communities, all contributing largely to the instruction, comfort, and happiness of man, are as nothing compared to the social, and moral revolution, which must inevitably follow in their train. By opening up the lines of communication and intercourse between man and man, they are already rapidly breaking down the barriers of ignorance, and isolation. And ignorance and isolation have hitherto been the greatest enemies with which the human race has had to contend. Hitherto humanity has had no lines on which it could advance with accelerated speed and rapidity. The printing press has done much, the railways have done more, and all the subsequent and recent discoveries in the transit, and locomotion, whether of thought or material, are merely the mechanical lines on which will ultimately run the social order and harmony of the race. The main arteries of this immense network are already laid, the smaller arteries have yet to be supplied, but when they are perfected and complete, the life-blood of knowledge, sympathy, and goodwill, will circulate freely through them all, and the human race will stand revealed, not as hitherto in separate units, or in isolated nations and communities, ignorant of, afraid of, and at war with one another, but as an organic entity—one and indivisible—with every part essential to the harmony and proper working of the whole.

It is the want of means of communication that has so long retarded education, and that has for centuries kept back, and impeded the development of the higher faculties of man. Isolation and ignorance are the harbours of fear, arrogance, and hate, they obstruct any sort of growth, and revolt against the idea of change. But the schoolmaster has been abroad, and education has at last got a firm grip on humanity. There can be no going back, that grip will never be relaxed. I am here using the word education in no pedantic, but in its widest and most catholic sense. Education can be misapplied, and what is education to one man may be poison to another. The world it must be remembered is entering on a new era, the centre of political gravity is shifting, and men's minds are taking on a different orientation.

One often hears very well meaning, but it must be confessed, very ignorant people, loudly asserting that education is the curse of the age. Why life without education would not be worth the living! The transitional stage may be in some respects disquieting, all transitional stages are. Misdirected education, and education of a certain sort may tend for a time to breed discontent, to unfit men for this and for that, to throw things generally out of gear, and worst offence of all it tends to rob the few of the subservience and slavery of the many. But that does not affect its ultimate and general beneficence. Just as a bird must moult its feathers, before it can put on a new plumage, so must humanity keep on moulting again and again, to maintain its healthy equilibrium.

And if people will not believe in the blessings of education it can be brought home to them by a very simple illustration.

Which among the nations of the world at this day are the most prosperous and the most happy, speaking in a large and general sense. Are they to be found among the peoples of Asia, Russia, China, India, and the rest, where education as we understand it is practically unknown, or among the Western peoples of England, Germany, and America. The answer can hardly be doubtful. Is not the East already crying out for the knowledge of the West. Does it not, more and more, welcome with open arms the missionary, the doctor, the statesman, and the man of science, to point out to them the way, and guide them in the various paths of salvation.

Education has taken a firm hold on the world, and the privileged and exclusive classes, will no more be able to shake it off their shoulders, than Sindbad could the old man of the sea. It tends to elevate the democracy, and that great army is already on the march, and numbers in its ranks the flower of the race. Many people shrink from the word democrat, but they need not be so desperately afraid; a democrat is by no means synonymous with a "*sansculotte*" of the French revolution. A true democracy should really be an inverted aristocracy and nothing more. Nor does democracy necessarily imply the destruction of aristocracy. There must always from the very nature of the case be an aristocracy, whether of birth, mind, imagination, or money. The most that socialism could effect against it would be to alter somewhat its dress and shift the venue of its operations.

If man, as Darwin's teaching seems to imply is merely a piece of animated matter flitting to and fro for an hour like a gadfly in the sunshine of life, "*cadit quaestio*," there is an end of the matter. But if man has a future and is something more, then man and his race are capable of almost indefinite expansion. And is man on the up grade or on the down. From a large and Darwinian point of view, and speaking of the race of man as a whole, man surely is advancing with considerable rapidity all along the line. There may be failures and backwardation in individual, and national life, this nation may go up and that down, Empires may rise and fall, there may be ebbs here, and flows there, but the tide of the whole race is advancing.

People speak at times without much warrant and very confidently of the degeneracy of this race and that. What sure data one would ask have they to go upon for that assertion? Are for instance the Englishmen of to-day, more decadent than those of a hundred years ago. There is no evidence to prove it. People who make that assertion, either have not read or have misread history altogether.

For almost every profession to-day, there are ten clever men, to the one of even fifty years ago. The mental capital of the race it can hardly be doubted has in that period multiplied many times over. And it is doubtful if its physique has materially deteriorated. The exigences of one age, such as factory life, and the weaknesses of another, such as drink, may have impoverished for a time its vitality, but so generous is nature, and so rich in recuperative power, that even three generations of fair living, would more than redress the balance.

But to leave the particular and return to the universal. Humanity so far from having reached its zenith, has hardly as an organic entity, yet risen above the horizon of time, and has yet a long journey to go before it reaches its meridian, and commences its decline.

And what has made this advance possible, and accelerated the speed of human development? Surely the great impulses that have been given at long intervals of time to physical and mental movement. People misread history when they talk of this great battle or that great battle, of the fall of one great man and the rise of another, of the success of one nation and the defeat of another, as being the real epoch-making events in the life of the race as a whole.

They may affect and powerfully affect a fraction of it for a time, but the great lines of cleavage and new departure which lie deeper, remain undetected and ignored. They are to be discovered in the several inventions, that tend to throw together more and more the bodies and minds of men. All things are double one against another, and strange paradox as it may appear, when this propelling power, which affected and acted upon the bodies of men, was the great instrument in bringing about and promoting war, when it affected and threw together their minds it became an equally effective instrument in the hands of peace.

The man who first mounted a horse, and by so doing accelerated communication between man and man, did more for the benefit of the race than all the learning and writing of antiquity. So it is with the inventors of the wheel, the oar, the rudder, and the sail, and so it is to come later down with the inventors of writing, of the printing press, the steam engine, the telegraph and so on. They were the great pioneers and agents, in bringing about an understanding between man and man, and nation and nation, and in enabling their minds to commingle. And once get thoroughly into touch all the brains of humanity, and the day cannot be far distant, when the swords will be turned into plough-shares, and universal peace will reign upon the earth. Take the case of the printing press alone. The great revolution it brought about in many directions, is best illustrated by its action in one, and no finer example of it could be given than that of Victor Hugo's celebrated description

DARWIN'S PHILOSOPHY

in his great novel "Notre Dame de Paris" of how the book killed the building. In it he says:—

"The printing press is an entirely new method of human expression, it is human thought putting off one garb, and clothing itself in another, it is a complete and definite change in the skin of the symbolic serpent, which since Adam represents intelligence.

"Under the form of printing, thought is more imperishable than ever; it is volatile, unseizable, indestructible. It mingles with the air. In the time of architecture it was a mountain, standing apart in time and space. Now it has become a flight of birds, stretching out its wings to the four winds, occupying at once space and time.

"We repeat it, who cannot perceive that this method of expression is far more indestructible. It passes from duration to immortality. One mortality. One can destroy a mass, how can one get rid of ubiquity? Let a deluge come, and when the mountain has long since disappeared under its waves, the birds would still fly, and while a single arch floated on the surface of its cataclysm, they would perch on it, swim with it, be present with it at the subsidence of the waters, and the new world which would emerge from this chaos, would realise hovering above it, winged and alive, the thought of a world engulfed.

"And when one reflects, that this method of expression is not only the most conservative, but the most simple, the most accommodating, the most practicable in every way that it draws no baggage in its train; that it journeys unencumbered; and when one contrasts thought compelled to express itself, in a building which sets in motion four or five other arts, a whole mountain of stone, a forest of wood, an entire army of workmen, with thought built up in a book, for which a little paper, a little ink, and a pen is sufficient, can one wonder that the human mind has abandoned architecture for printing?

"Cut sharply the bed of a river crossways below its level, the river will desert the bed.

"Again observe, how from the outset of the discovery of printing, architecture has little by little dried up, become atrophied and barren. One realises, that its water is abating, its spirit evaporating, and that people's thoughts are deserting her. In the fifteenth century this cooling process is almost imperceptible, printing is still too weak, and sucks, at most, from the still powerful building, the excess of its vitality. But from the sixteenth century, the malady of architecture is evident, the classic art suffers from being French; European indigenously it becomes Greek and Roman; from true and modern, pseudo-antique. It is this decadence, that one calls the renaissance. A decadence magnificent withal, for the old Gothic genius, that sun which is setting behind the giant press of Mayence, still sometimes penetrates with its last rays all that hybrid accumulation of Latin arcades and Corinthian colonnades.

"It is this setting sun that we take for an aurora.

"But from the moment, when architecture is no more than another art, when she is no longer, the art supreme, the art sovereign, the art absolute, she has no longer the power of monopolising the rest. They free themselves from her, and breaking her yoke, depart each one from her side. Each gains by the divorce. The separation ennobles them all. Sculpture becomes statuary, imagery painting, the canon music. One would liken it to an empire that breaks up at the death of an Alexander and whose provinces become kingdoms. From that day Raphael, Michael Angelo, Jean Gorjon, Palestrina, burst forth, those splendours of the sixteenth century.

"And with the arts, thought emancipates itself in every direction. The heresiarchs of the middle ages have already made large inroads on catholicism. The sixteenth century breaks the religious unity. Before printing, the reformation was but a schism, with it, it became a revolution. Take away the Press, heresy is enervated. Be it fatal or providential, Gutenberg is the precursor of Luther."

And all the other agents of motion above enumerated have been equally effective in their several directions.

There are only two courses open to humanity. It must proceed on the lines of sympathy, and good will, as laid down in the Gospels or fall back on the old lines of violence, barbarism, and reaction. The latter course is inconceivable, the former is the only alternative. The commercial interests of the world, would alone make this course imperative, and when once the net of commerce is thrown widely enough, and the meshes of that net are sufficiently fine, the most powerful and warlike fish in the sea of humanity will be unable either to break through, escape, or violate their captivity, to the disaster, and confusion of the rest.

The whole ethical future of the race has been outlined long ago in the precepts of the Gospel, and if the race of man advances at all upon those lines it is bound to proceed. Its teachings have anticipated all subsequent thought, or rather all subsequent thought is bound to acknowledge, however reluctantly the truth of its teaching, its universal applicability, nay, even its necessity. Many of its predictions which seemed impossible of fulfilment at the time, are already on the high road to realisation. But here I will only refer to three of them, as in a mundane and social sense they are perhaps more all-embracing than any. They relate respectively to the rules of sympathy, war, and socialism.

"The meek shall inherit the earth!" What! The meek inherit the earth! Let us remember when this was uttered, when the power of Rome was still at its height, when the glint was still resplendent on the armour of her legionaries, when might was right, when slavery was common, and meekness and humility were thrust ruthlessly to the wall. The British Empire of to-day is a living witness to the truth of the saying. The word meekness, is used rather in the sense of sympathy, and must not be confounded with weakness. It is not by means of its physical power and material resources though they are still considerable, that the British Empire of to-day holds a quarter of the human race in either political or moral allegiance. It is due to the sympathy and justice she extends to all people that come under her sway. Cut away those two qualities, and in a century her authority would disappear.

War, of course in any sense whether individual, or national, is entirely hostile to the spirit of Christianity.

Peace was the goal at which Christianity aimed though peace it did not immediately expect. Jerusalem had yet to be compassed about with armies, and there was to be war in all lands. But still peace was the goal, and peace in the long run will in all human probability be finally and universally assured. Something more than the mere seeds of peace are already apparent. The seeds are beginning to sprout, and bud in many directions, and the trees that are to come from those seeds, may obtain their full growth and majesty more speedily than was expected, and overshadow with their beneficence the whole earth, and at no very distant date. There are many indications of this.

War is becoming more scientific; it is regarded more and more, as a game of political and national necessity, rather than as a sporadic and spontaneous outburst of blood-letting. Its horrors are mitigated as far as science and humanity can mitigate them. The units which compose the hostile armies, have as a rule no more personal dislike to each other, than the units of rival cricket teams. The weapons manufactured by man are far more terrible factors, than the men who created them, indeed so terrible are they, that man will soon be waging war against the very weapons that he has created. The commercial interests of the whole world are too largely concerned to admit of its peace being violated merely as the result or at the caprice of this or that fraction of the whole. Arbitration is everywhere in the air and is the coming instrument by which all disputes will ere long, whether civil or military, be decided. It is doubtful if the peoples of the various nations, if left to themselves would ever make wars at all. If the electorate of any country were to be polled on the subject, and a secret ballot were to be taken, the chances are that ninety per cent. of the male population would cast their vote for peace, at any price short of national humiliation and extinction. Nearly all wars have been brought about, not by the will of the people but have been dictated by the caprice, ambition, and pride, of statesmen, soldiers, monarchs, and diplomatists. This can hardly be denied. The Napoleonic wars, the Crimean war, the Franco-German war, the Russo-Japanese war, all tell the same tale, and were all alike promoted by individuals, and were most assuredly not the spontaneous outcome of the people's will.

Much has been talked and written about the glory, and the ennobling influence of war, usually by people who have never experienced it. The personal element in war is receding more and more into the background, and even in war collectivism is beginning to supplant it. That old idea of " La gloire " in war, which reached its zenith under Napoleon, is fast fading away, and as a mere personal advertisement for some blood-thirsty butcher is never likely to be revived. As for its ennobling influence the only people it ever does ennoble are either the slaughtered, the wounded, or their relations, and they are usually the people who least require it.

The men who promote wars are as a rule too careful of their own skins, to enable the ennobling principle to come into operation, or to take effect upon themselves.

If people wish to be disillusioned of the glory of war, and to realise all that it implies, let them read Zola's novel " Debacle " wherein they will see the naked article with all its horrors unadorned.

Collectivism again as rightly understood is another of the great trunk lines on which humanity will have to proceed.

If " collectivism " is nothing more than mutual

assistance, and co-operation, and an equitable distribution of the profits of labour amongst those who produce them, then collectivism has the sanction of the Gospel and of every other true ethical scheme. It is nothing new. It is now, and has been for generations the first-born child of civilisation. But if by " collectivism " is meant that the units of the race can be collected, at the arbitrary pleasure of this or that authority, this or that government, or this or that imperial power, and be forced " willy nilly " and all that they possess, into some religious, political or charitable poor box, and be stereotyped and regulated for all time, then collectivism never has had, and never will have the sanction of sound ethics to support it.

Socialism as interpreted by some people is the bastard child, rather than the legitimate heir of true collectivism. It has behind it neither the sanction of the Gospel nor the human race. If the Gospel enjoins socialism at all, its injunction takes a purely voluntary form, and is free from any touch of compulsion.

There may be a text here and there, which if wrenched from its context and entirely misapplied, may appear to give it some countenance. Such texts as " Sell all that thou hast and give to the poor " are rather personal tests, than the promulgation of economic truth. And in its compulsory aspect Christianity repudiates it, and washes its hands of it altogether.

"Man, who made me a ruler or a judge over thee," is its final word on the subject.

But compulsory socialism, as unavoidable socialism, is no new theory. It is as old as the human race. The whole of the great continent of Asia is peopled by socialists and has been from time immemorial. For if by socialism, is meant equality of opportunity, and equality of possession, then ninety-five per cent. of the peoples of that vast area, have always been and from the very necessities of the case, always must remain socialists.

It is only when you reach the civilised, educated, and advancing communities, that the peaks of inequality, become more and more apparent, and begin to show themselves above this dead and stagnant sea.

If your true socialist really desires socialism, he can do no better than retire at once into Asia where he can enjoy its blessings undisturbed and to the full.

What socialists really desire, is not that every man should revel in a certain fifty pounds a year, but that every man should enjoy fifty thousand. And if they can show humanity how that blessed result can be obtained, humanity will give them their due and pronounce on them a blessing rather than a curse.

And here I must bring my reflections on Darwin to a close. I have followed him through his teachings on the Law of Natural Selection, and the underlying philosophy which is its outcome and on which it rests. [Has he in any way substantiated his theory, or brought it within the region of a higher probability. I deny that they have any true efficacy or value, or that they are likely to confer a blessing on mankind.] His idea is surely unsound, misleading, and delusive. I dissent from his idea that man's improvement is limited to mere functional development; and I have endeavoured to show that a real progress along the whole line of his life is possible for man, and the lines upon which that advance, is likely to proceed. What will be the ultimate outcome of it all, and what humanity will be like a thousand years hence, he would be a bold man who would venture to predict.

But this much it may be safely asserted, that to indicate the true course, and steer correctly, the chariot of the sun, will need the combined efforts and co-operation of the whole, for if any man, or if any body of men, be they statesmen, philosophers, men of science, or theologians, were to attempt the task single-handed and alone, their fate would be the fate of Icarus and they would meet with the same calamity as he.

CHAPTER XVII

CONCLUSION

THERE is a story told in old English history, which has some bearing on the point, and may be within the recollection of some of my readers. When the Saxon king, king Edwin had gathered together his thanes and aldermen, to discuss the momentous question whether they should leave the gods of their fathers, and listen to the new teaching of Paullinus the Christian missionary bishop, one of the king's thanes arose and made this remarkable speech :—

" Truly the life of a man in this world, compared with that life whereof we wot, is on this wise. It is as when thou O King, art sitting at supper with thine Aldermen and Thanes in the time of winter, when the hearth is lighted in the midst and the hall is warm, but without the rains and the snow, are falling, and the winds are howling: then cometh a sparrow and flieth through the house, she cometh in by one door, and goeth out by another. Whiles she is in the house, she feeleth not the storm of winter, but yet, when a little moment of rest is passed, she fleeth again into the storm, and passeth away from our eyes. So it is with the life of man : it is but for a moment; what goeth afore it and what cometh after it, wot we not at all. Wherefore if these strangers can tell us aught, that we may know whence man cometh, and whither he goeth, let us hearken to them and follow their law." [1]

But another simile, and perhaps an equally felicitous one suggests itself to the mind.

The life, or soul of man is like a sunbeam. Precisely as a ray of light, when passing through a medium, and falling on a prism, is refracted and broken up, into its constituent elements, and we see on the prism, the many brilliant colours of which that ray is composed, and the dark lines that intervene between them all, and when the medium of refraction is removed, the broken rays immediately reunite again, in their pristine purity and again become absorbed into the fountain of life from which they sprang: so possibly it may be with the life of man. The ray of light in his " ego " or personality. The medium of refraction through which it passes is this life. Its distractions and cares, distort and split up man's nature, and we behold as in a prism the startling picture of the good and bad qualities of which it is composed. But let the hand of death, remove this distracting medium, and like the ray of light man's nature may resume again its original synthesis and harmony, and return back unimpaired to the fountain of life, from which it came.

But be that as it may we live in a momentous and

[1] Green's " History of the English People."

CONCLUSION 343

stirring age. Men's hearts are not so much failing them for fear, as agitated by anxiety, expectancy, and hope. All things are in one sense becoming new. In many ways men's minds are assuming a different attitude towards religion, science, nature, and the rest. They present themselves to man in fresh and sometimes in strange habiliments, and are varying and ubiquitous in their methods, and manifestation. There is a babel of voices all around, some crying this way and some that, some saying Lo here! and others lo there! some offering one panacea and some another, those behind cry forward, and those before cry back, till amid the din of conflicting opinions man is in danger of losing his bearings altogether, and any consistency in action still, less in thought, seems impossible even for an hour.

And when we look backward down the vista of past ages, or forward through the ever widening avenue of futurity, until we reach that point where reasons stop short, and the rays of man's imagination brilliant though they are, refuse any longer to give their light, and all beyond is darkness and obscurity: and when the soul of man faces naked and alone the thick darkness of impenetrable night, whither can it betake itself, and to whom can it turn.

It can but, nay it must, bow down its head in awe, and abasement and take refuge where its forefathers did before it and cry aloud with them " Lord thou hast been our refuge from one generation to another, before the mountains were brought forth or ever the earth and worlds were made thou art God from everlasting and world without end. Thou turnest man to destruction; and so far science is with the Psalmist—but unlike the Psalmist—science does not go on, and extend to man the assurance of immortal hope implied in the divine refrain "Come again ye children of men."

The words carry with them at once consolation and hope, and if there are any poor souls—and there must be thousands, perhaps in classes and amongst individuals whom one least suspects—so hard pressed in the battle of life, and so broken with disaster or suffering in one form or another, as to put seriously to themselves that terrible question of Shakespeare's "To be, or not to be," let them look up and take heart of hope from those wonderful words, "Come again, ye children of men"; it is better surely than to despair? The invitation is a standing one and lasts through this life, and let us hope beyond the portals of the grave.

> Men fade like leaves, they drop away
>   Beneath the forest shade;
> Others again succeed; but they
>   Are in oblivion laid!
> So spake the sire of Grecian song;
>   Through each succeeding age,
> The words are caught and borne along
>   By poet, saint, and sage![1]

[1] Williams.

For Product Safety Concerns and Information please contact our EU representative GPSR@taylorandfrancis.com
Taylor & Francis Verlag GmbH, Kaufingerstraße 24, 80331 München, Germany

www.ingramcontent.com/pod-product-compliance
Lightning Source LLC
Chambersburg PA
CBHW071758300426
44116CB00009B/1130